Peaks: Unfolding the Philosophical Landscapes of Deleuze and Guattari

Robin Crystal

Published by Am I Am, 2024.

PEAKS: UNFOLDING THE PHILOSOPHICAL LANDSCAPES OF DELEUZE AND GUATTARI
BY ROBIN CRYSTAL
AM I AM © 2024
LOS ANGELES, CALIFORNIA

TABLE OF CONTENTS

CHAPTER 1: RHIZOMATIC THINKING

1.   WHAT   IS   RHIZOMATIC   THINKING?   AN INTRODUCTION

2. RHIZOMES IN NATURE AND CULTURE: EXAMPLES AND INSIGHTS

3.   REVOLUTIONIZING   EDUCATION   WITH RHIZOMATIC THINKING

4. TECHNOLOGY AND THE RHIZOME: A SYMBIOTIC RELATIONSHIP

5.   EXPLORING   RHIZOMATIC   STRUCTURES   IN LITERATURE AND ART

6.   IMAGINING   THE   RHIZOME: FICTIONAL EXPLORATIONS

7. THE POWER OF THE RHIZOME IN SOCIAL MOVEMENTS

8. APPLYING RHIZOMATIC THINKING IN EVERYDAY LIFE

9. REFERENCES

CHAPTER 2: DETERRITORIALIZATION AND RETERRITORIALIZATION

10. INTRODUCTION TO DETERRITORIALIZATION AND RETERRITORIALIZATION

11. HISTORICAL EXAMPLES OF DETERRITORIALIZATION

12. HISTORICAL EXAMPLES OF RETERRITORIALIZATION

13. DETERRITORIALIZATION IN MODERN SOCIETY

14. RETERRITORIALIZATION IN MODERN SOCIETY

15. DETERRITORIALIZATION AND RETERRITORIALIZATION IN FICTION

16. THEORETICAL PERSPECTIVES ON DETERRITORIALIZATION AND RETERRITORIALIZATION

17. FUTURE IMPLICATIONS OF DETERRITORIALIZATION AND RETERRITORIALIZATION

18. REFERENCES

CHAPTER 3: ASSEMBLAGES

19 INTRODUCTION TO ASSEMBLAGES
  20. THEORETICAL FOUNDATIONS OF ASSEMBLAGES
  21. ASSEMBLAGES IN NATURE
  22. ASSEMBLAGES IN SOCIETY
  23. TECHNOLOGICAL ASSEMBLAGES
  24. CULTURAL ASSEMBLAGES
  25. ASSEMBLAGES IN FICTION
  26. ASSEMBLAGES IN CONTEMPORARY ART
  27. ASSEMBLAGES IN ORGANIZATIONAL THEORY
  28. FUTURE IMPLICATIONS OF ASSEMBLAGES
  29. REFERENCES

CHAPTER 4: BODY WITHOUT ORGANS

30. INTRODUCTION TO THE BODY WITHOUT ORGANS

31. THEATRICAL FOUNDATIONS OF THE BODY WITHOUT ORGANS

32. IMPLICATIONS OF THE BODY WITHOUT ORGANS IN CONTEMPORARY THOUGHT

33. THE BODY WITHOUT ORGANS IN ART AND PERFORMANCE

34. THE BODY WITHOUT ORGANS IN LITERATURE

35. THE BODY WITHOUT ORGANS IN FILM AND MEDIA

36. THE BODY WITHOUT ORGANS IN TECHNOLOGY AND CYBERCULTURE

37. THE BODY WITHOUT ORGANS IN CONTEMPORARY PHILOSOPHY

38. PRACTICAL APPLICATIONS OF THE BODY WITHOUT ORGANS

39. FUTURE DIRECTIONS FOR THE BODY WITHOUT ORGANS

40. REFERENCES

CHAPTER 5: SCHIZOANALYSIS

41. INTRODUCTION TO SCHIZOANALYSIS

42. THEORETICAL FOUNDATIONS OF SCHIZOANALYSIS

43. CORE CONCEPTS IN SCHIZOANALYSIS

44. SCHIZOANALYSIS IN SOCIAL AND CULTURAL CRITIQUE

45. PRACTICAL APPLICATIONS OF SCHIZOANALYSIS IN THERAPY

46. SCHIZOANALYSIS IN LITERATURE

47. SCHIZOANALYSIS IN FILM AND MEDIA

48. SCHIZOANALYSIS IN ART

49. SCHIZOANALYSIS AND POLITICAL THEORY

50. FUTURE DIRECTIONS FOR SCHIZOANALYSIS

51. REFERENCES

CHAPTER 1: RHIZOMATIC THINKING

1. WHAT IS RHIZOMATIC THINKING? AN INTRODUCTION

Gilles Deleuze and Félix Guattari, two of the most influential philosophers of the 20th century, introduced the concept of rhizomatic thinking in their collaborative works, particularly in "A Thousand Plateaus." Their radical ideas challenge conventional structures and propose new ways of understanding knowledge, society, and the world at large. The rhizome, as they describe it, serves as a metaphor for an alternative model of thought that contrasts sharply with traditional, hierarchical systems.

At its core, the concept of the rhizome originates from botany, referring to the underground stem of plants like ginger, bamboo, and ferns, which grows horizontally and can sprout new shoots and roots at various points. This botanical characteristic serves as a powerful metaphor for a non-hierarchical, interconnected network of knowledge and ideas. Unlike trees or roots that follow a linear, hierarchical structure with a central trunk and branching limbs, a rhizome spreads out in all directions, without a clear beginning or end. This model of thinking encourages us to move away from fixed points and linear progressions, embracing instead a multiplicity of connections and pathways.

One of the key characteristics of rhizomatic thinking is its non-hierarchical nature. Traditional models of thought, particularly in Western philosophy, often rely on hierarchical structures where knowledge is organized in a top-down manner. There is a clear, dominant narrative or central point from which all other ideas stem. In contrast, rhizomatic thinking rejects this vertical organization in favor of a horizontal, decentralized network. In a rhizomatic structure, no single idea or point of view is privileged over another. Instead, all elements are equally important and interconnected, creating a web of relationships where each node can influence and be influenced by many others.

Another essential aspect of rhizomatic thinking is the presence of multiple entry and exit points. In hierarchical models, there is often a single, prescribed path to understanding or navigating a system of knowledge. Rhizomatic structures, however, allow for numerous points of entry and exit, reflecting the diverse ways in which individuals can engage with and interpret information. This multiplicity ensures that knowledge is not confined to a linear progression but can be accessed, understood, and utilized in various ways, depending on the context and the individual's perspective.

Connectivity and heterogeneity are also fundamental to rhizomatic thinking. In a rhizomatic structure, connections between different points are paramount, and these connections are not limited to homogeneous elements. Instead, rhizomatic thinking embraces diversity and the interrelation of heterogeneous elements. This means that disparate ideas, disciplines, and perspectives can come together to form a cohesive whole, reflecting the complexity and richness of the world we live in. By fostering connections between diverse elements, rhizomatic thinking encourages innovation, creativity, and a more holistic understanding of complex phenomena.

The concept of a-signifying rupture is another crucial characteristic of rhizomatic thinking. A-signifying ruptures refer to the points at which a rhizomatic structure can break and yet continue to thrive and grow in new directions. Unlike hierarchical systems, which can be severely disrupted or rendered dysfunctional by the breakdown of a key component, rhizomatic structures are resilient and adaptable. When a part of the rhizome is disrupted, it can regenerate and reconfigure itself, often in unexpected ways. This adaptability makes rhizomatic thinking particularly relevant in today's rapidly changing world, where flexibility and resilience are essential.

The significance of rhizomatic thinking lies in its ability to challenge and transform traditional structures. By rejecting hierarchical models, rhizomatic thinking opens up new possibilities for understanding and engaging with the world. It encourages us to move beyond fixed categories and linear progressions, embracing instead a more dynamic and interconnected approach to knowledge and experience. This shift has profound implications for various fields, including education, technology, and social organization.

In education, for example, rhizomatic thinking challenges the traditional, standardized approaches to teaching and learning. Conventional education systems often rely on a hierarchical model, where knowledge is transmitted from teacher to student in a linear fashion. This model can be limiting, as it tends to privilege certain types of knowledge and ways of knowing while marginalizing others. Rhizomatic thinking, on the other hand, promotes a more open and inclusive approach to education. It encourages students to explore multiple pathways, make connections between different subjects, and engage in collaborative learning. This approach not only enhances creativity and critical thinking but also fosters a more inclusive and democratic learning environment.

In the realm of technology, rhizomatic thinking can be seen in the development and proliferation of networked technologies, such as the internet and social media. These technologies exemplify the principles of rhizomatic structures, with their decentralized, interconnected networks and multiple points of entry and exit. The internet, for instance, is a vast, rhizomatic network where information flows in all directions, and users can access and contribute content from numerous points around the globe. This has transformed the way we communicate, share knowledge, and build communities, breaking down traditional hierarchies and enabling new forms of social organization.

Social movements also benefit from rhizomatic thinking. Traditional social movements often rely on hierarchical structures, with clear leadership and a centralized strategy. While effective in certain contexts, this approach can also be limiting and susceptible to disruption. Rhizomatic social movements, by contrast, operate through decentralized networks, where power and decision-making are distributed across many nodes. This allows for greater flexibility, resilience, and the ability to adapt to changing circumstances. Movements such as Occupy Wall Street and Black Lives Matter exemplify this rhizomatic approach, using networked technologies and decentralized organization to mobilize and sustain their efforts.

The importance of rhizomatic thinking extends beyond specific applications in education, technology, and social movements. It represents a broader shift in how we understand and engage with the world. By embracing the principles of connectivity, heterogeneity, and adaptability, rhizomatic thinking offers a more nuanced and comprehensive approach to knowledge and experience. It encourages us to move beyond rigid structures and fixed categories, fostering a more inclusive and dynamic way of thinking and being.

Rhizomatic thinking, as articulated by Deleuze and Guattari, offers a powerful alternative to traditional, hierarchical models of thought. By emphasizing non-hierarchical structures, multiple entry and exit points, connectivity and heterogeneity, and a-signifying ruptures, rhizomatic thinking challenges conventional ways of understanding and engaging with the world. Its significance lies in its ability to transform various fields, including education, technology, and social organization, promoting a more inclusive, dynamic, and resilient approach to knowledge and experience. As we navigate an increasingly complex and interconnected world, the principles of rhizomatic thinking provide valuable insights and tools for fostering innovation, creativity, and social change.

2. RHIZOMES IN NATURE AND CULTURE: EXAMPLES AND INSIGHTS

In both natural and cultural contexts, the concept of the rhizome offers a profound metaphor for understanding complex, interconnected systems. Rhizomes, as understood in biology, refer to the underground stems of plants such as ginger, bamboo, and ferns. These structures spread horizontally, sending out roots and shoots from their nodes, creating a network that is resilient, adaptable, and capable of rapid growth. This natural phenomenon provides a rich analogy for exploring similar structures in cultural and social systems.

Biological rhizomes are fascinating because of their unique growth patterns and the advantages they confer to the plants that utilize them. Unlike traditional root systems that grow downward and are primarily concerned with anchoring the plant and absorbing nutrients, rhizomes spread laterally, often just below the surface of the soil. This growth habit allows plants to cover large areas quickly and efficiently. For example, bamboo, one of the fastest-growing plants in the world, uses its rhizomatic network to expand rapidly, often outcompeting other plants for space and resources. This horizontal spread also enables the plant to survive and thrive even when parts of the network are damaged. Each node on a rhizome can potentially generate a new plant, making the system highly resilient and capable of regeneration.

The resilience and adaptability of rhizomatic structures in nature can be seen in how they allow plants to exploit diverse environmental conditions. Rhizomes can navigate through various soil types, bypass obstacles, and take advantage of spatial opportunities that vertical growth patterns might miss. This flexibility is not only a survival strategy but also a means of proliferating in a range of habitats. The interconnectedness of the rhizome means that nutrients and water can be shared across the network, supporting the entire system even if some parts are less resource-rich. This interconnected support system mirrors how certain social and cultural networks function.

In the realm of culture, the metaphor of the rhizome becomes a powerful tool for understanding non-hierarchical, decentralized systems. One of the most prominent examples is the internet. The internet's structure is fundamentally rhizomatic, with its decentralized network of nodes (computers, servers, and devices) that connect and communicate without a central governing authority. This design ensures that information can flow in multiple directions, offering resilience against failures. If one part of the network goes down, data can reroute through other nodes, much like how a biological rhizome can continue to grow and thrive even when parts of it are damaged.

This rhizomatic nature of the internet has profound implications for how information is shared and consumed. Unlike traditional media, which operates through centralized channels where information flows from a single source to many recipients, the internet allows for a more democratic and participatory form of communication. Anyone with access can contribute to the network, creating content, sharing ideas, and engaging in discussions. This has led to the proliferation of diverse voices and perspectives, challenging traditional power structures and enabling new forms of social organization.

Social movements also exhibit rhizomatic characteristics. Movements like Occupy Wall Street and Black Lives Matter are not led by a single figure or centralized leadership. Instead, they consist of numerous interconnected groups and individuals who share common goals but operate independently. This decentralized structure makes the movements more resilient and adaptable. They can quickly respond to changing circumstances, localize their actions to specific contexts, and sustain momentum even when facing external pressures. The horizontal spread of these movements allows them to cover a wide range of issues and reach diverse communities, much like how a rhizome spreads and adapts to different environmental conditions.

Meme culture is another example of rhizomatic thinking in action. Memes are units of cultural information that spread rapidly through social networks, often evolving and mutating as they go. The spread of memes is not linear or controlled by a central authority; instead, it is chaotic and decentralized. Each iteration of a meme can give rise to new variations, which in turn generate further iterations. This process of constant transformation and proliferation mirrors the growth patterns of biological rhizomes. Memes thrive on connectivity and heterogeneity, drawing on diverse cultural references and appealing to various audiences. Their success lies in their ability to adapt and resonate with different contexts, much like how rhizomes navigate and thrive in varied environments.

The rhizomatic nature of internet networks, social movements, and meme culture illustrates several key principles of rhizomatic thinking: non-hierarchical organization, multiple entry and exit points, connectivity, heterogeneity, and resilience. These principles challenge traditional hierarchical structures and offer new ways of understanding and engaging with complex systems.

Non-hierarchical organization, a core principle of rhizomatic thinking, is evident in the decentralized nature of the internet and social movements. Unlike hierarchical systems that rely on top-down control and clear lines of authority, rhizomatic structures distribute power and influence across many nodes. This decentralization fosters greater participation and inclusivity, as individuals and groups can contribute and influence the system without needing to go through a central authority. In social movements, this allows for a diversity of tactics and strategies, as different groups can pursue their own approaches while still contributing to the overall goals of the movement.

Multiple entry and exit points, another key principle, are crucial for the flexibility and adaptability of rhizomatic systems. On the internet, users can enter and exit the network at countless points, accessing information, sharing content, and engaging with others in myriad ways. This multiplicity of points of engagement ensures that the network remains open and accessible, accommodating a wide range of activities and interactions. In social movements, multiple entry points allow individuals to join and leave the movement as needed, contributing in ways that suit their abilities and circumstances. This flexibility helps sustain the movement over time, as it can continually renew itself with new participants and ideas.

Connectivity and heterogeneity are fundamental to the success of rhizomatic systems. The strength of a rhizome lies in its connections, with each node linked to many others, creating a robust network that can withstand disruptions. In cultural contexts, connectivity allows for the rapid spread of information and ideas, fostering innovation and creativity. Heterogeneity, the diversity of elements within the network, ensures that the system can draw on a wide range of resources and perspectives. This diversity is crucial for adapting to changing conditions and addressing complex challenges. In meme culture, for example, the diversity of cultural references and the connectivity of social networks enable memes to evolve and spread quickly, resonating with different audiences and contexts.

Resilience, a defining feature of rhizomatic systems, is evident in their ability to withstand and adapt to disruptions. Biological rhizomes can regenerate and continue to grow even when parts are damaged. Similarly, the decentralized nature of the internet and social movements ensures that they can recover from setbacks and continue to function. This resilience is crucial in a rapidly changing world, where adaptability and flexibility are essential for survival and success.

The analysis of natural and cultural rhizomes underscores the transformative potential of rhizomatic thinking. By embracing non-hierarchical organization, multiple entry and exit points, connectivity, heterogeneity, and resilience, we can develop more dynamic and inclusive ways of understanding and engaging with complex systems. This shift in perspective has profound implications for various fields, from technology and education to social organization and cultural production.

In technology, the principles of rhizomatic thinking can inform the design and development of more resilient and adaptable networks. By prioritizing decentralization, connectivity, and heterogeneity, we can create systems that are better equipped to handle disruptions and accommodate diverse needs. In education, adopting a rhizomatic approach can foster more inclusive and participatory learning environments, where students are encouraged to explore multiple pathways and make connections across different subjects. This can enhance creativity, critical thinking, and the ability to navigate complex challenges.

In social organization, rhizomatic thinking offers new models for collective action and community building. By embracing decentralized and non-hierarchical structures, social movements can mobilize diverse groups and sustain momentum over time. This approach can also inform the development of more inclusive and democratic institutions, where power and influence are distributed more equitably.

In cultural production, the principles of rhizomatic thinking can inspire new forms of creativity and expression. By embracing connectivity and heterogeneity, artists and creators can draw on a wide range of influences and engage with diverse audiences. This can lead to the emergence of new genres, styles, and modes of expression that reflect the complexity and richness of contemporary culture.

The concept of the rhizome, as seen in both natural and cultural contexts, offers a powerful metaphor for understanding complex, interconnected systems. The principles of rhizomatic thinking—non-hierarchical organization, multiple entry and exit points, connectivity, heterogeneity, and resilience—challenge traditional hierarchical structures and open up new possibilities for innovation, creativity, and social change. By embracing these principles, we can develop more dynamic, inclusive, and resilient ways of understanding and engaging with the world around us. As we navigate an increasingly complex and interconnected world, the insights gained from the study of rhizomes in nature and culture provide valuable tools for fostering a more adaptive and equitable society.

3.   REVOLUTIONIZING   EDUCATION   WITH RHIZOMATIC THINKING

Traditional education models have long been characterized by hierarchical structures and standardized approaches. These systems often prioritize a top-down method of teaching, where knowledge flows from the teacher to the student in a linear fashion. This model emphasizes uniformity, measurable outcomes, and a fixed curriculum, aiming to produce standardized results across diverse student populations. While this approach has its merits, such as ensuring a consistent baseline of knowledge and skills, it also has significant limitations. It can stifle creativity, limit critical thinking, and fail to accommodate the diverse needs and interests of individual learners. In contrast, rhizomatic education offers a revolutionary alternative that embraces the complexity and interconnectedness of learning.

Rhizomatic education, inspired by the philosophical concepts of Gilles Deleuze and Félix Guattari, challenges the traditional hierarchical model. It draws on the metaphor of the rhizome, a plant structure that grows horizontally and forms a network of interconnected nodes. Unlike a tree, which has a clear trunk and branches, a rhizome spreads out in multiple directions without a central point of authority. This metaphor translates into an educational model that is non-hierarchical, flexible, and dynamic, allowing for multiple entry and exit points, diverse connections, and continuous growth and adaptation.

In a traditional classroom, the teacher is often seen as the central authority, dispensing knowledge to passive students. The curriculum is predetermined, and assessments are standardized, focusing on the acquisition of specific facts and skills. This model can be effective in ensuring that all students receive a similar education, but it can also be rigid and exclusionary. It often fails to engage students who think differently or have unique interests, and it can discourage exploration and innovation. In contrast, rhizomatic education views learning as an active, participatory process where students and teachers co-create knowledge. The roles of teacher and student are fluid, with both parties engaging in a collaborative learning journey.

One of the most striking examples of rhizomatic education in practice is the use of Massive Open Online Courses (MOOCs). MOOCs are online courses that are open to anyone with internet access, offering a diverse array of subjects and learning experiences. They exemplify rhizomatic principles by providing multiple entry points for learners from different backgrounds and with varying levels of expertise. Students can engage with the material at their own pace, choose which topics to focus on, and connect with other learners through discussion forums and collaborative projects. This decentralized approach allows for a rich tapestry of learning experiences, driven by the interests and motivations of the participants rather than a rigid curriculum.

Self-directed learning platforms, such as Khan Academy and Coursera, also embody rhizomatic education. These platforms offer a wide range of courses and resources, enabling learners to pursue their interests and goals independently. Unlike traditional education models that follow a linear progression, self-directed learning allows students to chart their own paths, exploring topics in depth and making connections across disciplines. This approach fosters a sense of ownership and agency in learners, encouraging them to take responsibility for their education and engage more deeply with the material.

The impact of implementing rhizomatic thinking in education can be profound. One of the most significant benefits is the promotion of lifelong learning. Traditional education systems often treat learning as a finite process, culminating in a degree or certification. In contrast, rhizomatic education views learning as an ongoing journey, with no fixed endpoint. This perspective encourages learners to continue exploring and growing throughout their lives, adapting to new challenges and opportunities. By fostering a mindset of curiosity and continuous improvement, rhizomatic education helps individuals remain adaptable and resilient in a rapidly changing world.

Another key benefit is the development of critical thinking and problem-solving skills. Rhizomatic education encourages learners to question assumptions, explore multiple perspectives, and make connections between disparate ideas. This approach nurtures higher-order thinking skills that are essential for navigating complex, real-world problems. In a traditional classroom, the emphasis on standardized testing and rote memorization can limit opportunities for critical thinking and creativity. Rhizomatic education, by contrast, creates an environment where exploration and innovation are valued, helping students develop the skills they need to think critically and creatively.

Furthermore, rhizomatic education promotes inclusivity and diversity. Traditional education models often struggle to accommodate the diverse needs and interests of students, leading to disengagement and inequity. Rhizomatic approaches, with their emphasis on multiple entry points and flexible pathways, are better suited to support diverse learners. By allowing students to engage with material in ways that are meaningful to them, rhizomatic education can help bridge gaps in achievement and create a more equitable learning environment. This inclusivity extends to the types of knowledge and perspectives that are valued, embracing a wider range of cultural and intellectual traditions.

However, implementing rhizomatic thinking in education also presents challenges. One of the primary challenges is the need for a cultural shift in how we view education. Traditional models are deeply entrenched, and moving towards a more flexible, decentralized approach requires a significant change in mindset for educators, administrators, and policymakers. There may be resistance to abandoning established methods and metrics of success, particularly in systems that rely heavily on standardized testing and accountability measures. Overcoming this resistance requires advocacy, education, and the demonstration of the effectiveness of rhizomatic approaches.

Another challenge is ensuring access and equity in rhizomatic learning environments. While MOOCs and self-directed learning platforms offer incredible opportunities, they also require access to technology and internet connectivity, which can be barriers for some students. Additionally, the self-directed nature of rhizomatic learning can be daunting for individuals who are accustomed to more structured environments or who need additional support to succeed. To address these challenges, it is important to provide resources and support systems that help all learners access and benefit from rhizomatic education.

Moreover, assessing learning outcomes in a rhizomatic context can be complex. Traditional education relies on standardized assessments to measure student progress and achievement. Rhizomatic education, with its emphasis on personalized learning journeys and diverse outcomes, requires new methods of assessment that capture the richness and complexity of the learning process. This might include portfolio-based assessments, peer reviews, and other forms of qualitative evaluation that reflect the holistic nature of rhizomatic learning.

Teacher training and professional development are also critical for the successful implementation of rhizomatic education. Educators need to be equipped with the skills and knowledge to facilitate learning in a decentralized, student-centered environment. This includes understanding the principles of rhizomatic thinking, mastering new technologies, and developing strategies to support diverse learners. Ongoing professional development and collaborative learning opportunities for teachers can help build a community of practice that embraces and advances rhizomatic education.

Rhizomatic thinking offers a revolutionary approach to education that challenges traditional hierarchical and standardized models. By embracing non-hierarchical structures, multiple entry and exit points, and the interconnectedness of knowledge, rhizomatic education fosters a more inclusive, dynamic, and resilient learning environment. Case studies of MOOCs and self-directed learning platforms illustrate the potential of rhizomatic approaches to promote lifelong learning, critical thinking, and inclusivity. However, implementing rhizomatic thinking in education also presents challenges, including the need for cultural shifts, ensuring access and equity, developing new methods of assessment, and providing teacher training. Despite these challenges, the transformative potential of rhizomatic education is immense, offering new possibilities for how we understand and engage with learning in an increasingly complex and interconnected world. As we continue to explore and refine these approaches, rhizomatic thinking can help create more adaptable, innovative, and equitable educational systems that better prepare learners for the future.

4. TECHNOLOGY AND THE RHIZOME: A SYMBIOTIC RELATIONSHIP

The concept of the rhizome, as articulated by Gilles Deleuze and Félix Guattari, offers a compelling framework for understanding the dynamics of networked technologies. The rhizome metaphor, which originates from the horizontal growth patterns of certain plants, emphasizes non-hierarchical structures, multiple entry and exit points, and interconnected nodes. This model is particularly apt for describing the architecture and function of modern technologies such as the internet, blockchain, and social media. These technologies not only exemplify rhizomatic principles but also highlight the symbiotic relationship between technology and the rhizome.

The internet is perhaps the most prominent example of a rhizomatic structure in the technological realm. Unlike traditional centralized networks, the internet operates as a decentralized, global network of interconnected nodes. Each node in this network can connect to multiple other nodes, allowing for the free flow of information in all directions. This decentralization ensures that the internet remains resilient and adaptable; if one part of the network fails, data can be rerouted through other nodes, maintaining the overall integrity of the system. This non-hierarchical and flexible architecture is a direct embodiment of rhizomatic principles, enabling a diverse array of activities, from communication and commerce to education and entertainment.

Blockchain technology further exemplifies rhizomatic principles through its decentralized ledger system. In a blockchain, information is stored across a distributed network of computers, known as nodes, rather than in a single centralized database. Each transaction or piece of data is recorded in a block, which is then linked to previous blocks, forming a chain. This structure ensures transparency, security, and immutability, as altering a single block would require changing all subsequent blocks, an impractically difficult task. Blockchain's decentralization prevents any single entity from exerting control over the entire network, fostering a more democratic and resilient system. This technology has found applications in various fields, including finance (e.g., cryptocurrencies like Bitcoin), supply chain management, and even voting systems, where trust and security are paramount.

Social media platforms also reflect rhizomatic structures through their interconnected and user-generated content networks. Unlike traditional media, which relies on a top-down dissemination model, social media allows users to create, share, and engage with content in a decentralized manner. Platforms like Twitter, Facebook, and Instagram operate through networks of users who interact with each other, forming complex webs of connections. These interactions can propagate information rapidly across the network, creating viral phenomena and enabling real-time communication on a global scale. The non-hierarchical nature of social media means that anyone can contribute to the discourse, democratizing content creation and distribution.

To understand how rhizomatic principles manifest in specific technologies, it is useful to examine detailed case studies. Wikipedia, the free online encyclopedia, is a prime example of a rhizomatic knowledge system. Unlike traditional encyclopedias, which are curated by a select group of experts, Wikipedia is a collaborative platform where anyone can contribute, edit, or update articles. This open-access model allows for the continuous growth and evolution of content, reflecting the dynamic nature of knowledge. The decentralized and non-hierarchical structure of Wikipedia ensures that diverse perspectives are represented, and the content is constantly refined through collective effort. This rhizomatic approach to knowledge creation and dissemination has made Wikipedia one of the most comprehensive and up-to-date information resources available.

Another illustrative case study is the peer-to-peer (P2P) file-sharing network BitTorrent. BitTorrent operates by breaking files into small pieces and distributing them across multiple nodes in the network. Users download these pieces from various sources and reassemble them on their devices. This decentralized approach makes the network highly efficient and resilient, as the availability of files does not depend on a single server. The more users participate in the network, the faster and more robust it becomes, exemplifying the rhizomatic principle of interconnectedness and collective growth.

Cryptocurrencies like Bitcoin offer a compelling case study of rhizomatic financial systems. Bitcoin's underlying technology, blockchain, creates a decentralized ledger of transactions that is maintained by a network of nodes, rather than a central authority. This structure ensures transparency and security, as each transaction is verified by the network and recorded in a block. Bitcoin's rhizomatic nature allows for peer-to-peer transactions without intermediaries, reducing costs and increasing access to financial services. The decentralized and transparent nature of blockchain technology has the potential to revolutionize traditional financial systems, making them more inclusive and equitable.

Looking to the future, technological developments are likely to further embrace rhizomatic structures, driven by the need for greater resilience, adaptability, and inclusivity. One promising area is the development of decentralized autonomous organizations (DAOs). DAOs are organizations governed by smart contracts on a blockchain, operating without centralized control. Decisions within a DAO are made through collective voting by stakeholders, ensuring a democratic and transparent governance process. This rhizomatic approach to organizational structure could transform how businesses and institutions operate, promoting more equitable and participatory models of governance.

The Internet of Things (IoT) is another area where rhizomatic principles are set to play a significant role. IoT involves the interconnection of everyday objects, from household appliances to industrial machinery, through the internet. These objects, equipped with sensors and communication capabilities, form a decentralized network that can collect and share data in real-time. The rhizomatic nature of IoT networks allows for greater flexibility and efficiency, as devices can communicate directly with each other without relying on a central hub. This can lead to smarter, more responsive systems in various domains, including smart homes, healthcare, and industrial automation.

Artificial intelligence (AI) and machine learning are also poised to benefit from rhizomatic structures. Traditional AI systems often rely on centralized data processing, which can be limiting in terms of scalability and adaptability. However, decentralized AI, which leverages the power of distributed networks, can process data and make decisions in a more flexible and resilient manner. By distributing the computational load across a network of nodes, decentralized AI can handle larger datasets, adapt to changing conditions, and provide more robust and scalable solutions. This rhizomatic approach to AI could lead to significant advancements in fields such as autonomous vehicles, personalized medicine, and smart city infrastructure.

In education, the rise of decentralized learning platforms and collaborative knowledge networks reflects a move towards rhizomatic structures. These platforms leverage the power of the internet to connect learners and educators across the globe, facilitating the exchange of knowledge and resources. Decentralized learning models, such as those employed by MOOCs and peer-to-peer learning communities, promote a more inclusive and participatory approach to education. By breaking down traditional hierarchies and enabling learners to take control of their educational journeys, these rhizomatic systems foster lifelong learning and adaptability.

Moreover, advancements in virtual and augmented reality (VR/AR) technologies are set to create new rhizomatic experiences. VR and AR can create immersive environments where users interact with digital content and each other in real-time. These technologies enable the creation of decentralized virtual spaces where users can collaborate, learn, and socialize without the constraints of physical location. The rhizomatic nature of these virtual environments promotes diverse interactions and the co-creation of content, offering new possibilities for education, entertainment, and socialization.

The development of decentralized energy systems also exemplifies the potential of rhizomatic structures. Traditional energy grids are centralized, with power generated at large plants and distributed through a hierarchical network. In contrast, decentralized energy systems rely on multiple small-scale generators, such as solar panels and wind turbines, distributed across a network. These systems can generate and store energy locally, reducing reliance on central power plants and increasing resilience. By enabling communities to produce and manage their own energy, decentralized systems promote sustainability and energy independence.

The symbiotic relationship between technology and the rhizome highlights the transformative potential of decentralized, interconnected systems. Networked technologies such as the internet, blockchain, and social media exemplify rhizomatic principles, fostering resilience, adaptability, and inclusivity. Detailed case studies of technologies like Wikipedia, BitTorrent, and Bitcoin illustrate how rhizomatic structures can revolutionize knowledge dissemination, file sharing, and financial systems. Looking to the future, technological developments in areas such as DAOs, IoT, AI, education, VR/AR, and decentralized energy systems are set to further embrace rhizomatic principles. By leveraging the power of interconnected networks, these innovations can create more resilient, equitable, and dynamic systems, transforming how we interact with technology and each other. As we continue to explore and develop these rhizomatic structures, we unlock new possibilities for a more adaptable and interconnected world.

5. EXPLORING RHIZOMATIC STRUCTURES IN LITERATURE AND ART

Rhizomatic thinking, as conceptualized by Gilles Deleuze and Félix Guattari, has had a profound influence on literature and art, inspiring works that embody principles of interconnectedness, non-linearity, and multiplicity. This framework offers a dynamic way to explore and understand the complexities of human creativity. In literature, works like James Joyce's "Finnegans Wake" and hypertext literature exemplify rhizomatic structures, while in the realm of art, movements such as surrealism and postmodernism capture the essence of rhizomatic thinking. By examining these examples, we can see how rhizomatic principles foster innovation and open new creative avenues for artists and writers.

James Joyce's "Finnegans Wake" stands as a monumental example of rhizomatic literature. Published in 1939, this novel breaks away from traditional narrative structures, presenting a complex, circular narrative that defies linear reading. The text is characterized by its dense language, intricate wordplay, and multiplicity of meanings, reflecting the non-hierarchical and interconnected nature of a rhizome. Joyce's work challenges readers to engage with the text in a non-linear fashion, allowing them to enter and exit the narrative at multiple points, much like navigating a rhizomatic structure. This approach not only reflects the complexity of human consciousness but also encourages a more active and participatory form of reading, where meaning is co-created by the reader and the text.

Hypertext literature, which emerged with the advent of digital technology, further exemplifies rhizomatic principles. Hypertext fiction is a genre that uses digital links to create a non-linear reading experience, allowing readers to navigate the narrative through various interconnected paths. Works such as Michael Joyce's "afternoon, a story" and Shelley Jackson's "Patchwork Girl" leverage hypertext to create a multiplicity of narratives, where the reader's choices determine the unfolding of the story. This form of literature embodies the rhizomatic idea of multiple entry and exit points, offering a decentralized and participatory approach to storytelling. The interconnected nodes of a hypertext narrative mirror the structure of a rhizome, highlighting the fluidity and adaptability of the text.

In the realm of art, surrealism is a movement that embodies rhizomatic principles. Surrealist artists like Salvador Dalí, Max Ernst, and René Magritte sought to explore the unconscious mind and challenge conventional perceptions of reality. Their works often feature dreamlike scenes, unexpected juxtapositions, and a fluid blending of the real and the imaginary. These characteristics reflect the interconnected and non-hierarchical nature of rhizomatic thinking, where disparate elements are brought together to create new meanings and associations. Surrealist art encourages viewers to engage with their own subconscious and explore the multiple layers of interpretation, much like navigating a rhizome.

Postmodernism, another significant movement in art and literature, also reflects rhizomatic principles. Postmodern works often reject the idea of a single, authoritative narrative, embracing instead a plurality of voices and perspectives. Artists and writers such as Jean-Michel Basquiat, Cindy Sherman, and Thomas Pynchon employ techniques like pastiche, fragmentation, and intertextuality to create works that are open-ended and multifaceted. This approach aligns with the rhizomatic idea of connectivity and heterogeneity, where multiple influences and ideas are interwoven to form a complex and dynamic whole. Postmodern art and literature invite viewers and readers to actively engage with the work, constructing their own meanings from the interplay of elements.

The creative potential of rhizomatic thinking is vast, offering artists and writers new ways to innovate and push the boundaries of their mediums. By embracing the principles of interconnectedness, non-linearity, and multiplicity, creators can develop works that reflect the complexity of contemporary life and encourage more active engagement from audiences.

One way artists and writers can use rhizomatic thinking to innovate is by exploring non-linear narratives and structures. Traditional storytelling often follows a linear progression, with a clear beginning, middle, and end. Rhizomatic narratives, on the other hand, allow for multiple pathways and entry points, reflecting the complexity and unpredictability of real life. By creating works that can be experienced in various orders and from different perspectives, artists and writers can offer audiences a more immersive and participatory experience. This approach not only challenges conventional storytelling but also reflects the interconnected nature of human experiences.

Collaboration and interdisciplinarity are other areas where rhizomatic thinking can foster innovation. The interconnected nature of a rhizome encourages the blending of different disciplines and the collaboration of diverse voices. Artists and writers can work together across mediums, drawing on each other's strengths and perspectives to create multifaceted works. This collaborative approach reflects the rhizomatic principle of connectivity, where the whole is enriched by the diverse contributions of its parts. By breaking down the boundaries between disciplines, creators can develop works that are more reflective of the interconnected and interdependent world we live in.

Another innovative potential of rhizomatic thinking lies in the use of technology. Digital tools and platforms offer new possibilities for creating and experiencing art and literature. Virtual reality (VR) and augmented reality (AR) technologies, for example, can create immersive environments that engage multiple senses and allow for interactive storytelling. These technologies can transform the way audiences experience narratives, making them active participants in the creation of meaning. The decentralized nature of digital platforms also allows for greater collaboration and participation, enabling creators to reach wider audiences and engage with them in new and meaningful ways.

Rhizomatic thinking also encourages the exploration of themes related to multiplicity and hybridity. In a world that is increasingly interconnected and diverse, artists and writers can use rhizomatic principles to explore the complexities of identity, culture, and experience. By embracing multiplicity, creators can develop works that reflect the diverse and fluid nature of contemporary life. This approach not only enriches the work itself but also promotes a more inclusive and nuanced understanding of the world.

The potential for innovation through rhizomatic thinking is further exemplified by the rise of participatory art and literature. In participatory works, the audience is not just a passive observer but an active collaborator in the creation of the work. This approach aligns with the rhizomatic principle of multiple entry and exit points, allowing audiences to engage with the work in various ways and contribute their own perspectives. Participatory works can take many forms, from interactive installations and performance art to collaborative writing projects and online platforms. By involving the audience in the creative process, artists and writers can create more dynamic and responsive works that resonate with diverse experiences and viewpoints.

The rhizomatic approach also offers a framework for exploring and addressing social and political issues. The interconnected nature of a rhizome reflects the complexities and interdependencies of social systems, encouraging creators to explore these dynamics in their work. By highlighting the connections between different issues and perspectives, artists and writers can develop works that promote greater understanding and empathy. This approach can also empower audiences to see themselves as part of a larger, interconnected community, encouraging collective action and social change.

In conclusion, rhizomatic thinking offers a rich and dynamic framework for exploring and understanding literature and art. Works like James Joyce's "Finnegans Wake" and hypertext literature exemplify the non-linear, interconnected nature of rhizomatic structures, challenging traditional narratives and engaging readers in new ways. Artistic movements like surrealism and postmodernism embody rhizomatic principles through their embrace of multiplicity and interconnectedness, inviting viewers to explore new associations and meanings. The creative potential of rhizomatic thinking is vast, offering artists and writers new ways to innovate and push the boundaries of their mediums. By embracing the principles of interconnectedness, non-linearity, and multiplicity, creators can develop works that reflect the complexity of contemporary life and encourage more active engagement from audiences. Through collaboration, the use of technology, and the exploration of themes related to multiplicity and hybridity, artists and writers can create works that are more inclusive, dynamic, and reflective of our interconnected world. The rhizomatic approach also offers a powerful framework for exploring social and political issues, promoting greater understanding and collective action. As we continue to navigate an increasingly complex and interconnected world, rhizomatic thinking provides valuable tools and insights for fostering innovation and creativity in literature and art.

6. IMAGINING THE RHIZOME: FICTIONAL EXPLORATIONS

Rhizomatic thinking, as articulated by Gilles Deleuze and Félix Guattari, offers a compelling framework for reimagining how fiction can be structured and understood. In contrast to traditional, linear narratives that follow a clear beginning, middle, and end, rhizomatic fiction embraces interconnectedness, non-linearity, and multiplicity. This approach to storytelling reflects the complexity of human experience and challenges readers to engage with narratives in more dynamic and participatory ways. By exploring conceptual fiction through the lens of rhizomatic thinking, we can uncover new possibilities for how stories are told and experienced.

Conceptual fiction, which prioritizes ideas and structures over conventional plot and character development, is particularly well-suited to illustrating rhizomatic thinking. In a rhizomatic narrative, the story does not unfold in a straightforward, linear manner. Instead, it branches out in multiple directions, allowing readers to enter and exit the narrative at various points. This non-hierarchical structure mirrors the way rhizomes grow, with each node connecting to many others, creating a network of relationships rather than a single, dominant path. By embracing this approach, fiction can better capture the fluidity and interconnectedness of real-life experiences, where events and ideas are often intertwined in complex ways.

One way to illustrate rhizomatic thinking in fiction is through the use of fragmented narratives. These stories are composed of seemingly disjointed scenes or chapters that may not follow a chronological order. Instead, they are linked thematically or through recurring motifs, allowing readers to piece together the narrative in a non-linear fashion. For example, consider a story that follows multiple characters in different locations and time periods, with each chapter focusing on a different perspective. As the narrative progresses, connections between the characters and events emerge, creating a web of relationships that the reader must navigate.

A short fictional piece that exemplifies this approach might begin with a scene set in a bustling city, where a young artist named Lena is preparing for her first gallery exhibition. The narrative then shifts to a small village decades earlier, where a carpenter named Miguel is crafting a beautiful wooden sculpture. In another chapter, we meet a scientist named Aisha, who is conducting research on the impact of urbanization on local ecosystems. As the story unfolds, readers discover that Lena's artwork is inspired by Miguel's sculpture, which she found in an antique shop, and Aisha's research includes a case study on the village where Miguel lived. Through these interconnections, the story creates a rich tapestry of themes related to art, heritage, and environmental change, inviting readers to explore the relationships between different elements of the narrative.

Another example of rhizomatic fiction can be found in hypertext literature, where digital links allow readers to navigate the story in multiple directions. A hypertext narrative might begin with a central event, such as a mysterious disappearance, and then provide links to various documents, interviews, and personal accounts related to the case. Readers can choose which links to follow, creating their own path through the narrative and uncovering different aspects of the story based on their choices. This interactive approach not only reflects the interconnected nature of a rhizome but also engages readers as active participants in the construction of meaning.

For instance, a hypertext story could revolve around the disappearance of a renowned archaeologist named Dr. Harper during an expedition in the Amazon rainforest. The narrative might include links to Dr. Harper's journal entries, emails to her colleagues, news articles about the expedition, and interviews with local villagers. Each document provides a piece of the puzzle, and readers can follow different threads to uncover various theories and perspectives on what happened to Dr. Harper. By allowing readers to explore the narrative in a non-linear way, the story mirrors the complexity and uncertainty of real-life investigations, where information is often incomplete and open to interpretation.

Rhizomatic fiction can also challenge readers' perceptions of structure and narrative by incorporating multiple voices and perspectives. In a traditional narrative, the story is often told from a single point of view, with a clear distinction between the protagonist and other characters. Rhizomatic fiction, however, blurs these boundaries by giving equal weight to different voices and allowing multiple characters to share their experiences. This approach reflects the rhizomatic principle of non-hierarchical organization, where no single perspective dominates the narrative.

A story that exemplifies this approach might follow a community living in a coastal town threatened by rising sea levels. Each chapter is narrated by a different character, including a fisherman, a schoolteacher, a teenage activist, and an elderly resident. Through their diverse perspectives, the narrative explores the impact of climate change on the community, highlighting the interconnectedness of their experiences and the collective efforts to adapt and survive. By presenting multiple voices, the story encourages readers to consider the broader implications of environmental issues and the ways in which individual actions and experiences are linked.

Rhizomatic fiction also opens up possibilities for exploring themes of identity and transformation. Traditional narratives often focus on the development of a single character, following a linear progression from one state to another. In contrast, rhizomatic fiction can present identity as fluid and multifaceted, with characters undergoing continuous change and reinvention. This approach reflects the rhizomatic idea of growth and adaptation, where connections and transformations are constant and ongoing.

A short story that illustrates this concept might follow a protagonist named Alex, who experiences a series of life-changing events that lead to multiple reinventions of their identity. The narrative could be structured around key moments in Alex's life, such as moving to a new city, changing careers, and discovering a hidden talent for music. Each chapter explores a different aspect of Alex's identity, with recurring themes and motifs creating connections between the various stages of their journey. By presenting identity as a rhizomatic process, the story challenges readers to rethink traditional notions of selfhood and embrace the fluidity of personal growth.

Analyzing these examples of rhizomatic fiction reveals how they reflect and challenge readers' perceptions of structure and narrative. Traditional narratives often rely on a clear, linear progression, with a focus on plot and character development. Rhizomatic fiction, however, disrupts these conventions by embracing non-linearity, interconnectedness, and multiplicity. This approach not only reflects the complexity of real-life experiences but also encourages readers to engage with the narrative in more active and participatory ways.

By presenting fragmented narratives, hypertext structures, multiple voices, and fluid identities, rhizomatic fiction invites readers to piece together meaning and make connections between different elements of the story. This process of active engagement mirrors the way we navigate the complexities of the real world, where information and experiences are often interconnected and multifaceted. In doing so, rhizomatic fiction challenges readers to think critically about the nature of storytelling and the ways in which narratives can reflect the interconnectedness of human experiences.

Furthermore, rhizomatic fiction offers a space for exploring alternative forms of storytelling that break away from conventional norms. By experimenting with structure, perspective, and theme, writers can push the boundaries of the medium and create works that resonate with contemporary audiences. This innovative approach to fiction not only enriches the literary landscape but also provides new opportunities for readers to engage with stories in meaningful and transformative ways.

In conclusion, rhizomatic thinking provides a powerful framework for reimagining fiction, offering new possibilities for how stories are structured and experienced. Through the exploration of conceptual fiction, fragmented narratives, hypertext literature, multiple voices, and fluid identities, rhizomatic fiction reflects the complexity and interconnectedness of human experience. By challenging traditional notions of structure and narrative, these stories invite readers to engage with the text in more dynamic and participatory ways, fostering a deeper understanding of the interconnected nature of our world. As writers continue to experiment with rhizomatic principles, the potential for innovation and transformation in fiction remains vast, opening up new avenues for creative expression and storytelling.

7. THE POWER OF THE RHIZOME IN SOCIAL MOVEMENTS

The concept of the rhizome, as developed by Gilles Deleuze and Félix Guattari, provides a powerful framework for understanding and analyzing social movements. A rhizome is a root system that grows horizontally, forming a network of interconnected nodes without a central axis. This metaphor highlights the principles of non-hierarchical organization, multiplicity, and connectivity, which can be observed in various social movements throughout history and in contemporary times. By examining historical examples such as Occupy Wall Street and decentralized grassroots movements, as well as modern movements like Black Lives Matter and climate activism, we can gain insights into the effectiveness of rhizomatic approaches in achieving social change.

Historical examples of rhizomatic structures in social movements can be traced back to the decentralized and grassroots nature of many significant uprisings. The Civil Rights Movement in the United States during the 1950s and 1960s, for instance, showcased elements of rhizomatic organization. While there were prominent leaders such as Martin Luther King Jr., the movement was fundamentally driven by local grassroots efforts. Community organizations, churches, and student groups across the country acted independently yet remained interconnected through shared goals and mutual support. This decentralized approach allowed the movement to be resilient and adaptive, responding to local contexts while maintaining a cohesive push for systemic change.

The Occupy Wall Street movement, which began in 2011, is another prominent example of a rhizomatic social movement. Inspired by the Arab Spring and other global protests, Occupy Wall Street emerged as a response to economic inequality and corporate influence in politics. The movement was characterized by its leaderless structure, horizontal organization, and emphasis on direct democracy.

Participants gathered in public spaces, most notably Zuccotti Park in New York City, to create a physical manifestation of their networked, decentralized approach. Decisions were made through general assemblies, where all participants had an equal voice. This rhizomatic structure allowed the movement to spread rapidly to cities across the world, each with its own local adaptations while remaining connected to the broader Occupy ethos.

Decentralized grassroots movements have also been pivotal in environmental activism. The anti-nuclear movement of the 1970s and 1980s, for example, consisted of numerous local groups advocating against nuclear power and weapons. These groups operated independently but were united by their common cause, sharing information and strategies through informal networks. This non-hierarchical structure enabled the movement to be flexible and responsive, capable of mobilizing large numbers of people for protests and direct actions while avoiding centralized control that could be targeted by authorities.

Modern social movements continue to embody rhizomatic characteristics, leveraging digital technology to enhance their decentralized and interconnected nature. The Black Lives Matter (BLM) movement, founded in 2013 in response to the acquittal of Trayvon Martin's killer, exemplifies these principles. BLM operates as a decentralized network of chapters and affiliated organizations, each focusing on issues relevant to their local communities. The movement's use of social media and digital platforms has been instrumental in amplifying its message, coordinating actions, and fostering a sense of global solidarity. By remaining decentralized, BLM has been able to adapt to changing circumstances, maintain resilience against repression, and engage a diverse array of participants.

Climate activism also illustrates the power of rhizomatic structures. Movements such as Extinction Rebellion and Fridays for Future demonstrate how decentralized organization can effectively mobilize people around the world. Extinction Rebellion, founded in the UK in 2018, employs a decentralized model where local groups organize autonomously while adhering to shared principles and strategies. This approach allows for a high degree of adaptability and innovation, as groups can experiment with different tactics and learn from each other. Similarly, Fridays for Future, inspired by Greta Thunberg's school strikes for climate, has grown into a global movement with millions of participants. The decentralized nature of the movement enables young people from diverse backgrounds to take action in their own communities, connected by a common cause but not constrained by a rigid hierarchy.

The effectiveness of rhizomatic approaches in social movements can be analyzed through their strengths and weaknesses. One of the primary strengths of rhizomatic organization is its resilience. Decentralized structures are less vulnerable to disruption because they do not rely on a single leader or central authority. If one node is suppressed or dismantled, the rest of the network can continue to function. This resilience is crucial in the face of state repression or co-optation, as it allows movements to sustain momentum and adapt to changing conditions.

Another strength of rhizomatic approaches is their inclusivity and participatory nature. By rejecting hierarchical structures, these movements encourage broader participation and empower individuals to take initiative. This inclusivity fosters a sense of ownership and commitment among participants, as they are not merely following directives from a central authority but actively shaping the movement's direction. The horizontal organization also facilitates the exchange of ideas and strategies, promoting innovation and creativity.

Rhizomatic movements are also adept at leveraging digital technology to enhance their connectivity and reach. Social media platforms, messaging apps, and online forums enable decentralized networks to communicate, coordinate, and share information in real-time. This digital connectivity amplifies the movement's message, mobilizes supporters, and creates a sense of global solidarity. The ability to rapidly disseminate information and organize actions across diverse geographies is a significant advantage in the digital age.

However, rhizomatic approaches also face challenges. One potential weakness is the lack of centralized leadership, which can sometimes lead to difficulties in decision-making and coordination. Without a clear hierarchy, it can be challenging to achieve consensus or implement cohesive strategies. This can result in fragmentation or internal conflicts, as different nodes within the network pursue divergent goals or tactics. Additionally, the absence of centralized leadership can make it harder to present a unified front or negotiate with external actors, such as governments or media organizations.

Another challenge is the risk of co-optation or dilution of the movement's message. The decentralized nature of rhizomatic movements means that they can be more easily influenced by external forces or infiltrated by individuals with differing agendas. This can lead to a dilution of the movement's core principles or a shift away from its original goals. Ensuring consistency and coherence across a decentralized network requires ongoing communication and reinforcement of shared values.

Despite these challenges, the strengths of rhizomatic approaches often outweigh their weaknesses, particularly in the context of contemporary social movements. The resilience, inclusivity, and adaptability of rhizomatic structures make them well-suited to addressing complex, multifaceted issues in a rapidly changing world. By embracing non-hierarchical organization and leveraging digital technology, rhizomatic movements can mobilize diverse populations, sustain momentum, and drive meaningful social change.

The power of the rhizome in social movements lies in its ability to foster interconnectedness and adaptability. Historical examples like the Civil Rights Movement, Occupy Wall Street, and decentralized grassroots movements demonstrate the effectiveness of non-hierarchical organization in achieving social change. Modern movements such as Black Lives Matter and climate activism continue to build on these principles, using digital technology to enhance their reach and impact. While rhizomatic approaches face challenges related to decision-making and message coherence, their strengths in resilience, inclusivity, and innovation make them powerful tools for mobilizing and sustaining social movements.

In conclusion, the rhizomatic structure offers a compelling framework for understanding and organizing social movements. By emphasizing non-hierarchical organization, connectivity, and adaptability, rhizomatic movements can effectively mobilize diverse populations and drive meaningful social change. Historical and modern examples illustrate the power of these principles in practice, highlighting both the strengths and challenges of rhizomatic approaches. As social movements continue to evolve in response to new challenges and opportunities, the rhizome provides a valuable model for fostering resilience, inclusivity, and innovation in the pursuit of a more just and equitable world.

8. APPLYING RHIZOMATIC THINKING IN EVERYDAY LIFE

Rhizomatic thinking, inspired by the work of philosophers Gilles Deleuze and Félix Guattari, presents a unique approach to understanding and navigating the world. Unlike traditional, hierarchical structures that follow a linear progression, rhizomatic thinking embraces interconnectedness, multiplicity, and non-linearity. This perspective can be profoundly beneficial when applied to everyday life, influencing personal development, business practices, and innovation. By incorporating rhizomatic principles, individuals and organizations can foster adaptability, creativity, and resilience.

In personal development, rhizomatic thinking encourages individuals to see their growth and learning as a dynamic, interconnected process. Instead of viewing personal and professional development as a linear path with a clear beginning and end, rhizomatic thinking suggests that growth is continuous and multifaceted. This perspective allows individuals to explore various interests and skills simultaneously, creating a more holistic and adaptable approach to self-improvement.

One way to incorporate rhizomatic thinking into personal development is by embracing lifelong learning. This involves continuously seeking new knowledge and experiences, rather than adhering to a fixed curriculum or career path. For instance, a professional might pursue interests outside their immediate field, such as learning a new language, taking up a hobby like painting, or studying a different discipline. These activities can enrich their primary work by bringing new perspectives and skills that enhance creativity and problem-solving abilities. By seeing learning as a rhizomatic process, individuals can connect diverse areas of knowledge and apply them in innovative ways.

Another aspect of personal development influenced by rhizomatic thinking is the ability to navigate and adapt to change. In a rapidly changing world, being flexible and open to new possibilities is crucial. Rhizomatic thinking encourages individuals to see change not as a disruption but as an opportunity for growth and transformation. This mindset can be particularly beneficial in professional settings where industries and job roles are constantly evolving. By cultivating a rhizomatic approach, professionals can adapt more quickly to new technologies, market demands, and organizational changes.

In business and innovation, rhizomatic principles can lead to more dynamic and resilient organizations. Businesses that adopt rhizomatic thinking are better equipped to handle complexity and uncertainty, as they emphasize connectivity, decentralization, and flexibility. These principles can be seen in various innovative business models and practices that prioritize collaboration, networked structures, and adaptive strategies.

One example of a business that utilizes rhizomatic principles is the technology company Google. Google's organizational structure encourages innovation through its emphasis on cross-functional teams and a flat hierarchy. Employees are encouraged to collaborate across departments, sharing knowledge and expertise to develop new products and services. This approach reflects the rhizomatic principle of interconnectedness, where different nodes (teams and individuals) contribute to the overall growth and innovation of the company. Additionally, Google's practice of allowing employees to spend a portion of their time on personal projects fosters a culture of continuous learning and exploration, aligning with the rhizomatic idea of multiple entry and exit points in the learning process.

Another example is the open-source software movement, which exemplifies rhizomatic thinking through its decentralized and collaborative nature. Open-source projects, such as the Linux operating system, are developed by communities of contributors from around the world. These projects are not controlled by a single entity but grow through the contributions of many individuals who share their code, ideas, and improvements. This decentralized approach allows for rapid innovation and adaptation, as the collective intelligence of the community drives the development process. The open-source model demonstrates how rhizomatic principles can lead to more resilient and innovative technological solutions.

To foster a rhizomatic mindset, both individuals and organizations can adopt several practical strategies. One key strategy is to prioritize connectivity and collaboration. This involves creating environments where diverse ideas and perspectives can intersect and interact. In professional settings, this might mean forming cross-functional teams, encouraging open communication, and fostering a culture of knowledge sharing. In personal life, individuals can seek out diverse social networks, engage in interdisciplinary learning, and participate in collaborative projects.

Another strategy is to embrace flexibility and adaptability. Rhizomatic thinking requires a willingness to explore new paths and adjust to changing circumstances. This can be achieved by setting flexible goals, remaining open to new opportunities, and continuously reassessing and adjusting strategies based on feedback and changing conditions. In a business context, this might involve adopting agile methodologies, which prioritize iterative development and responsiveness to change, over rigid planning and control.

Encouraging experimentation and innovation is also crucial for fostering a rhizomatic mindset. This involves creating spaces where failure is seen as a natural part of the learning process and where new ideas can be tested and refined. For individuals, this might mean taking on new challenges, trying out different approaches to problem-solving, and learning from both successes and failures. For organizations, it can involve creating innovation labs, supporting intrapreneurship, and rewarding creative risk-taking.

Developing a rhizomatic mindset also involves cultivating curiosity and a love of learning. This means seeking out new knowledge and experiences, questioning assumptions, and staying open to different perspectives. In professional development, this might involve pursuing continuous education, attending conferences and workshops, and reading broadly across different fields. In personal development, it can mean exploring new hobbies, traveling, and engaging in lifelong learning.

In addition to these strategies, adopting digital tools and platforms can support rhizomatic thinking. Technology offers numerous ways to connect, collaborate, and learn in a decentralized and flexible manner. Social media, online learning platforms, and collaborative tools like Slack and Trello enable individuals and teams to work together across distances and disciplines. These tools facilitate the kind of interconnected, adaptive, and collaborative processes that are at the heart of rhizomatic thinking.

Furthermore, mindfulness and reflective practices can help individuals integrate rhizomatic thinking into their daily lives. Mindfulness involves paying attention to the present moment with curiosity and openness, which can enhance awareness and adaptability. Reflective practices, such as journaling or meditation, allow individuals to process their experiences, identify patterns, and explore connections between different aspects of their lives. These practices support a rhizomatic approach by encouraging continuous self-awareness and growth.

In conclusion, rhizomatic thinking offers a transformative approach to personal development, business practices, and innovation. By embracing principles of interconnectedness, multiplicity, and non-linearity, individuals and organizations can navigate complexity and change more effectively. In personal development, rhizomatic thinking encourages continuous learning, adaptability, and the integration of diverse interests and skills. In business and innovation, it fosters resilient and dynamic organizations that prioritize collaboration, flexibility, and creativity. Practical strategies for fostering a rhizomatic mindset include prioritizing connectivity and collaboration, embracing flexibility and adaptability, encouraging experimentation and innovation, cultivating curiosity and a love of learning, leveraging digital tools, and practicing mindfulness and reflection. By applying rhizomatic principles in everyday life, we can create more vibrant, adaptive, and interconnected ways of living and working, better suited to the complexities of the modern world.

9. REFERENCES

Gilles Deleuze and Félix Guattari introduced the concept of the rhizome in their seminal work "A Thousand Plateaus: Capitalism and Schizophrenia" (1987). This book elaborates on the principles of rhizomatic thinking, contrasting it with traditional, hierarchical models of thought. The metaphor of the rhizome illustrates the potential for decentralized, interconnected, and adaptive structures in both natural and cultural contexts.

In "A Thousand Plateaus," Deleuze and Guattari (1987) write:

"A rhizome has no beginning or end; it is always in the middle, between things, interbeing, intermezzo. The tree is filiation, but the rhizome is alliance, uniquely alliance" (p. 25).

This passage captures the essence of rhizomatic thinking, emphasizing its non-hierarchical and interconnected nature.

For additional scholarly perspectives, consider the following sources:

1. Buchanan, I. (2000). "Deleuze and Guattari's Anti-Oedipus: A Reader's Guide". London: Continuum.

This book provides a comprehensive overview of Deleuze and Guattari's ideas, including their development of rhizomatic thinking. Buchanan explains how their philosophy challenges conventional structures and promotes new ways of understanding and organizing knowledge.

2. Massumi, B. (1987). "Notes on the Translation and Acknowledgments." In G. Deleuze & F. Guattari, "A Thousand Plateaus: Capitalism and Schizophrenia" (pp. xv-xvi). Minneapolis: University of Minnesota Press.

Brian Massumi's notes offer valuable insights into the translation and interpretation of Deleuze and Guattari's work. He highlights the significance of the rhizome metaphor and its implications for various disciplines.

3. Parr, A. (Ed.). (2005). "The Deleuze Dictionary." Edinburgh: Edinburgh University Press.

This dictionary provides definitions and explanations of key concepts in Deleuze's philosophy, including rhizomatic thinking. It is a useful resource for understanding the broader context of their ideas and how they can be applied to different fields.

4. Bogue, R. (2003). "Deleuze on Literature." London: Routledge.

Ronald Bogue's work explores how Deleuze's concepts, including rhizomatic thinking, can be applied to literary studies. This book provides examples of how rhizomatic structures can be identified and analyzed in literature, offering insights that are relevant to broader applications.

5. Colebrook, C. (2002). "Understanding Deleuze." Crows Nest, NSW: Allen & Unwin.

Claire Colebrook's book offers an accessible introduction to Deleuze's philosophy, including his collaboration with Guattari. It explains key concepts such as the rhizome and how they challenge traditional ways of thinking.

6. Lash, S. (2007). "Power after Hegemony: Cultural Studies in Mutation?" Theory, Culture & Society, 24(3), 55-78.

In this article, Scott Lash discusses the implications of Deleuze and Guattari's rhizomatic thinking for cultural studies and social theory. He explores how decentralized, networked structures can reshape power dynamics and cultural practices.

Applying rhizomatic thinking to personal development involves recognizing that growth and learning are not linear processes but rather interconnected and ongoing. Deleuze and Guattari's concept encourages individuals to explore diverse interests and skills simultaneously, fostering a more holistic approach to self-improvement. Embracing lifelong learning, as described by Deleuze and Guattari (1987), allows individuals to continuously seek new knowledge and experiences, enhancing their adaptability and creativity.

In business and innovation, rhizomatic principles can lead to more dynamic and resilient organizations. Google's cross-functional teams and flat hierarchy, as well as the open-source software movement exemplified by Linux, reflect the interconnectedness and decentralized nature of rhizomatic thinking. These examples demonstrate how businesses can foster innovation and adaptability by prioritizing collaboration and flexibility.

To foster a rhizomatic mindset, individuals and organizations can adopt several practical strategies. Prioritizing connectivity and collaboration, embracing flexibility and adaptability, encouraging experimentation and innovation, and cultivating curiosity and a love of learning are key strategies. Leveraging digital tools and practicing mindfulness and reflection can further support the integration of rhizomatic principles into everyday life.

By applying rhizomatic thinking, we can create more vibrant, adaptive, and interconnected ways of living and working. This approach is better suited to the complexities of the modern world, allowing individuals and organizations to navigate change and uncertainty more effectively. The works of Deleuze and Guattari, along with other scholarly sources, provide a solid foundation for understanding and implementing rhizomatic thinking in various contexts, ultimately fostering a more dynamic and resilient approach to personal and professional development.

CHAPTER 2:
DETERRITORIALIZATION AND RETERRITORIALIZATION

10. INTRODUCTION TO DETERRITORIALIZATION AND RETERRITORIALIZATION

Deterritorialization and reterritorialization are crucial concepts within the fields of cultural studies and globalization theory. These terms were notably developed and popularized by the French philosophers Gilles Deleuze and Félix Guattari in their works, particularly in "A Thousand Plateaus: Capitalism and Schizophrenia" (1987). Understanding these processes provides insight into how social, political, and cultural phenomena evolve, move, and adapt in our increasingly interconnected world.

Deterritorialization refers to the process by which a social, political, or cultural phenomenon loses its connection to a specific geographic location. This detachment can occur for various reasons, including technological advancements, economic shifts, or social changes that disrupt traditional associations between phenomena and places. In essence, deterritorialization represents a form of disembedding, where established ties to a particular territory are weakened or severed.

For instance, consider the way traditional cultural practices may become deterritorialized through the influence of global media. Practices that were once confined to specific locales are now accessible worldwide through television, the internet, and other forms of digital communication. This widespread dissemination allows cultural elements to travel far beyond their original geographic boundaries, reaching diverse audiences who may adopt or adapt these practices in new contexts.

Reterritorialization, on the other hand, is the process by which a deterritorialized phenomenon re-establishes a new connection with a different geographic location. After losing its original territorial association, the phenomenon adapts and integrates into a new environment, often undergoing transformation in the process. Reterritorialization reflects the dynamic nature of cultural and social practices, highlighting their ability to move, change, and establish new roots in different contexts.

An example of reterritorialization can be seen in the global spread of fast-food chains. Originally an American phenomenon, fast-food culture has spread worldwide, with major chains like McDonald's establishing outlets in numerous countries. In each new location, the fast-food model adapts to local tastes and preferences, incorporating regional dishes and flavors into their menus. This process illustrates how a cultural phenomenon can be reterritorialized, finding new expressions and associations in different geographic settings.

The importance of deterritorialization and reterritorialization in globalization and cultural studies cannot be overstated. These processes are central to understanding how cultures interact, transform, and coexist in an increasingly interconnected world. Globalization, characterized by the rapid movement of people, goods, information, and ideas across borders, facilitates the deterritorialization of cultural practices and their subsequent reterritorialization in new contexts.

In cultural studies, deterritorialization and reterritorialization help explain the complex dynamics of cultural exchange and hybridity. As cultural practices move and adapt, they often merge with local traditions, creating hybrid forms that reflect both global influences and local particularities. This hybridity is a hallmark of contemporary cultural landscapes, where identities and practices are continually reshaped through processes of deterritorialization and reterritorialization.

A key case study illustrating these concepts is the influence of global media on local cultures. Global media, encompassing television, film, music, and digital platforms, plays a significant role in disseminating cultural content across the world. This dissemination leads to the deterritorialization of cultural products, as they are no longer confined to their place of origin but are consumed and interpreted by global audiences.

For example, consider the global popularity of American television shows and films. These media products, created within the cultural context of the United States, are widely distributed and consumed around the world. In the process, they become deterritorialized, as their cultural content is separated from the geographic and social context of their origin. Audiences in different countries engage with these media products, interpreting them through their own cultural lenses and integrating aspects into their local contexts.

Reterritorialization occurs as these global media products are adapted and localized. Local media industries may produce their versions of popular American shows, tailoring content to reflect regional tastes, values, and social norms. This localization process is a form of reterritorialization, where the global media product is transformed and re-established within a new cultural and geographic setting. The success of shows like "The Office," which originated in the UK and was later adapted in the US and several other countries, exemplifies this process. Each adaptation reflects the cultural nuances and humor of its new context while retaining the core elements of the original show.

Moreover, the influence of global media on local cultures often results in the creation of hybrid cultural forms. These hybrids blend elements from the original media products with local traditions, creating unique expressions that resonate with local audiences. For instance, the genre of Bollywood films in India combines elements of traditional Indian storytelling, music, and dance with influences from Western cinema. This hybridity reflects the processes of deterritorialization and reterritorialization, as cultural elements move across borders and integrate into new contexts.

The impact of global media on local cultures also extends to language, fashion, and lifestyle. English, as the dominant language of global media, has become increasingly influential worldwide, affecting local languages and communication practices. Similarly, fashion trends disseminated through global media are adopted and adapted in various regions, resulting in diverse expressions of style that reflect both global influences and local identities.

While deterritorialization and reterritorialization facilitate cultural exchange and innovation, they also raise important questions about cultural homogenization and the loss of local traditions. Critics argue that the dominance of global media, particularly from Western countries, can lead to the erosion of local cultures and identities. The widespread consumption of American media, for example, may result in the adoption of Western values and lifestyles at the expense of indigenous cultural practices.

However, the processes of reterritorialization and cultural hybridity suggest that local cultures are not merely passive recipients of global influences. Instead, they actively engage with and reinterpret these influences, creating new cultural forms that reflect local identities and traditions. This active engagement demonstrates the resilience and adaptability of local cultures in the face of globalization.

To conclude, the concepts of deterritorialization and reterritorialization, as developed by Deleuze and Guattari, provide valuable insights into the dynamics of cultural exchange in an interconnected world. Deterritorialization involves the separation of cultural practices from their original geographic context, while reterritorialization describes their adaptation and integration into new environments. These processes are central to understanding globalization and cultural hybridity, highlighting the fluid and dynamic nature of cultural practices.

The influence of global media on local cultures serves as a compelling case study of these processes. As media products move across borders, they become deterritorialized and are subsequently reterritorialized through localization and adaptation. This interaction results in hybrid cultural forms that blend global influences with local traditions, reflecting the ongoing negotiation between global and local identities.

While concerns about cultural homogenization persist, the resilience and creativity of local cultures in reinterpreting global influences underscore the complex and dynamic nature of cultural exchange. By examining the processes of deterritorialization and reterritorialization, we can better understand how cultures interact, transform, and coexist in our increasingly interconnected world.

11.   HISTORICAL   EXAMPLES   OF DETERRITORIALIZATION

Deterritorialization, a concept articulated by Gilles Deleuze and Félix Guattari, refers to the process by which social, political, or cultural phenomena lose their association with a specific geographic location. Throughout history, various events and movements have exemplified this process, profoundly impacting societies and cultures. Exploring historical instances of deterritorialization provides insight into how such phenomena reshape the world, often leading to significant cultural and political shifts.

One of the earliest and most notable examples of deterritorialization is the spread of the Roman Empire. The Roman Empire, at its height, spanned large parts of Europe, North Africa, and the Middle East, encompassing a multitude of local cultures and societies. As the Romans expanded their territory, they brought with them their own social, political, and cultural practices, often displacing or assimilating local traditions.

The process of Romanization involved the introduction of Roman law, language (Latin), and customs to conquered territories. Local elites were often co-opted into the Roman administrative system, and Roman cities, complete with forums, baths, and amphitheaters, were established across the empire. While the Roman Empire brought infrastructure and administrative efficiency, it also led to the erosion of local identities and traditions. For instance, indigenous languages and practices were often supplanted by Latin and Roman customs, resulting in a loss of cultural diversity. This displacement of local cultures by Roman norms is a clear example of deterritorialization.

Another profound instance of deterritorialization occurred with the transatlantic slave trade. This brutal and dehumanizing trade forcibly removed millions of Africans from their homelands, transporting them to the Americas and other parts of the world. The cultural impact on African societies was immense, as entire communities were uprooted, and social structures were dismantled. The removal of individuals from their native lands and their placement into entirely different geographic and cultural contexts disrupted traditional ways of life and led to a significant loss of cultural heritage.

The deterritorialization caused by the transatlantic slave trade had lasting effects on both African and American societies. In Africa, the removal of a significant portion of the population, particularly young and able-bodied individuals, weakened many societies and economies. Traditional practices, knowledge, and cultural expressions were severely impacted as communities were torn apart. In the Americas, enslaved Africans were forced to adapt to new environments and cultures. Despite this, they managed to retain and transform elements of their cultural heritage, contributing to the rich cultural mosaic of the Americas. African music, dance, religion, and other cultural practices merged with local traditions, creating new hybrid forms that continue to influence cultures worldwide.

Colonialism represents another significant historical instance of deterritorialization. European powers, driven by economic, political, and ideological motivations, established colonies across Africa, Asia, and the Americas. The colonization process involved the imposition of European administrative systems, languages, religions, and cultural practices on indigenous populations. This imposition often led to the displacement and marginalization of indigenous cultures.

In many cases, colonial powers redrew territorial boundaries, grouping disparate ethnic and cultural groups within new political entities. This artificial territorial reorganization often ignored existing social and cultural divisions, leading to long-term conflicts and instability. The imposition of European educational systems, legal frameworks, and religious institutions further disrupted indigenous ways of life, resulting in a significant loss of cultural autonomy.

For example, in India, British colonial rule introduced English as the language of administration and education, significantly impacting local languages and cultural practices. Traditional forms of governance, economic systems, and social structures were altered or replaced by British models. This process of deterritorialization eroded indigenous cultures and identities, leading to a complex legacy that continues to influence Indian society today.

A case study that vividly illustrates the process of deterritorialization is the dissolution of the Ottoman Empire. At its peak, the Ottoman Empire was a vast and diverse multi-ethnic empire that controlled territories in the Middle East, North Africa, and southeastern Europe. The empire maintained a delicate balance of power among various ethnic, religious, and linguistic groups through a system of provincial autonomy and millet (religious community) governance. However, the decline and eventual dissolution of the Ottoman Empire in the early 20th century led to significant cultural and political shifts.

The collapse of the Ottoman Empire was precipitated by a combination of internal weaknesses and external pressures, including military defeats, nationalist movements, and European imperial ambitions. The aftermath of World War I and the subsequent treaties, particularly the Treaty of Sèvres and the Treaty of Lausanne, formalized the partitioning of Ottoman territories among European powers and newly emerging nation-states. This redrawing of boundaries and the creation of new political entities led to the deterritorialization of Ottoman cultural and political structures.

The dissolution of the Ottoman Empire had profound cultural impacts on the people within its former territories. Traditional Ottoman administrative and social systems were replaced by the institutions of the new nation-states or colonial powers. This often involved the imposition of new national identities and the suppression of diverse cultural practices that had been accommodated under Ottoman rule. For example, the establishment of the Republic of Turkey involved a concerted effort to create a homogeneous Turkish national identity, which included policies of language reform, secularization, and the suppression of ethnic and religious minorities.

In the Arab world, the dissolution of the Ottoman Empire and the subsequent colonial mandates led to significant cultural and political shifts. The imposition of European administrative systems and borders disrupted existing social and cultural networks. The creation of artificial states, such as Iraq and Syria, grouped together diverse ethnic and religious communities, leading to long-term tensions and conflicts. This deterritorialization of Ottoman cultural and political structures had lasting repercussions, contributing to the complex and often contentious political landscape of the modern Middle East.

The process of deterritorialization is not only a historical phenomenon but continues to shape contemporary societies. Globalization, characterized by the rapid movement of people, goods, information, and ideas across borders, facilitates the deterritorialization of cultural practices and their subsequent reterritorialization in new contexts. This ongoing dynamic underscores the fluid and interconnected nature of cultures in the modern world.

For example, the migration of people across borders, whether driven by economic opportunities, conflict, or environmental factors, often leads to the deterritorialization of cultural practices. Migrant communities bring their traditions, languages, and customs to new geographic locations, where they interact with and adapt to local cultures. This process can result in the creation of hybrid cultural forms that reflect both the migrants' heritage and the influences of their new environment.

Similarly, the global spread of technology and media has facilitated the deterritorialization of cultural content. Television shows, films, music, and digital platforms disseminate cultural products worldwide, allowing them to be consumed and interpreted by diverse audiences. This global dissemination often leads to the adaptation and localization of cultural content, as seen in the popularity of American television shows and films in different countries. Local media industries may produce their versions of popular global content, incorporating regional flavors and reflecting local cultural contexts.

The historical instances of deterritorialization, from the spread of the Roman Empire and the transatlantic slave trade to colonialism and the dissolution of the Ottoman Empire, highlight the transformative impact of these processes on societies and cultures. These examples underscore how the displacement of social, political, and cultural phenomena from their original geographic contexts leads to significant changes and adaptations.

Understanding deterritorialization and its effects is crucial for comprehending the complex dynamics of cultural exchange and globalization. These processes reveal the fluid and interconnected nature of cultural practices, demonstrating how they evolve and adapt in response to changing circumstances. By examining historical and contemporary instances of deterritorialization, we gain valuable insights into the ongoing negotiation between global and local identities, the resilience of cultural traditions, and the creation of new hybrid forms in our interconnected world.

12. HISTORICAL EXAMPLES OF RETERRITORIALIZATION

Reterritorialization is the process by which social, political, or cultural phenomena, after being deterritorialized or displaced from their original geographic contexts, establish new connections and identities in different locations. This concept, as articulated by Gilles Deleuze and Félix Guattari, highlights the dynamic nature of cultural and political identities as they adapt and reformulate in new settings. Examining historical instances of reterritorialization provides valuable insights into how nations, communities, and cultural practices have redefined themselves in the face of displacement and change.

One significant instance of reterritorialization is the re-establishment of national identities in post-colonial regions. During the colonial era, European powers imposed their control over vast territories in Africa, Asia, and the Americas, disrupting local governance, economies, and cultures. The end of colonial rule in the mid-20th century saw the emergence of new nation-states, which had to navigate the complex task of re-establishing national identities that had been suppressed or altered by colonial powers.

For example, India, after gaining independence from British rule in 1947, embarked on a process of reterritorialization. The new Indian state had to forge a cohesive national identity from a diverse and fragmented society composed of multiple languages, religions, and ethnic groups. This reterritorialization involved reviving and integrating indigenous cultural practices, languages, and traditions while also embracing modern democratic values. The Indian constitution, adopted in 1950, reflected this synthesis by promoting secularism, democracy, and social justice, aiming to unify the diverse population under a common national identity.

Similarly, many African nations faced the challenge of reterritorializing their identities post-independence. The arbitrary borders drawn by colonial powers often grouped disparate ethnic and cultural groups within single political entities, leading to tensions and conflicts. Post-colonial leaders sought to re-establish national identities that could unite their populations. In Ghana, for instance, Kwame Nkrumah, the country's first prime minister and president, promoted the idea of Pan-Africanism, advocating for unity among African nations and the revival of African cultural heritage. This reterritorialization process aimed to forge a collective identity that transcended colonial divisions and celebrated the continent's shared history and aspirations.

The reformation of European borders post-World War II presents another significant example of reterritorialization. The devastation of the war and the subsequent political upheavals led to the redrawing of national boundaries and the re-establishment of political identities. The partitioning of Germany into East and West, the creation of new states like Yugoslavia and Czechoslovakia, and the shifting borders of Poland are all instances where reterritorialization played a crucial role in reshaping national identities and political landscapes.

In Germany, the post-war reterritorialization process was particularly complex. Following the defeat of Nazi Germany, the country was divided into occupation zones controlled by the Allied powers. This division eventually led to the establishment of two separate states: the Federal Republic of Germany (West Germany) and the German Democratic Republic (East Germany). Each state underwent a distinct reterritorialization process, with West Germany aligning itself with Western democratic values and market economies, while East Germany adopted Soviet-style socialism. The fall of the Berlin Wall in 1989 and the subsequent reunification of Germany in 1990 marked another phase of reterritorialization, as the country sought to integrate its divided populations and reconcile differing political and social systems into a unified national identity.

The rise of nationalistic movements in formerly colonized regions further illustrates the process of reterritorialization. In the wake of colonial rule, many countries experienced a surge of nationalist sentiments as they sought to reclaim their sovereignty and cultural heritage. These movements often involved a deliberate reassertion of indigenous languages, customs, and historical narratives that had been marginalized or suppressed during colonial times.

In Algeria, the struggle for independence from French colonial rule, which culminated in 1962, was deeply rooted in the reterritorialization of national identity. The Algerian War of Independence was not only a political and military struggle but also a cultural reawakening. The National Liberation Front (FLN), which led the independence movement, emphasized the importance of reclaiming Algerian culture and identity. Post-independence, Algeria undertook efforts to revive Arabic and Berber languages, promote traditional music and art, and reassert its Islamic heritage as central to the national identity.

A particularly compelling case study of reterritorialization is the formation of Israel and the re-establishment of Jewish cultural and religious practices. The establishment of the State of Israel in 1948 represents a significant instance of reterritorialization, as Jewish people from around the world returned to their ancestral homeland after centuries of diaspora.

The Zionist movement, which emerged in the late 19th century, sought to re-establish a Jewish homeland in Palestine. This movement was driven by the desire to create a safe haven for Jews facing persecution and to revive Jewish cultural and religious practices in a land with deep historical and spiritual significance. The Balfour Declaration of 1917, in which the British government expressed support for the establishment of a "national home for the Jewish people" in Palestine, marked a pivotal moment in the reterritorialization process.

The re-establishment of Jewish cultural and religious practices in Israel involved the revival of Hebrew as a spoken language. Hebrew, which had been primarily a liturgical language for centuries, was revitalized and modernized to serve as the national language of the new state. This linguistic reterritorialization was instrumental in unifying diverse Jewish communities from different parts of the world.

The establishment of kibbutzim (collective farms) and moshavim (cooperative agricultural communities) also played a significant role in the reterritorialization of Jewish identity. These communal settlements were based on principles of collective ownership, social equality, and self-reliance, reflecting both traditional Jewish values and modern socialist ideals. The kibbutzim, in particular, became symbols of the pioneering spirit and the connection to the land, central to the Zionist vision.

Moreover, the reterritorialization of Jewish identity in Israel involved the integration of diverse Jewish customs and traditions. Jews from Europe, the Middle East, North Africa, and other regions brought with them their unique cultural practices, which were woven into the fabric of Israeli society. This blending of traditions created a vibrant and multifaceted national culture that reflected the global Jewish diaspora's diversity.

The process of reterritorialization in Israel also involved significant challenges and conflicts. The establishment of the state led to the displacement of Palestinian Arabs, resulting in ongoing conflict and complex political dynamics. The reterritorialization of Jewish identity in Israel has thus been marked by both the revival of cultural and religious practices and the contentious realities of nation-building in a historically and politically fraught region.

Examining these historical instances of reterritorialization reveals the dynamic and multifaceted nature of identity formation in response to displacement and change. The re-establishment of national identities in post-colonial regions, the reformation of European borders post-World War II, the rise of nationalistic movements, and the formation of Israel all demonstrate how communities and nations navigate the complexities of reterritorialization.

These processes highlight the resilience and adaptability of cultural and political identities. They show how identities can be redefined and revitalized in new contexts, drawing on historical legacies, collective memories, and contemporary realities. The reterritorialization of identity involves not only reclaiming and reviving cultural practices but also adapting them to new environments and integrating diverse influences.

Understanding the historical instances of reterritorialization provides valuable insights into the broader dynamics of cultural and political change. It underscores the importance of considering both historical legacies and contemporary contexts in the analysis of identity formation. As societies continue to experience displacement and transformation, the processes of reterritorialization will remain central to the ongoing negotiation and redefinition of cultural and political identities.

In conclusion, reterritorialization is a crucial process in the formation and reformation of cultural and political identities. Historical instances such as the re-establishment of national identities post-colonialism, the reformation of European borders post-World War II, the rise of nationalistic movements, and the formation of Israel illustrate the dynamic nature of this process. These examples demonstrate how communities and nations navigate the complexities of identity formation, drawing on historical legacies, collective memories, and contemporary realities to redefine themselves in new contexts. Understanding these processes provides valuable insights into the broader dynamics of cultural and political change, highlighting the resilience and adaptability of identities in response to displacement and transformation.

13. DETERRITORIALIZATION IN MODERN SOCIETY

Deterritorialization, as defined by Gilles Deleuze and Félix Guattari, refers to the process by which social, political, or cultural phenomena lose their association with a specific geographic location. In contemporary society, this concept is especially pertinent as the forces of globalization, digital communication, and multinational corporations increasingly blur the boundaries that once defined local cultures and economies. Understanding how deterritorialization manifests in modern society reveals the complex dynamics of cultural exchange, identity formation, and economic integration.

One of the most profound manifestations of deterritorialization in contemporary society is the influence of the internet and digital communication on local cultures. The internet has created a global platform where information, ideas, and cultural products can be shared instantaneously across vast distances. This digital interconnectedness has significantly altered how cultures interact and evolve, leading to the blending and reshaping of cultural identities.

Social media platforms like Facebook, Instagram, and Twitter enable individuals from diverse backgrounds to connect, share experiences, and participate in global conversations. These platforms facilitate the dissemination of cultural practices and trends, allowing them to spread rapidly and be adopted by people worldwide. For instance, fashion trends, music genres, and slang terms that originate in one part of the world can quickly gain popularity in other regions, creating a globalized cultural landscape. This phenomenon illustrates the deterritorialization of culture, as local practices and identities become influenced and transformed by global digital interactions.

The rise of digital communication also impacts how people consume media. Streaming services like Netflix and Spotify offer access to a vast array of global content, breaking down geographic barriers to entertainment. Viewers can watch films and TV shows from different countries, while music fans can listen to artists from around the world. This access to diverse cultural products fosters a more interconnected global culture, where local traditions and global influences continuously interact and reshape one another.

Globalization, characterized by the movement of people, ideas, and goods across borders, further exemplifies deterritorialization in modern society. The increased mobility of individuals through migration, travel, and international work has led to the blending of cultures and the creation of multicultural societies. Migrants bring their cultural practices, languages, and traditions to new geographic contexts, where they interact with and adapt to local cultures. This movement results in the deterritorialization of cultural identities, as they become less tied to specific places and more influenced by diverse experiences and environments.

For example, the diaspora communities that form in major cities around the world are prime examples of cultural deterritorialization. In cities like New York, London, and Toronto, neighborhoods are often characterized by their multicultural composition, with residents hailing from various parts of the globe. These communities maintain cultural practices from their countries of origin while also adopting and influencing the local culture. The result is a rich tapestry of hybrid identities that reflect the interconnected nature of modern society.

The movement of ideas and knowledge is another critical aspect of globalization that drives deterritorialization. Academic institutions, research collaborations, and international conferences facilitate the exchange of ideas and innovations across borders. This flow of knowledge contributes to the global intellectual landscape, where ideas are no longer confined to their place of origin but are shared, adapted, and built upon worldwide. This process enhances the collective understanding and fosters innovation, as diverse perspectives and expertise come together to address global challenges.

The impact of multinational corporations on local economies and cultures is a significant factor in the deterritorialization process. Multinational corporations operate in multiple countries, bringing with them standardized products, business practices, and corporate cultures. This presence can profoundly influence local economies and cultural landscapes, often leading to the homogenization of consumer experiences and the erosion of local traditions.

Retail giants like Walmart and fast-food chains like McDonald's exemplify how multinational corporations contribute to deterritorialization. These companies offer standardized products and services that are consistent across different geographic locations, reducing the distinctiveness of local markets. For example, the presence of McDonald's in various countries means that consumers worldwide can experience a similar menu and dining environment, regardless of their location. While this standardization provides convenience and familiarity, it also diminishes the uniqueness of local culinary traditions and dining experiences.

The influence of multinational corporations extends to local labor markets and business practices. The entry of these corporations into local economies often leads to the adoption of global business models and practices, which can displace traditional ways of working and doing business. Small, local businesses may struggle to compete with the resources and efficiencies of multinational corporations, leading to economic and cultural shifts in local communities. This process reflects the deterritorialization of local economies, as they become integrated into the global market and influenced by international corporate practices.

A compelling case study of deterritorialization in modern society is the global spread of fast food culture and its effects on traditional diets. Fast food, characterized by its convenience, standardization, and affordability, has become a ubiquitous part of the global culinary landscape. The proliferation of fast-food chains like McDonald's, KFC, and Burger King illustrates how a cultural practice that originated in one country can spread worldwide, influencing local eating habits and dietary preferences.

The global spread of fast food has had a significant impact on traditional diets in many regions. In countries with rich culinary traditions, the introduction of fast food often leads to changes in eating habits, particularly among younger generations. The convenience and affordability of fast food make it an attractive option for busy urban dwellers, leading to its widespread adoption. However, this shift in dietary preferences can have adverse effects on health and cultural heritage.

In many developing countries, the rise of fast food has been linked to an increase in diet-related health issues, such as obesity, diabetes, and cardiovascular diseases. Traditional diets, which often emphasize fresh, locally sourced ingredients and balanced meals, are increasingly being replaced by fast food, which tends to be high in calories, fat, and sugar. This nutritional transition illustrates the deterritorialization of dietary practices, as global fast-food culture displaces local culinary traditions and contributes to changing health patterns.

The cultural impact of fast food extends beyond dietary habits. The presence of fast-food chains in different countries often brings with it the values and lifestyles associated with fast food culture. For example, the fast-paced, convenience-oriented nature of fast food reflects broader societal shifts towards efficiency and instant gratification. This cultural shift can influence local customs and social practices, such as family meals and communal dining, which may become less common as fast food becomes more prevalent.

However, the process of deterritorialization through fast food is not one-sided. Many fast-food chains adapt their menus to reflect local tastes and preferences, a process known as glocalization. For instance, McDonald's in India offers vegetarian options like the McAloo Tikki burger, while in Japan, it serves items like the Teriyaki Burger. This adaptation illustrates how global cultural practices can be reterritorialized, integrating local elements and creating new hybrid forms that resonate with local consumers. This dynamic process highlights the interplay between global and local influences, where deterritorialization leads to the re-establishment of cultural practices in new contexts.

In conclusion, deterritorialization manifests in contemporary society through various mechanisms, including the influence of the internet and digital communication, globalization, and the impact of multinational corporations. These forces contribute to the displacement and transformation of local cultures, economies, and identities, creating a complex and interconnected global landscape. The case study of the global spread of fast food culture exemplifies how cultural practices can become deterritorialized, influencing traditional diets and social customs worldwide. Understanding these processes provides valuable insights into the ongoing negotiation between global and local identities in our increasingly interconnected world. As cultures continue to interact and evolve, the dynamics of deterritorialization and reterritorialization will remain central to the analysis of contemporary society.

14. RETERRITORIALIZATION IN MODERN SOCIETY

Reterritorialization, a concept advanced by Gilles Deleuze and Félix Guattari, describes the process by which cultural, social, or political phenomena, after being displaced or deterritorialized, establish new associations and identities in different geographic contexts. In contemporary society, reterritorialization manifests in various ways as local cultures and identities resurge, adapt global influences, and are supported by governmental policies aimed at cultural preservation. This dynamic interplay between global and local forces is vividly illustrated in the rise of regionalism within the European Union (EU) and the emphasis on local governance.

One significant example of reterritorialization in modern society is the resurgence of local cultures and identities in the face of globalization. As global forces increasingly permeate everyday life, there is a concurrent revival of local traditions and identities as communities seek to preserve their unique cultural heritage. This resurgence often emerges as a reaction to the perceived homogenization brought about by globalization, where local practices and values are at risk of being overshadowed by dominant global trends.

In various parts of the world, indigenous communities have been at the forefront of reterritorializing their cultural identities. In Canada, for instance, First Nations, Inuit, and Métis peoples have actively worked to reclaim and revive their languages, traditions, and governance systems. Government initiatives, such as the Truth and Reconciliation Commission and policies supporting indigenous education and language preservation, have played a crucial role in this process. By integrating traditional knowledge and practices into contemporary settings, these communities are re-establishing their cultural identities within the modern Canadian state, thereby illustrating reterritorialization.

Another manifestation of reterritorialization is the adaptation and integration of global influences into local traditions. Globalization facilitates the movement of ideas, goods, and people across borders, leading to the infusion of global elements into local cultures. Rather than merely adopting these influences, many communities creatively integrate them, resulting in new hybrid cultural forms that reflect both local and global identities.

The culinary world offers a rich example of this process. The global spread of sushi, originally a Japanese dish, provides a clear illustration. In countries around the world, sushi has been adapted to local tastes and ingredients, resulting in unique variations such as the California roll in the United States, which uses avocado and crab. This adaptation demonstrates how a global cultural product can be reterritorialized to align with local preferences, creating a new cultural expression that resonates with local consumers while retaining its global origins.

Similarly, music genres like hip-hop have undergone reterritorialization as they spread globally. Originating in the Bronx, New York, hip-hop has been adopted and transformed by artists worldwide, blending with local musical traditions and social contexts. In France, for instance, hip-hop has merged with French urban culture, addressing local social issues and incorporating French language and musical styles. This reterritorialization process has resulted in a distinct form of French hip-hop that maintains the genre's global essence while reflecting local cultural dynamics.

Government policies play a pivotal role in promoting cultural preservation and revival, thereby facilitating reterritorialization. Recognizing the value of cultural diversity, many governments implement policies aimed at preserving and revitalizing local cultures and traditions. These policies often support initiatives in education, the arts, and community development, ensuring that cultural heritage is maintained and adapted to contemporary contexts.

In South Korea, the government's efforts to preserve and promote traditional culture through the "Cultural Properties Protection Law" exemplify reterritorialization supported by policy. This law, established in 1962, aims to protect and promote intangible cultural heritage, such as traditional music, dance, and crafts. The government provides funding and resources to practitioners of these arts, encouraging the transmission of skills and knowledge to younger generations. By integrating these traditions into modern cultural expressions, South Korea has successfully reterritorialized its cultural heritage, ensuring its continued relevance in a globalized world.

In Europe, the rise of regionalism within the European Union (EU) provides a compelling case study of reterritorialization and the emphasis on local governance. The EU, while promoting economic integration and political cooperation among its member states, also recognizes the importance of regional identities and local governance. This recognition is reflected in policies and initiatives that support regional development and cultural preservation.

The EU's commitment to regionalism is evident in its cohesion policy, which aims to reduce disparities between regions and promote balanced development. Through structural funds and investment programs, the EU supports regional initiatives that enhance economic growth, social inclusion, and cultural heritage. These efforts enable regions to leverage their unique assets and identities, fostering a sense of pride and ownership among local populations.

Catalonia in Spain exemplifies the reterritorialization of regional identity within the EU framework. Catalonia has a distinct cultural and linguistic identity, with a strong tradition of regional autonomy. In recent years, there has been a resurgence of Catalan culture and identity, driven by a combination of grassroots movements and supportive government policies. The promotion of the Catalan language in education, media, and public life has been central to this revival. Additionally, cultural festivals, literature, and music celebrating

Catalan heritage have flourished, reinforcing the region's unique identity within the broader Spanish state and the EU.

The reterritorialization of regional identity is also evident in Scotland. Following the devolution of powers from the United Kingdom to the Scottish Parliament in 1999, Scotland has experienced a cultural and political renaissance. The Scottish government has actively promoted Scottish culture, language, and heritage through various initiatives, such as supporting Gaelic language education and funding cultural festivals like the Edinburgh International Festival. These efforts have strengthened Scotland's regional identity and fostered a sense of distinctiveness within the UK and the EU.

The emphasis on local governance within the EU framework supports the reterritorialization of regional identities by empowering regions to make decisions that reflect their unique cultural, social, and economic contexts. This approach not only enhances regional development but also promotes cultural diversity and the preservation of local traditions.

Reterritorialization in modern society illustrates the dynamic interplay between global and local forces, where local cultures and identities resurge, adapt global influences, and are supported by governmental policies aimed at cultural preservation. This process is evident in the resurgence of local cultures and identities in the face of globalization, where communities reclaim and revive their cultural heritage to maintain their distinctiveness.

The adaptation and integration of global influences into local traditions further demonstrate reterritorialization. As global cultural products and practices spread, they are often reinterpreted and incorporated into local contexts, resulting in new hybrid forms that reflect both local and global identities. This dynamic process underscores the resilience and adaptability of cultures in a globalized world.

Government policies play a crucial role in facilitating reterritorialization by promoting cultural preservation and revival. By supporting initiatives in education, the arts, and community development, governments ensure that cultural heritage is maintained and adapted to contemporary contexts. These policies enable communities to preserve their unique identities while participating in the global cultural exchange.

The rise of regionalism within the European Union provides a compelling case study of reterritorialization and the emphasis on local governance. The EU's commitment to regional development and cultural preservation empowers regions to leverage their unique assets and identities, fostering a sense of pride and ownership among local populations. The examples of Catalonia and Scotland illustrate how regions can reterritorialize their identities within the broader framework of the EU, promoting cultural diversity and local governance.

In conclusion, reterritorialization in modern society is a multifaceted process that involves the resurgence of local cultures and identities, the adaptation of global influences, and the support of government policies. This process highlights the dynamic interplay between global and local forces, demonstrating the resilience and adaptability of cultures in a rapidly changing world. By examining examples of reterritorialization, such as the resurgence of local cultures, the integration of global influences, and the rise of regionalism within the EU, we gain valuable insights into how communities navigate and redefine their identities in contemporary contexts. These insights underscore the importance of cultural preservation and the role of local governance in fostering vibrant, diverse, and resilient societies.

15.   DETERRITORIALIZATION   AND RETERRITORIALIZATION IN FICTION

Deterritorialization and reterritorialization are powerful concepts that can be vividly explored through fiction. In literature and media, these processes often serve as central themes that drive narratives, particularly in genres such as science fiction, post-apocalyptic fiction, and dystopian fiction. These genres allow for the exploration of how cultures, societies, and identities are displaced and subsequently redefined in new contexts. A compelling case study of these themes can be found in "The Expanse" series, which offers a rich depiction of human migration and cultural integration in space.

Science fiction frequently uses the concept of space colonization as a form of deterritorialization. As humanity expands beyond Earth, the process of establishing colonies on other planets and moons inherently involves the displacement of familiar cultural, social, and political norms. Space colonization narratives often explore the challenges and opportunities that arise when human societies detach from their terrestrial origins and adapt to new environments.

In many science fiction works, the act of leaving Earth and settling in space prompts characters and societies to rethink their identities and organizational structures. For instance, in Kim Stanley Robinson's "Mars Trilogy," the colonization of Mars involves significant cultural and societal changes. As the Martian settlers develop new ways of living suited to their harsh environment, they gradually detach from Earth's traditions and create a unique Martian identity. This narrative illustrates deterritorialization as the settlers' original cultural practices are displaced by the need to adapt to their new home.

Similarly, in "The Expanse" series by James S.A. Corey, the colonization of the asteroid belt and outer planets serves as a backdrop for exploring themes of deterritorialization. The Belters, inhabitants of the asteroid belt, develop distinct cultural practices, languages, and identities that reflect their separation from Earth and Mars. This cultural evolution exemplifies deterritorialization, as the Belters' way of life is shaped by the unique challenges of living in space.

Post-apocalyptic fiction provides a fertile ground for examining reterritorialization, the process by which new societal norms and structures are established following a catastrophic event. In these narratives, the collapse of existing social orders forces survivors to create new communities and ways of life, often from the remnants of their previous societies.

One of the most prominent examples of reterritorialization in post-apocalyptic fiction is Cormac McCarthy's "The Road." In this bleak narrative, a father and son navigate a devastated landscape, struggling to survive amidst the ruins of civilization. As they encounter other survivors and remnants of the old world, they must constantly adapt and redefine their understanding of morality, trust, and survival. The process of reterritorialization is evident as the characters attempt to establish new norms and values in a world where traditional societal structures have collapsed.

Another example can be found in "The Walking Dead" series, where survivors of a zombie apocalypse must form new communities to navigate their radically changed world. Throughout the series, characters establish various forms of governance, social organization, and cultural practices as they seek stability and security. The fluctuating nature of these new societal norms highlights the ongoing process of reterritorialization, as survivors continuously adapt to their environment and the evolving threats they face.

Dystopian fiction often portrays the displacement of traditional cultures by authoritarian regimes, providing a stark illustration of deterritorialization. In these narratives, oppressive governments impose new social orders that disrupt and displace existing cultural and social practices. The struggle to maintain or reclaim cultural identity in the face of such regimes is a central theme in many dystopian works.

George Orwell's "1984" is a quintessential example of this dynamic. In the novel, the totalitarian regime of Oceania exerts control over all aspects of life, including language, history, and personal relationships. The Party's manipulation of truth and suppression of dissent leads to the deterritorialization of traditional cultural practices and identities. The protagonist, Winston Smith, grapples with the loss of his personal and cultural history as he navigates a society where individual identity is subsumed by the state's ideology.

Margaret Atwood's "The Handmaid's Tale" similarly explores the displacement of traditional cultures by an authoritarian regime. The theocratic government of Gilead imposes strict social and cultural norms, stripping individuals of their previous identities and roles. Women, in particular, are reterritorialized into rigidly defined categories, such as Handmaids, Wives, and Marthas, with little agency or autonomy. The protagonist, Offred, resists this reterritorialization by clinging to memories of her former life and seeking small acts of rebellion.

"The Expanse" series offers a rich case study for analyzing the interplay of deterritorialization and reterritorialization in a fictional context. Set in a future where humanity has colonized the solar system, the series explores themes of migration, cultural integration, and political conflict. The diverse settings of Earth, Mars, and the Belt provide a backdrop for examining how human societies evolve and adapt in new environments.

In "The Expanse," the colonization of the asteroid belt and outer planets leads to significant cultural and social changes. The Belters, who inhabit the asteroid belt, develop distinct cultural practices and identities that reflect their unique environment. Their language, Belter Creole, incorporates elements from various Earth languages, symbolizing the blend of cultures among the Belter population. This linguistic evolution exemplifies deterritorialization, as the Belters' original languages and cultural practices are displaced and transformed by their new context.

The series also explores the reterritorialization of these new identities as Belters seek recognition and autonomy. Throughout the series, the Belters' struggle for political representation and self-determination highlights their efforts to reterritorialize their cultural identity within the broader framework of the solar system's political landscape. This reterritorialization process is marked by the creation of new symbols, traditions, and social structures that reflect the Belters' distinct identity and aspirations.

The Martian colony in "The Expanse" provides another example of reterritorialization. As the descendants of Earth's settlers, Martians develop a strong sense of identity centered around their vision of transforming Mars into a habitable planet. This shared goal fosters a collective cultural identity that is distinct from Earth, emphasizing values such as discipline, cooperation, and technological innovation. The Martian society's adaptation to their environment and their efforts to terraform Mars illustrate the reterritorialization of their cultural and social norms.

"The Expanse" also addresses the broader theme of cultural integration in space. The interactions between Earth, Mars, and the Belt highlight the complexities of cultural exchange and adaptation. Characters navigate the challenges of bridging cultural divides and finding common ground amidst political tensions and historical grievances. This dynamic interplay of cultures exemplifies both deterritorialization and reterritorialization, as characters and societies continually adapt to new environments and contexts.

In conclusion, deterritorialization and reterritorialization are powerful concepts that are vividly explored in fiction, particularly in genres such as science fiction, post-apocalyptic fiction, and dystopian fiction. These narratives provide a lens through which to examine how cultures, societies, and identities are displaced and subsequently redefined in new contexts. The exploration of space colonization in science fiction, the re-establishment of societal norms in post-apocalyptic narratives, and the displacement of traditional cultures in dystopian fiction all illustrate these processes.

"The Expanse" series offers a rich case study for analyzing deterritorialization and reterritorialization, depicting human migration and cultural integration in space. The series explores the evolution of distinct cultural identities among the Belters, Martians, and Earthers, highlighting the dynamic interplay of cultural exchange and adaptation. Through its depiction of political conflict, cultural integration, and identity formation, "The Expanse" provides valuable insights into the complex processes of deterritorialization and reterritorialization in a fictional context. These narratives not only entertain but also provoke thought about the resilience and adaptability of human cultures in the face of change and displacement.

16.   THEORETICAL   PERSPECTIVES   ON DETERRITORIALIZATION   AND RETERRITORIALIZATION

Deterritorialization and reterritorialization are pivotal concepts developed by Gilles Deleuze and Félix Guattari in their influential work "A Thousand Plateaus: Capitalism and Schizophrenia" (1987). These processes are essential for understanding the dynamic and fluid nature of cultural, social, and political identities in contemporary society. By providing a theoretical framework for these concepts, we can explore their role in postmodern and postcolonial theory, as well as engage with critiques and debates within academic circles. A case study on the application of these concepts to contemporary globalization will further illustrate their relevance and impact.

Deleuze and Guattari's theories on deterritorialization and reterritorialization are foundational to their broader philosophical project, which challenges traditional, hierarchical models of thought. Deterritorialization refers to the process by which social, political, or cultural phenomena lose their fixed association with a specific geographic location. This can occur through various means, such as the movement of people, the spread of ideas, or technological advancements. Deterritorialization disrupts established structures and boundaries, creating a sense of fluidity and displacement.

Reterritorialization, on the other hand, is the process by which deterritorialized phenomena re-establish new associations with different geographic or conceptual spaces. This involves adapting and integrating into new contexts, leading to the formation of new identities and structures. Reterritorialization reflects the resilience and adaptability of cultural and social practices as they navigate changing environments.

In postmodern theory, deterritorialization and reterritorialization are crucial for understanding the fragmentation and fluidity of contemporary identities. Postmodernism rejects grand narratives and fixed structures, emphasizing instead the multiplicity of perspectives and the instability of meaning. Deterritorialization aligns with this perspective by highlighting the ways in which traditional boundaries and categories are disrupted and redefined. In a postmodern world, identities are no longer tied to stable, singular locations but are constantly shifting and evolving through interactions with diverse influences.

Jean-François Lyotard, a prominent postmodern theorist, discusses the decline of metanarratives in his work "The Postmodern Condition" (1979). He argues that grand narratives, which once provided coherent frameworks for understanding the world, have lost their credibility in the face of pluralism and fragmentation. Deterritorialization captures this shift by illustrating how established structures and meanings are destabilized, leading to a proliferation of localized and contingent narratives. Reterritorialization, in turn, reflects the process by which these new narratives and identities are constructed in response to changing conditions.

In postcolonial theory, deterritorialization and reterritorialization are essential for analyzing the impact of colonialism and globalization on cultural identities. Colonialism involved the deterritorialization of indigenous cultures, as colonial powers imposed their languages, religions, and administrative systems on colonized populations. This displacement disrupted traditional cultural practices and social structures, leading to a loss of autonomy and identity.

Postcolonial theorists such as Homi K. Bhabha and Edward Said have explored the ways in which colonized peoples navigate the legacy of colonialism. Bhabha's concept of hybridity, for instance, highlights the creation of new cultural forms that emerge from the interaction between colonizer and colonized. These hybrid identities are a result of reterritorialization, as indigenous cultures adapt and integrate elements of colonial influence to create new, syncretic practices. Reterritorialization in this context involves reclaiming and redefining cultural identities in ways that reflect both the impact of colonialism and the agency of colonized peoples.

Edward Said's seminal work "Orientalism" (1978) examines how Western representations of the East have constructed and perpetuated colonial power dynamics. Said's analysis reveals how cultural identities are shaped by discursive practices that reflect and reinforce colonial hierarchies. Deterritorialization in this framework involves the displacement of indigenous cultural narratives by colonial representations, while reterritorialization involves the effort to reclaim and reassert indigenous voices and perspectives within the global discourse.

Within academic circles, the concepts of deterritorialization and reterritorialization have generated significant debate and critique. Some scholars argue that these concepts risk oversimplifying complex cultural dynamics by focusing too narrowly on processes of displacement and adaptation. Critics contend that the emphasis on fluidity and hybridity can obscure the persistence of structural inequalities and power imbalances that shape cultural interactions.

Moreover, some scholars challenge the notion that deterritorialization necessarily leads to positive or liberating outcomes. For instance, the deterritorialization of labor markets through globalization has resulted in precarious working conditions and economic exploitation for many workers in developing countries. Reterritorialization in this context often involves integrating into exploitative global supply chains, raising questions about the equity and sustainability of such processes.

Despite these critiques, deterritorialization and reterritorialization remain valuable analytical tools for examining the complexities of contemporary globalization. The case study of globalization provides a concrete application of Deleuze and Guattari's concepts, illustrating their relevance in understanding the shifting dynamics of cultural, social, and economic practices.

Globalization, characterized by the increased movement of people, goods, information, and capital across borders, exemplifies deterritorialization on a grand scale. Traditional boundaries between nations, cultures, and economies are increasingly permeable, leading to the displacement and reconfiguration of identities and practices. The spread of information technology, global trade, and transnational migration all contribute to this process.

The global spread of information technology, particularly the internet, is a key driver of deterritorialization. Digital communication platforms enable the instantaneous exchange of ideas and cultural products across vast distances, disrupting established cultural boundaries. Social media platforms like Facebook, Twitter, and Instagram facilitate the dissemination of cultural practices and trends, allowing them to reach global audiences. This digital interconnectedness exemplifies deterritorialization, as local cultures and identities become influenced by global interactions.

Reterritorialization in the context of globalization involves the adaptation and integration of global influences into local contexts. For example, the global popularity of K-pop, South Korean pop music, illustrates how local cultural products can achieve global reach and influence. K-pop's success involves adapting Western pop music elements while retaining distinct Korean cultural aspects, creating a hybrid form that resonates with both local and international audiences. This process reflects reterritorialization, as K-pop integrates global influences into its cultural identity and establishes new associations within the global music industry.

The movement of people through transnational migration also exemplifies deterritorialization and reterritorialization. Migrants often experience deterritorialization as they leave their home countries and adapt to new cultural and social environments. This displacement involves navigating new cultural norms, languages, and social structures. Reterritorialization occurs as migrants integrate into their host societies, creating new hybrid identities that reflect both their cultural heritage and their new environment. Diaspora communities, such as those in major urban centers like New York and London, illustrate this process as they maintain cultural traditions while also adapting to the local context.

Multinational corporations play a significant role in the deterritorialization and reterritorialization of economic practices. These corporations operate across multiple countries, standardizing products, services, and business practices. This standardization can lead to the homogenization of consumer experiences, as global brands offer consistent products worldwide. For example, fast-food chains like McDonald's provide a uniform dining experience across different countries, reflecting the deterritorialization of local culinary practices.

Reterritorialization in this context involves adapting global business models to local markets. Multinational corporations often modify their products and marketing strategies to align with local preferences and cultural norms. McDonald's, for instance, offers region-specific menu items that cater to local tastes, such as the McAloo Tikki burger in India or the Teriyaki Burger in Japan. This adaptation reflects reterritorialization, as global corporations integrate local elements into their offerings, creating a hybrid consumer experience.

The theoretical framework provided by Deleuze and Guattari's concepts of deterritorialization and reterritorialization offers valuable insights into the dynamic processes shaping contemporary globalization. These concepts help us understand how cultural, social, and economic practices are displaced and redefined in new contexts, highlighting the fluidity and adaptability of identities in a globalized world.

While critiques of these concepts emphasize the need to consider structural inequalities and power dynamics, the framework remains a powerful tool for analyzing the complexities of globalization. By examining how local cultures and identities resurge, adapt global influences, and navigate the interplay between global and local forces, we can gain a deeper understanding of the processes that shape our interconnected world.

In conclusion, deterritorialization and reterritorialization provide a theoretical lens through which to analyze the shifting dynamics of contemporary society. Deleuze and Guattari's concepts illuminate the ways in which identities and practices are displaced and redefined, offering a nuanced understanding of cultural, social, and economic interactions. The application of these concepts to contemporary globalization reveals the complex interplay between global and local forces, highlighting the resilience and adaptability of human societies in the face of change. As we continue to navigate the challenges and opportunities of globalization, these theoretical perspectives remain essential for understanding the processes that shape our world.

17. FUTURE IMPLICATIONS OF DETERRITORIALIZATION AND RETERRITORIALIZATION

Deterritorialization and reterritorialization are dynamic processes that have significantly shaped cultural and social territories throughout history. As we look to the future, it is essential to speculate on the trajectory of these processes, particularly in the context of technological advancements, climate change, and the evolution of national and cultural identities in an increasingly globalized world. By exploring these themes, we can gain insights into how these processes might continue to influence and reshape our societies. A compelling case study in this regard is the potential reterritorialization of climate refugees and the formation of new cultural identities.

Technological advancements are poised to play a crucial role in the future of deterritorialization and reterritorialization. The rapid pace of innovation in areas such as artificial intelligence, virtual reality, and biotechnology is likely to further blur the boundaries between physical and digital spaces, leading to new forms of cultural and social territories.

One significant area where technological advancements are driving deterritorialization is through the proliferation of virtual and augmented reality technologies. These technologies enable users to create and inhabit virtual worlds, where geographic boundaries are rendered irrelevant. In these digital spaces, individuals can interact, collaborate, and share experiences in ways that transcend physical location. This shift has the potential to transform how we perceive and engage with cultural and social territories, leading to the emergence of new, deterritorialized communities and identities.

For example, virtual reality platforms like VRChat and Second Life allow users to create avatars and participate in immersive digital environments. These platforms facilitate the formation of virtual communities that are not bound by geographic constraints. Users from different parts of the world can come together to share interests, collaborate on projects, and build relationships. This digital deterritorialization challenges traditional notions of community and identity, as individuals navigate and integrate multiple virtual and physical spaces.

Artificial intelligence (AI) and machine learning also contribute to deterritorialization by reshaping how we access and consume information. AI algorithms curate personalized content for users, tailoring news, entertainment, and social media feeds to individual preferences. This personalized curation creates echo chambers where individuals are exposed to specific perspectives and cultural content, regardless of their geographic location. While this can foster a sense of connection and belonging, it also raises concerns about cultural homogenization and the erosion of diverse viewpoints.

Biotechnology advancements, such as genetic engineering and biohacking, further complicate the landscape of deterritorialization. These technologies enable individuals to modify their physical bodies and biological identities, challenging traditional notions of human identity and territory. As biohacking communities emerge and individuals experiment with enhancing their physical and cognitive abilities, new forms of identity and community may arise, detached from traditional geographic and cultural anchors.

Climate change is another critical factor that will drive deterritorialization and reterritorialization in the future. The accelerating impacts of climate change, including rising sea levels, extreme weather events, and resource scarcity, are expected to force large-scale migrations and alter geographic and cultural landscapes. These changes will necessitate the redefinition of cultural and social territories as communities adapt to new environmental realities.

One significant implication of climate change is the displacement of populations from vulnerable regions. Coastal areas, small island nations, and regions prone to extreme weather events are particularly at risk. As people are forced to leave their homes and seek refuge in safer areas, the process of deterritorialization will disrupt established cultural and social identities. These climate refugees will need to reterritorialize in new locations, creating opportunities for the formation of new cultural identities and communities.

The reterritorialization of climate refugees will involve the integration of displaced populations into host communities. This integration process will be complex and multifaceted, requiring efforts to preserve cultural heritage while fostering new hybrid identities. Host communities will need to adapt to the influx of new residents, incorporating diverse cultural practices and perspectives into their social fabric. This reterritorialization process will shape the future of cultural and social territories, highlighting the resilience and adaptability of human societies in the face of environmental change.

Predictions on the evolution of national and cultural identities in a globalized world must consider the interplay between technological advancements, climate change, and migration. As deterritorialization and reterritorialization continue to shape cultural and social landscapes, national and cultural identities will likely become more fluid and hybridized.

In a globalized world, the concept of the nation-state is increasingly challenged by transnational flows of people, ideas, and goods. National identities, traditionally tied to geographic boundaries and shared cultural heritage, are becoming more porous and inclusive. The rise of multiculturalism and the increasing prominence of diaspora communities contribute to the redefinition of national identities. These identities will continue to evolve as individuals navigate multiple cultural affiliations and form connections across borders.

Cultural identities will also become more dynamic and multifaceted. The blending of global and local influences will give rise to new hybrid cultural forms that reflect the interconnectedness of contemporary societies. This process of cultural reterritorialization will involve the integration of diverse traditions, languages, and practices, creating rich and complex cultural landscapes.

The case study of climate refugees offers a tangible example of how deterritorialization and reterritorialization might play out in the future. As climate change forces people to migrate, the resulting cultural integration and adaptation processes will shape new identities and communities.

For instance, the displacement of populations from Pacific island nations due to rising sea levels will necessitate the reterritorialization of these communities in new geographic locations. Countries such as New Zealand and Australia, which are likely destinations for climate refugees, will need to develop policies and frameworks to support their integration. This process will involve preserving the cultural heritage of Pacific island communities while fostering new, hybrid identities that reflect the blending of indigenous and host cultures.

The reterritorialization of climate refugees will also require addressing social, economic, and political challenges. Ensuring access to education, healthcare, and employment opportunities for displaced populations will be critical for successful integration. Additionally, fostering social cohesion and addressing potential conflicts between host and refugee communities will be essential for building inclusive and resilient societies.

Technological advancements can play a role in facilitating the reterritorialization of climate refugees. Digital platforms and tools can support cultural preservation and adaptation by providing spaces for virtual communities and cultural exchange. For example, digital storytelling projects and online cultural archives can help displaced populations maintain connections to their cultural heritage while adapting to new environments.

Moreover, technology can support the economic integration of climate refugees by providing access to remote work opportunities and online education. Digital skills training and access to the internet can empower displaced individuals to participate in the global economy and build new livelihoods.

In conclusion, the future trajectory of deterritorialization and reterritorialization will be shaped by technological advancements, climate change, and the evolving dynamics of globalization. These processes will continue to disrupt and redefine cultural and social territories, leading to the formation of new identities and communities. The integration of global influences into local traditions and the resurgence of local cultures in response to global challenges will contribute to the dynamic interplay between deterritorialization and reterritorialization.

The case study of climate refugees highlights the complex and multifaceted nature of these processes. As climate change forces people to migrate, the reterritorialization of displaced populations will involve preserving cultural heritage, fostering new hybrid identities, and addressing social, economic, and political challenges. Technological advancements can support these efforts by providing tools for cultural preservation, economic integration, and social cohesion.

Ultimately, the resilience and adaptability of human societies will be key to navigating the future implications of deterritorialization and reterritorialization. By embracing the dynamic and fluid nature of cultural and social territories, we can build inclusive and resilient communities that thrive in an interconnected and rapidly changing world. Understanding and anticipating these processes will be essential for policymakers, scholars, and communities as they work to address the challenges and opportunities of the future.

18. REFERENCES

Deterritorialization and reterritorialization are significant concepts developed by Gilles Deleuze and Félix Guattari, primarily in their influential work "A Thousand Plateaus: Capitalism and Schizophrenia" (1987). These processes have been extensively discussed in various academic books and journal articles, providing a robust theoretical framework for understanding cultural, social, and political dynamics in contemporary society. Here are some key references that delve into these concepts:

1. Deleuze, G., & Guattari, F. (1987). "A Thousand Plateaus: Capitalism and Schizophrenia." Minneapolis: University of Minnesota Press.

This seminal work by Deleuze and Guattari introduces and elaborates on the concepts of deterritorialization and reterritorialization, providing the foundational framework for these processes. The book explores how social, political, and cultural phenomena are continuously displaced and redefined in various contexts.

2. Bhabha, H. K. (1994). "The Location of Culture." London: Routledge.

Homi K. Bhabha's work on postcolonial theory discusses concepts related to deterritorialization and reterritorialization, particularly through his analysis of hybridity and cultural negotiation. Bhabha explores how colonized peoples navigate and redefine their identities in response to colonial displacement.

3. Said, E. W. (1978). "Orientalism." New York: Pantheon Books.

Edward Said's "Orientalism" examines how Western representations of the East have constructed and perpetuated colonial power dynamics. The book provides insights into the processes of deterritorialization and reterritorialization as they relate to cultural identities and discursive practices.

4. Lyotard, J. F. (1984). "The Postmodern Condition: A Report on Knowledge." Minneapolis: University of Minnesota Press.

Jean-François Lyotard's exploration of postmodernity highlights the decline of metanarratives and the fragmentation of cultural identities. His work aligns with the concept of deterritorialization, as it emphasizes the destabilization of established structures and meanings.

5. Brenner, N., Jessop, B., Jones, M., & MacLeod, G. (Eds.). (2003). "State/Space: A Reader." Malden, MA: Blackwell Publishing.

This edited volume includes essays that discuss the implications of deterritorialization and reterritorialization in the context of state space and globalization. The contributors analyze how these processes affect political, economic, and social structures.

6. Ong, A., & Collier, S. J. (Eds.). (2005). "Global Assemblages: Technology, Politics, and Ethics as Anthropological Problems." Malden, MA: Blackwell Publishing.

This collection of essays examines the interplay between globalization and local practices, focusing on how technological advancements and political changes drive processes of deterritorialization and reterritorialization. The book provides case studies from various regions, highlighting the dynamic nature of cultural and social territories.

7. Hardt, M., & Negri, A. (2000). "Empire." Cambridge, MA: Harvard University Press.

Michael Hardt and Antonio Negri's "Empire" explores the global dynamics of power and control, discussing how contemporary forms of imperialism involve deterritorialization and reterritorialization. The authors analyze the shifting nature of sovereignty and cultural identity in the context of globalization.

8. Appadurai, A. (1996). "Modernity at Large: Cultural Dimensions of Globalization." Minneapolis: University of Minnesota Press.

Arjun Appadurai's work on globalization discusses the cultural flows and disjunctures that drive deterritorialization and reterritorialization. He introduces the concept of "scapes" to describe the various dimensions of global cultural interactions.

9. Grosz, E. (1994). "Volatile Bodies: Toward a Corporeal Feminism." Bloomington: Indiana University Press.

Elizabeth Grosz's feminist theory engages with Deleuze and Guattari's ideas, exploring how deterritorialization and reterritorialization relate to the body and identity. Her work examines the fluidity and multiplicity of corporeal experiences.

10. Harvey, D. (1989). "The Condition of Postmodernity: An Enquiry into the Origins of Cultural Change." Oxford: Blackwell.

David Harvey's analysis of postmodernity includes discussions of spatial reconfiguration and the impacts of globalization on cultural and social territories. He explores how processes of deterritorialization and reterritorialization shape contemporary urban and cultural landscapes.

CHAPTER 3: ASSEMBLAGES

19 INTRODUCTION TO ASSEMBLAGES

An assemblage is a concept that refers to a collection or gathering of heterogeneous elements that interact and form a functional whole. It is a dynamic and flexible framework that encompasses various components, ranging from material objects to social practices, institutions, and discourses. The concept emphasizes the interconnectedness and interdependence of these elements, highlighting how their interactions create emergent properties and patterns that cannot be reduced to the sum of their parts.

The philosophical origins of the concept of assemblages can be traced back to the work of Gilles Deleuze and Félix Guattari, particularly in their seminal text "A Thousand Plateaus: Capitalism and Schizophrenia" (1987). Deleuze and Guattari's theory of assemblages, or "agencements" in French, provides a novel way of thinking about the complexity and fluidity of social, cultural, and political phenomena. Their ideas draw from a rich intellectual tradition that includes elements of structuralism, post-structuralism, and systems theory.

Deleuze and Guattari's theory of assemblages emerged as a critique of traditional hierarchical and essentialist models of understanding social and cultural phenomena. They sought to move beyond binary oppositions and fixed categories, proposing instead a more nuanced and dynamic approach. Assemblages are characterized by their capacity for constant change, reconfiguration, and adaptation. They are composed of diverse elements that can come together in different ways, forming temporary and contingent arrangements.

Assemblages are not fixed or static entities but are always in a state of becoming. This process-oriented perspective emphasizes the importance of interactions, flows, and transformations. Elements within an assemblage are not bound by rigid structures but are connected through complex networks of relations. These relations can be material, such as physical objects and technologies, or immaterial, such as ideas, beliefs, and social practices. The interactions between these elements give rise to new properties and patterns, making assemblages inherently dynamic and unpredictable.

The concept of assemblages has gained significant importance in various fields, including sociology, anthropology, and philosophy. In sociology, assemblages offer a way to understand the complexity of social life by focusing on the interactions and connections between different elements. This approach allows sociologists to move beyond reductionist explanations and consider the emergent properties of social phenomena. For example, urban sociology can use the concept of assemblages to analyze how diverse elements such as architecture, infrastructure, social practices, and economic activities come together to shape the dynamics of urban spaces.

In anthropology, assemblages provide a framework for studying cultural practices and institutions. Anthropologists can use this concept to explore how different elements, such as rituals, artifacts, symbols, and social norms, interact to create and sustain cultural systems. Assemblages allow for a more holistic understanding of culture, recognizing the interplay between material and immaterial aspects. This approach is particularly useful for analyzing cultural change and adaptation, as it emphasizes the fluid and contingent nature of cultural assemblages.

In philosophy, the concept of assemblages challenges traditional metaphysical notions of fixed essences and stable identities. Deleuze and Guattari's theory of assemblages is rooted in a process-oriented ontology that prioritizes becoming over being. This perspective has influenced various strands of contemporary philosophy, including post-structuralism, new materialism, and speculative realism. Assemblages provide a way to think about the interconnectedness of different entities and the emergent properties that arise from their interactions.

Deleuze and Guattari's theory of assemblages is central to their broader philosophical project, which seeks to understand the complexity and multiplicity of reality. In "A Thousand Plateaus," they introduce the concept of the rhizome as a metaphor for the interconnected and non-hierarchical nature of assemblages. Rhizomes, like assemblages, are characterized by their capacity for growth, adaptation, and transformation. They contrast rhizomes with arborescent (tree-like) structures, which represent hierarchical and linear models of organization.

According to Deleuze and Guattari, assemblages are composed of two main dimensions: the "machinic" and the "collective assemblage of enunciation." The machinic dimension refers to the material and technical components of an assemblage, including physical objects, technologies, and infrastructure. These elements interact to produce certain functions and effects. The collective assemblage of enunciation, on the other hand, encompasses the immaterial aspects, such as language, discourses, and social practices. It involves the ways in which meaning is produced, communicated, and circulated within an assemblage.

A key feature of assemblages is their capacity for deterritorialization and reterritorialization. Deterritorialization involves the displacement or disruption of established relations and structures within an assemblage. It can occur through various processes, such as technological innovations, social movements, or environmental changes. Reterritorialization, in contrast, involves the re-establishment of new relations and structures. This dynamic interplay between deterritorialization and reterritorialization is central to the fluid and adaptive nature of assemblages.

The concept of assemblages has been applied to various contemporary issues and phenomena. For example, in the study of globalization, assemblages provide a framework for analyzing the complex and interconnected nature of global networks. Researchers can explore how different elements, such as transnational corporations, financial markets, migration flows, and communication technologies, come together to shape the dynamics of globalization. This approach allows for a more nuanced understanding of the multiple and contingent processes that constitute globalization.

In the field of political ecology, assemblages are used to analyze the interactions between human and non-human actors in environmental systems. Researchers can examine how different elements, such as ecosystems, technologies, policies, and social practices, interact to produce environmental outcomes. This approach emphasizes the interdependence of social and ecological systems and the importance of considering both human and non-human agency.

The concept of assemblages also has significant implications for understanding power and agency. Traditional models of power often focus on hierarchical structures and centralized control. In contrast, the assemblage framework highlights the distributed and relational nature of power. Power is not concentrated in a single entity but is dispersed across the different elements and interactions within an assemblage. This perspective allows for a more complex and dynamic understanding of power relations.

A case study that illustrates Deleuze and Guattari's theory of assemblages is the analysis of urban environments. Cities can be seen as complex assemblages composed of diverse elements, including buildings, infrastructure, technologies, social practices, and economic activities. These elements interact in various ways, producing the emergent properties and dynamics of urban life.

Urban assemblages are characterized by their capacity for constant change and adaptation. For example, technological innovations, such as the introduction of smart technologies and digital platforms, can lead to the deterritorialization of established urban practices and structures. These changes create new possibilities for interaction, communication, and governance within the city. Reterritorialization occurs as new relations and structures are established, integrating the technological innovations into the urban assemblage.

The concept of assemblages allows for a more holistic and integrated analysis of urban environments. Researchers can explore how different elements, such as transportation systems, housing policies, social networks, and cultural practices, interact to shape the dynamics of the city. This approach moves beyond reductionist explanations and considers the emergent properties of urban assemblages.

In conclusion, the concept of assemblages provides a powerful theoretical framework for understanding the complexity and fluidity of social, cultural, and political phenomena. Originating from the work of Deleuze and Guattari, assemblages emphasize the interconnectedness and interdependence of diverse elements. They challenge traditional hierarchical and essentialist models, offering a more nuanced and dynamic perspective.

Assemblages have significant implications for various fields, including sociology, anthropology, and philosophy. They provide a way to analyze the emergent properties of social life, the interactions between material and immaterial elements, and the processes of deterritorialization and reterritorialization. By focusing on the relational and process-oriented nature of reality, assemblages offer valuable insights into the complexity and multiplicity of contemporary issues and phenomena. The case study of urban environments illustrates how the concept of assemblages can be applied to analyze the dynamic and adaptive nature of cities. Understanding assemblages is crucial for navigating and addressing the challenges and opportunities of an increasingly interconnected and complex world.

20. THEORETICAL FOUNDATIONS OF ASSEMBLAGES

The concept of assemblages, as developed by Gilles Deleuze and Félix Guattari, provides a sophisticated and dynamic framework for understanding the complexity and fluidity of various phenomena in contemporary society. This theoretical foundation emphasizes the interconnectedness and interdependence of diverse elements, highlighting how these interactions give rise to emergent properties that cannot be reduced to the sum of their parts. To gain a deeper understanding of this concept, it is essential to explore Deleuze and Guattari's work on assemblages, compare assemblages with traditional structures or systems, and examine the role of heterogeneity and multiplicity in forming assemblages. Additionally, a case study comparing assemblages with traditional organizational structures in companies will illustrate these theoretical principles in practice.

Deleuze and Guattari's work on assemblages is primarily articulated in their influential text "A Thousand Plateaus: Capitalism and Schizophrenia" (1987). In this work, they introduce the concept of assemblages, or "agencements" in French, as a way to move beyond hierarchical and essentialist models of understanding social, cultural, and political phenomena. Assemblages are characterized by their capacity for constant change, reconfiguration, and adaptation. They are composed of diverse elements that come together in various ways to form temporary and contingent arrangements.

Assemblages are not fixed or static entities but are always in a state of becoming. This process-oriented perspective emphasizes the importance of interactions, flows, and transformations. Elements within an assemblage are not bound by rigid structures but are connected through complex networks of relations. These relations can be material, such as physical objects and technologies, or immaterial, such as ideas, beliefs, and social practices. The interactions between these elements give rise to new properties and patterns, making assemblages inherently dynamic and unpredictable.

One of the key contributions of Deleuze and Guattari's theory is their critique of traditional structures or systems. Traditional models often rely on hierarchical and linear organization, where elements are arranged in a top-down fashion, and their roles and functions are predefined. These models tend to emphasize stability, control, and predictability, often at the expense of flexibility and innovation.

In contrast, assemblages emphasize the importance of heterogeneity and multiplicity. Heterogeneity refers to the diversity of elements that make up an assemblage, including different types of actors, materials, and practices. Multiplicity refers to the various ways these elements can come together and interact, creating a range of possible configurations. This focus on heterogeneity and multiplicity allows assemblages to adapt and respond to changing conditions, making them more resilient and innovative than traditional structures.

Assemblages are also characterized by their capacity for deterritorialization and reterritorialization. Deterritorialization involves the displacement or disruption of established relations and structures within an assemblage. It can occur through various processes, such as technological innovations, social movements, or environmental changes. Reterritorialization, in contrast, involves the re-establishment of new relations and structures. This dynamic interplay between deterritorialization and reterritorialization is central to the fluid and adaptive nature of assemblages.

The role of heterogeneity and multiplicity in forming assemblages is crucial for understanding their dynamic nature. Heterogeneity ensures that an assemblage is composed of a diverse range of elements, each bringing its unique properties and capabilities. This diversity allows for a greater range of interactions and potential configurations, enhancing the assemblage's adaptability and resilience.

Multiplicity refers to the various ways these heterogeneous elements can come together and interact. This concept highlights the non-linear and contingent nature of assemblages, where different combinations of elements can produce different outcomes. The emphasis on multiplicity allows for a more nuanced understanding of how assemblages function and evolve, recognizing the importance of context and contingency in shaping their dynamics.

To illustrate these theoretical principles in practice, it is useful to compare assemblages with traditional organizational structures in companies. Traditional organizational structures are typically hierarchical, with clearly defined roles and responsibilities arranged in a top-down fashion. These structures emphasize stability, control, and predictability, often through standardized procedures and centralized decision-making.

In contrast, organizational assemblages are characterized by their flexibility, adaptability, and emphasis on innovation. These organizations are composed of diverse elements, including employees, technologies, processes, and external stakeholders. The interactions between these elements are dynamic and contingent, allowing the organization to respond more effectively to changing conditions.

For example, consider a traditional manufacturing company with a hierarchical structure. In this company, decision-making is centralized, with managers at the top making key decisions and directing the activities of lower-level employees. Roles and responsibilities are clearly defined, and procedures are standardized to ensure efficiency and control.

Now, compare this with a technology startup operating as an organizational assemblage. In this startup, decision-making is more decentralized, with teams and individuals given greater autonomy to make decisions and experiment with new ideas. The organization is composed of diverse elements, including software developers, designers, marketing professionals, and external partners. These elements interact in various ways, creating a range of possible configurations and outcomes.

The startup's emphasis on heterogeneity and multiplicity allows it to adapt more quickly to changes in the market, experiment with new technologies, and innovate more effectively. For example, if a new technological trend emerges, the startup can quickly reconfigure its teams and processes to capitalize on the opportunity. This adaptability contrasts with the traditional manufacturing company, which may be slower to respond due to its rigid hierarchical structure and standardized procedures.

The dynamic nature of organizational assemblages also allows for more effective integration of new technologies and practices. In the startup, new technologies can be incorporated into existing processes and workflows in various ways, creating new opportunities for innovation and improvement. In contrast, the traditional manufacturing company may struggle to integrate new technologies due to its standardized procedures and centralized decision-making.

Another key difference between assemblages and traditional structures is the approach to power and control. In traditional hierarchical structures, power is concentrated at the top, with managers exerting control over lower-level employees. This top-down approach can limit creativity and innovation, as employees may be less motivated to experiment and take risks.

In organizational assemblages, power is more distributed, with teams and individuals given greater autonomy to make decisions and take initiative. This distribution of power encourages creativity and innovation, as employees feel more empowered to experiment and pursue new ideas. The dynamic interactions between different elements of the assemblage create opportunities for emergent properties and patterns, enhancing the organization's overall adaptability and resilience.

The comparison between assemblages and traditional organizational structures highlights the advantages of adopting an assemblage approach in contemporary companies. By emphasizing heterogeneity, multiplicity, and dynamic interactions, organizational assemblages can respond more effectively to changing conditions, integrate new technologies and practices, and foster a culture of creativity and innovation.

In conclusion, the theoretical foundations of assemblages, as developed by Deleuze and Guattari, provide a sophisticated and dynamic framework for understanding the complexity and fluidity of various phenomena in contemporary society. Assemblages emphasize the interconnectedness and interdependence of diverse elements, highlighting how these interactions give rise to emergent properties that cannot be reduced to the sum of their parts.

By comparing assemblages with traditional structures or systems, we can appreciate the advantages of adopting an assemblage approach, particularly in terms of adaptability, resilience, and innovation. The emphasis on heterogeneity and multiplicity allows assemblages to respond more effectively to changing conditions and integrate new technologies and practices.

The case study comparing assemblages with traditional organizational structures in companies illustrates these theoretical principles in practice. Organizational assemblages, with their flexible and dynamic nature, offer significant advantages over traditional hierarchical structures, particularly in terms of fostering creativity, innovation, and adaptability.

Understanding the theoretical foundations of assemblages is crucial for navigating and addressing the challenges and opportunities of an increasingly interconnected and complex world. By adopting an assemblage approach, organizations and individuals can better respond to the dynamic and contingent nature of contemporary society, enhancing their ability to innovate and thrive in a rapidly changing environment.

21. ASSEMBLAGES IN NATURE

Assemblages, a concept developed by Gilles Deleuze and Félix Guattari, refer to collections of heterogeneous elements that interact and form functional wholes. This framework is particularly useful for understanding the complexity and interdependence of natural systems. In nature, assemblages are evident in ecosystems, where living organisms interact with each other and their physical environments to create dynamic, interconnected networks. This discussion will explore ecosystems as assemblages, the interaction of biotic (living) and abiotic (non-living) components, the role of symbiotic relationships in forming natural assemblages, and provide a detailed case study of coral reefs as complex assemblages of marine life.

Ecosystems represent some of the most profound examples of natural assemblages. An ecosystem is a biological community of interacting organisms and their physical environment. It encompasses all living things (biotic components) and non-living things (abiotic components) in a particular area, functioning together as a unit. These components form intricate networks of relationships that drive the processes essential for life, such as energy flow, nutrient cycling, and ecosystem regulation.

The interaction of biotic and abiotic components in an ecosystem illustrates the concept of assemblages. Biotic components include plants, animals, fungi, and microorganisms, each playing specific roles within the ecosystem. For instance, plants (producers) convert solar energy into chemical energy through photosynthesis, providing a primary energy source for herbivores (primary consumers). Herbivores, in turn, become prey for carnivores (secondary consumers), creating a complex web of energy transfer.

Abiotic components, such as sunlight, water, air, soil, and minerals, provide the physical context in which biotic components live and interact. These non-living elements influence the growth, reproduction, and survival of living organisms. For example, the availability of sunlight and water directly affects plant growth, which in turn impacts the food supply for herbivores and subsequently the entire food web. Soil composition and nutrient availability also play critical roles in determining the types of plants that can thrive in an area, influencing the structure and diversity of the ecosystem.

The interactions between biotic and abiotic components create feedback loops that regulate ecosystem functions. For instance, plants influence the carbon cycle by absorbing carbon dioxide during photosynthesis and releasing oxygen. Decomposers, such as bacteria and fungi, break down dead organic matter, returning nutrients to the soil and maintaining soil fertility. These interactions highlight the interconnectedness and interdependence of ecosystem components, characteristic of assemblages.

Symbiotic relationships are essential for forming and maintaining natural assemblages. Symbiosis refers to the close and often long-term interaction between different biological species. These relationships can be mutualistic (both species benefit), commensalistic (one species benefits without affecting the other), or parasitic (one species benefits at the expense of the other). Symbiotic relationships enhance the stability and resilience of ecosystems by fostering cooperation and resource sharing among species.

Mutualistic relationships are particularly significant in natural assemblages. For example, the relationship between flowering plants and pollinators (such as bees, birds, and bats) is a classic mutualistic interaction. Plants provide nectar as a food source for pollinators, while pollinators assist in the plant's reproductive process by transferring pollen from one flower to another. This mutualism enhances the reproductive success of plants and ensures a food supply for pollinators, contributing to the stability and diversity of the ecosystem.

Another example of mutualism is the relationship between mycorrhizal fungi and plant roots. Mycorrhizal fungi colonize plant roots and extend their hyphae into the soil, increasing the surface area for nutrient and water absorption. In return, the fungi receive carbohydrates produced by the plant through photosynthesis. This relationship enhances plant growth and resilience, particularly in nutrient-poor soils, and supports a diverse range of plant species within the ecosystem.

Parasitic relationships, though often seen as negative, also play a crucial role in natural assemblages. Parasites can regulate host populations, preventing any single species from becoming too dominant and promoting biodiversity. For example, the presence of parasites in a predator population can limit their numbers, reducing the predation pressure on prey species and allowing a more diverse range of species to coexist.

Commensalistic relationships, where one species benefits while the other is unaffected, also contribute to the complexity of natural assemblages. An example is epiphytic plants, such as orchids, which grow on the surfaces of trees. The epiphytes benefit by gaining access to sunlight without harming the host tree, adding to the structural complexity and biodiversity of the ecosystem.

A detailed case study of coral reefs illustrates the complexity and functionality of natural assemblages. Coral reefs are among the most diverse and productive ecosystems on Earth, often referred to as the "rainforests of the sea." They are formed by the calcium carbonate skeletons of coral polyps, tiny marine animals that live in colonies. Coral reefs provide habitat, food, and protection for a vast array of marine life, creating a complex web of interactions.

Coral reefs are exemplary assemblages due to the intricate relationships between their biotic and abiotic components. The primary builders of coral reefs are coral polyps, which form symbiotic relationships with zooxanthellae, photosynthetic algae living within their tissues. The algae provide the corals with nutrients produced through photosynthesis, while the corals offer the algae a protected environment and access to sunlight. This mutualistic relationship is crucial for the growth and health of coral reefs, as the energy produced by the algae enables the corals to build their calcium carbonate skeletons.

In addition to corals and zooxanthellae, coral reefs support a diverse range of organisms, including fish, mollusks, crustaceans, sponges, and seaweeds. These organisms interact in various ways, creating a complex network of relationships. Fish, for instance, play essential roles in coral reef ecosystems by controlling algal growth, preying on invertebrates, and serving as prey for larger predators. Herbivorous fish, such as parrotfish and surgeonfish, graze on algae, preventing them from overgrowing and smothering the corals. Predatory fish, such as groupers and snappers, help maintain the balance of species within the reef by preying on smaller fish and invertebrates.

The abiotic components of coral reefs, such as water temperature, light availability, and nutrient levels, significantly influence their structure and function. Coral reefs thrive in warm, clear, and nutrient-poor waters, where the conditions are optimal for coral growth and zooxanthellae photosynthesis. Changes in these abiotic factors, such as increased water temperature or pollution, can have profound impacts on coral reef health and resilience. For example, elevated water temperatures can cause coral bleaching, a phenomenon where corals expel their symbiotic algae, leading to a loss of color and vital nutrients. Prolonged bleaching events can result in coral mortality and the degradation of the reef ecosystem.

Coral reefs also exhibit symbiotic relationships beyond corals and zooxanthellae. Cleaner fish and shrimp provide cleaning services to larger fish by removing parasites and dead skin from their bodies. This mutualistic interaction benefits the cleaner species by providing them with a food source, while the cleaned fish gain health benefits from parasite removal. These relationships contribute to the overall health and stability of the coral reef assemblage.

Human activities, such as overfishing, pollution, and climate change, pose significant threats to coral reef assemblages. Overfishing disrupts the balance of species within the reef, leading to the decline of key functional groups, such as herbivores and predators. Pollution from agricultural runoff, sewage, and plastic waste introduces harmful substances into the reef environment, affecting water quality and the health of marine organisms. Climate change, through rising sea temperatures and ocean acidification, exacerbates coral bleaching and reduces the ability of corals to build their skeletons.

Conservation efforts aimed at protecting coral reef assemblages focus on mitigating these threats and promoting the resilience of the reefs. Marine protected areas (MPAs) restrict human activities, such as fishing and coastal development, to safeguard critical habitats and allow ecosystems to recover. Restoration projects involve active interventions, such as coral gardening and transplantation, to replenish degraded reefs and enhance their capacity to withstand environmental stressors. Public awareness and education campaigns aim to reduce pollution and promote sustainable practices, encouraging individuals and communities to take action in protecting coral reefs.

In conclusion, assemblages provide a powerful framework for understanding the complexity and interdependence of natural systems. Ecosystems, as assemblages of living organisms and their environments, illustrate the dynamic interactions between biotic and abiotic components. Symbiotic relationships play a crucial role in forming and maintaining natural assemblages, enhancing their stability and resilience. Coral reefs serve as a compelling case study, showcasing the intricate relationships and interactions that characterize these diverse and productive ecosystems. By recognizing the importance of assemblages in nature, we can better appreciate the interconnectedness of life and the need for holistic approaches to conservation and environmental management.

22. ASSEMBLAGES IN SOCIETY

Assemblages, as conceptualized by Gilles Deleuze and Félix Guattari, offer a framework for understanding the dynamic and interconnected nature of various phenomena. In social contexts, assemblages form through the interactions of individuals, organizations, and technologies, creating complex networks that are constantly evolving. This discussion explores how social networks, urban environments, and the forces of globalization contribute to the formation of social assemblages, with a detailed case study on the rise of smart cities and their integration of technology, people, and services.

Social networks are prime examples of assemblages in society. They consist of individuals, organizations, and technologies that interact to form intricate webs of relationships and communication. Social networks are not static; they are dynamic systems that evolve as new connections are made and old ones dissolve. The interactions within these networks generate emergent properties that shape social behavior, influence public opinion, and drive collective action.

The digital age has profoundly transformed social networks by introducing new technologies that facilitate communication and connectivity. Platforms such as Facebook, Twitter, and LinkedIn enable individuals to connect with others across vast distances, creating global networks that transcend traditional geographic boundaries. These digital platforms function as assemblages, bringing together diverse elements such as users, software algorithms, data, and hardware infrastructure. The interactions within these networks are shaped by both human agency and technological mediation, resulting in complex patterns of information flow and social influence.

For instance, social media platforms allow users to share content, form groups, and participate in discussions, creating virtual communities based on shared interests or goals. These online communities often have significant real-world impacts, such as organizing social movements, influencing political campaigns, or fostering professional collaborations. The assemblage of individuals, digital tools, and communication practices within social networks highlights the interconnectedness and interdependence of these elements in shaping social phenomena.

Urban environments also exemplify the concept of assemblages, characterized by the interplay of infrastructure, people, and policies. Cities are dynamic systems where diverse elements interact to create complex urban landscapes. The physical infrastructure of a city, including buildings, roads, public transportation, and utilities, forms the backbone of urban life. However, the functioning of a city relies on more than just its physical components; it also depends on the people who inhabit and navigate these spaces, as well as the policies and regulations that govern urban activities.

Urban assemblages are shaped by the interactions between these various elements. For example, the design and layout of urban infrastructure influence patterns of movement and social interaction. Public transportation systems connect different parts of a city, facilitating the flow of people and goods. Zoning laws and urban planning policies determine the distribution of residential, commercial, and industrial areas, impacting economic activities and social dynamics. The presence of public spaces such as parks and plazas provides venues for social gatherings, cultural events, and civic engagement.

The complexity of urban assemblages is further heightened by the diversity of urban populations. Cities are often characterized by a mix of different cultural, ethnic, and socioeconomic groups, each contributing to the richness of urban life. The interactions between these groups, along with their engagement with the physical and institutional infrastructure of the city, create a constantly evolving urban landscape. This dynamic interplay highlights the importance of considering multiple perspectives and factors in understanding urban assemblages.

Globalization has also played a crucial role in forming new social assemblages. The increased movement of people, goods, information, and capital across borders has led to the creation of transnational networks and interconnected communities. Globalization facilitates the deterritorialization of social and cultural practices, allowing them to spread and adapt in new contexts. As a result, new assemblages emerge, characterized by the blending of local and global influences.

One significant impact of globalization is the rise of transnational communities, where individuals maintain connections with multiple countries and cultures. These communities often form through migration, trade, or digital communication, creating networks that span across different geographic regions. For example, diasporic communities, such as the Indian diaspora in the United States or the Chinese diaspora in Southeast Asia, maintain strong ties with their countries of origin while integrating into their host societies. These transnational assemblages are shaped by the interactions between cultural traditions, economic activities, and social networks, resulting in hybrid identities and practices.

The integration of global markets has also led to the formation of economic assemblages that connect producers, consumers, and intermediaries across different countries. Global supply chains, for instance, involve complex networks of manufacturers, suppliers, logistics providers, and retailers, each contributing to the production and distribution of goods. These economic assemblages are influenced by various factors, including trade policies, technological innovations, and consumer preferences, creating a dynamic and interconnected global economy.

The rise of smart cities provides a compelling case study of how assemblages form through the integration of technology, people, and services. Smart cities use digital technologies to enhance urban living, improve efficiency, and promote sustainability. The concept of a smart city involves the integration of various technological systems, such as data analytics, the Internet of Things (IoT), and artificial intelligence, with urban infrastructure and services.

In a smart city, different elements come together to form a cohesive and functional whole. Sensors and IoT devices collect data on various aspects of urban life, such as traffic flow, energy consumption, air quality, and waste management. This data is then analyzed using advanced algorithms to provide insights and optimize city operations. For example, smart traffic management systems can adjust traffic signals in real time to reduce congestion and improve mobility. Smart grids can balance energy supply and demand, enhancing energy efficiency and reducing environmental impact.

The people who live and work in smart cities are also integral to these assemblages. Citizens interact with smart technologies through various interfaces, such as mobile apps, online platforms, and public kiosks. These interactions enable them to access information, participate in decision-making, and benefit from improved services. For instance, smart city apps can provide real-time updates on public transportation schedules, alert residents to environmental hazards, or facilitate access to municipal services.

Policies and governance frameworks play a crucial role in shaping smart city assemblages. Effective governance is necessary to ensure that the deployment of smart technologies aligns with the goals of sustainability, inclusivity, and equity. Policies related to data privacy, cybersecurity, and public participation are essential for building trust and fostering citizen engagement. Additionally, collaboration between different stakeholders, including government agencies, private companies, and civil society organizations, is vital for the successful implementation of smart city initiatives.

The case of Singapore illustrates how smart city assemblages integrate technology, people, and services. Singapore's Smart Nation initiative aims to leverage digital technologies to improve urban living and drive economic growth. The city-state has implemented various smart technologies across different sectors, such as transportation, healthcare, and public safety.

In transportation, Singapore has deployed a comprehensive smart traffic management system that uses data from sensors and cameras to monitor traffic conditions and optimize traffic flow. The system provides real-time information to drivers and public transportation users, helping to reduce congestion and improve mobility. Additionally, the city has implemented a smart parking system that guides drivers to available parking spaces, reducing the time spent searching for parking and minimizing traffic disruptions.

In healthcare, Singapore has introduced telemedicine services and health monitoring devices to enhance patient care and accessibility. Telemedicine platforms allow patients to consult with healthcare professionals remotely, reducing the need for physical visits and improving convenience. Health monitoring devices, such as wearable sensors, enable continuous monitoring of vital signs, providing valuable data for personalized healthcare and early intervention.

Public safety in Singapore is also enhanced through smart technologies. The city-state has implemented an extensive network of surveillance cameras and sensors to monitor public spaces and detect potential security threats. Data from these devices is analyzed using artificial intelligence to identify suspicious activities and support law enforcement efforts. Additionally, smart technologies are used in emergency response systems to improve coordination and efficiency during crises.

The success of Singapore's Smart Nation initiative highlights the potential of smart city assemblages to enhance urban living and address complex challenges. The integration of technology, people, and services in a cohesive and functional whole demonstrates the dynamic and interconnected nature of assemblages. By leveraging the power of data and digital technologies, smart cities can optimize urban operations, promote sustainability, and improve the quality of life for residents.

In conclusion, assemblages provide a powerful framework for understanding the formation and dynamics of social contexts. Social networks, urban environments, and globalization all contribute to the creation of complex and interconnected assemblages. The rise of smart cities illustrates how the integration of technology, people, and services can enhance urban living and address contemporary challenges. By recognizing the importance of assemblages in society, we can better understand the interconnectedness of social phenomena and develop strategies to foster resilience, innovation, and sustainability in our communities.

23. TECHNOLOGICAL ASSEMBLAGES

Technological assemblages represent a dynamic integration of various elements, including devices, software, data, and user interactions, which together form complex systems with emergent properties. These assemblages are characterized by their interconnectedness, adaptability, and the ability to evolve over time. This discussion will explore the concept of technological assemblages, focusing on the Internet of Things (IoT), the integration of hardware, software, and data in modern technology, the role of user interaction, and a detailed case study of autonomous vehicles.

The Internet of Things (IoT) is a quintessential example of a technological assemblage. IoT refers to the network of interconnected devices that communicate and share data with each other, often via the internet. These devices range from everyday household items like smart thermostats and refrigerators to industrial machinery and infrastructure systems. The IoT ecosystem is composed of sensors, actuators, communication protocols, data analytics, and cloud computing, all working together to create a seamless flow of information and control.

In an IoT assemblage, sensors play a crucial role by collecting data from the physical environment. These sensors can monitor various parameters, such as temperature, humidity, motion, and light. Actuators, on the other hand, perform actions based on the data received, such as adjusting the thermostat or turning on lights. Communication protocols enable devices to share data and commands, often through wireless networks like Wi-Fi, Bluetooth, or Zigbee. Cloud computing and data analytics platforms process and analyze the data, providing insights and enabling automated decision-making.

The integration of hardware, software, and data is fundamental to the functioning of modern technological assemblages. Hardware components, such as sensors and actuators, provide the physical interface with the environment. These devices are embedded with software that controls their operations and facilitates communication. The software can range from embedded firmware to complex operating systems and applications. Data generated by these devices is transmitted to central servers or cloud platforms, where it is stored, processed, and analyzed.

For instance, in a smart home IoT assemblage, hardware components like smart speakers, security cameras, and smart locks interact with software applications that control their functions. Data collected by these devices, such as voice commands, video footage, and entry logs, is sent to cloud platforms for processing. The integration of hardware, software, and data enables various functionalities, such as voice-activated controls, remote monitoring, and automated security alerts.

Data plays a critical role in technological assemblages, acting as the glue that binds different elements together. Data collected from devices is used to generate insights, optimize performance, and enable new functionalities. For example, in industrial IoT applications, data from sensors monitoring machinery can be analyzed to predict maintenance needs, reducing downtime and improving efficiency. In healthcare, wearable devices collect data on vital signs, which can be analyzed to monitor patients' health and provide personalized care.

User interaction is another crucial component in shaping technological assemblages. Users interact with devices and systems through various interfaces, such as touchscreens, voice commands, and mobile applications. These interactions influence how the technology operates and adapts to user needs. User feedback and behavior data are often used to refine algorithms, improve user experience, and develop new features.

In the context of smart homes, user interaction can significantly shape the assemblage. For example, users may customize their smart lighting systems to adjust based on their preferences and routines. Voice assistants like Amazon Alexa or Google Assistant enable users to control devices through voice commands, creating a more intuitive and seamless experience. User data, such as preferred lighting settings or frequently used commands, can be analyzed to personalize the system further and improve its functionality.

The role of user interaction is also evident in the development of machine learning algorithms. Machine learning models are trained on large datasets that include user behavior and preferences. These models learn to recognize patterns and make predictions, which can then be applied to enhance the user experience. For instance, recommendation systems used by streaming services like Netflix or Spotify analyze user interactions to suggest content tailored to individual preferences.

A detailed case study of autonomous vehicles highlights the complexity and interdependence of technological assemblages. Autonomous vehicles, or self-driving cars, are advanced systems that integrate sensors, algorithms, and user inputs to navigate and operate without human intervention. These vehicles rely on a combination of hardware, software, and data to perceive the environment, make decisions, and control the vehicle's movements.

Sensors are a critical component of autonomous vehicles, providing the necessary data to perceive the environment. These sensors include cameras, lidar (light detection and ranging), radar, and ultrasonic sensors. Cameras capture visual information, lidar provides detailed 3D maps of the surroundings, radar detects objects' speed and distance, and ultrasonic sensors assist with close-range detection. The integration of these sensors allows the vehicle to create a comprehensive understanding of its environment.

The data collected by sensors is processed by sophisticated algorithms, which are at the heart of autonomous vehicle technology. These algorithms include computer vision, machine learning, and sensor fusion techniques. Computer vision algorithms analyze camera images to identify objects, lane markings, and traffic signs. Machine learning models, trained on vast amounts of driving data, predict the behavior of other road users and make decisions based on the vehicle's surroundings. Sensor fusion algorithms combine data from multiple sensors to create a coherent and accurate representation of the environment.

The integration of hardware, software, and data in autonomous vehicles enables them to perform complex tasks, such as lane-keeping, obstacle avoidance, and route planning. The vehicle's control system uses the processed data to make real-time decisions and execute maneuvers. For example, if the sensors detect an obstacle in the vehicle's path, the control system can calculate an alternative route and steer the vehicle accordingly.

User interaction also plays a significant role in the operation and acceptance of autonomous vehicles. While fully autonomous vehicles aim to operate without human intervention, user inputs are still crucial in certain scenarios. For instance, users may set destinations, adjust driving preferences, or take over control in specific situations. The interaction between the user and the vehicle is facilitated through interfaces such as touchscreens, voice commands, and mobile applications.

User feedback and data are essential for improving autonomous vehicle technology. Data collected from user interactions, such as driving habits and preferences, can be used to refine algorithms and enhance the user experience. Additionally, feedback on the vehicle's performance and behavior can inform updates and improvements to the system.

The development and deployment of autonomous vehicles also involve a broader assemblage of stakeholders, including automotive manufacturers, technology companies, regulatory bodies, and infrastructure providers. Collaboration between these stakeholders is crucial for addressing technical, legal, and societal challenges. For example, regulatory frameworks must be established to ensure the safety and reliability of autonomous vehicles, while infrastructure providers may need to upgrade roads and communication systems to support vehicle-to-infrastructure communication.

The case study of autonomous vehicles illustrates the complexity and interdependence of technological assemblages. The integration of sensors, algorithms, and user inputs creates a system capable of navigating and operating in diverse environments. The interactions between hardware, software, data, and users highlight the dynamic nature of technological assemblages, where different elements come together to form a cohesive and functional whole.

In conclusion, technological assemblages represent a sophisticated integration of diverse elements, including devices, software, data, and user interactions. The Internet of Things exemplifies how interconnected devices form dynamic networks that enhance functionality and efficiency. The integration of hardware, software, and data is fundamental to modern technology, enabling advanced capabilities and new applications. User interaction shapes technological assemblages by influencing design, functionality, and user experience.

The case study of autonomous vehicles underscores the complexity and interdependence of technological assemblages. The integration of sensors, algorithms, and user inputs enables autonomous vehicles to perceive their environment, make decisions, and navigate without human intervention. The development and deployment of autonomous vehicles involve collaboration among various stakeholders, highlighting the broader assemblage that supports technological innovation.

Understanding technological assemblages is crucial for navigating the complexities of modern technology and addressing the challenges and opportunities it presents. By recognizing the interconnectedness and dynamic nature of these assemblages, we can develop more effective and adaptive technologies that enhance our lives and address pressing societal issues.

24. CULTURAL ASSEMBLAGES

Cultural assemblages refer to the dynamic and intricate formations that emerge when diverse cultural elements interact, blend, and coalesce into new, multifaceted expressions. These assemblages are not fixed or static; they are fluid and constantly evolving, reflecting the ongoing processes of cultural exchange and adaptation. This exploration will delve into the formation of cultural assemblages through the blending of different cultural elements in art, music, and literature, the role of migration and diaspora in creating new cultural assemblages, the impact of cultural hybridity on identity formation, and a detailed case study of the influence of African, European, and Indigenous cultures in shaping Latin American music.

Art, music, and literature are prime arenas where cultural assemblages manifest. These forms of creative expression often incorporate elements from various cultural traditions, creating rich tapestries that reflect the complexity and diversity of human experience. The blending of different cultural elements in these fields results in innovative and hybrid forms that challenge conventional boundaries and categories.

In art, cultural assemblages are evident in movements such as modernism and postmodernism, which often draw on a wide range of cultural references and influences. For example, Picasso's use of African masks and motifs in his groundbreaking works like "Les Demoiselles d'Avignon" illustrates how non-Western art forms can influence and transform Western artistic practices. This blending of cultural elements creates new visual languages that reflect the interconnectedness of global cultures.

In literature, cultural assemblages can be seen in the works of authors who draw on multiple cultural traditions to create rich and layered narratives. For instance, the novels of Salman Rushdie, such as "Midnight's Children" and "The Satanic Verses," blend elements of Indian, Islamic, and Western literary traditions. Rushdie's use of magical realism, a genre with roots in Latin American literature, further exemplifies how different cultural influences can come together to create innovative literary forms.

Music is perhaps the most prominent field where cultural assemblages are evident. Genres such as jazz, reggae, and hip-hop have emerged from the blending of different cultural traditions and have, in turn, influenced global musical landscapes. Jazz, for example, originated in the early 20th century in the United States, drawing on African American musical traditions, European harmonic structures, and Latin rhythms. The result is a dynamic and improvisational genre that has evolved and adapted to various cultural contexts worldwide.

Migration and diaspora play crucial roles in creating new cultural assemblages. The movement of people across borders brings different cultural traditions into contact, leading to the blending and hybridization of cultural practices. Diasporic communities maintain connections to their cultural heritage while also adapting to their new environments, creating rich and diverse cultural landscapes.

The African diaspora, resulting from the transatlantic slave trade, has had a profound impact on the formation of cultural assemblages in the Americas. African cultural traditions, including music, dance, religion, and cuisine, have blended with Indigenous and European influences to create new, hybrid forms. This blending is evident in various cultural practices, such as the syncretic religions of Vodou in Haiti and Candomblé in Brazil, which combine African spiritual practices with elements of Catholicism and Indigenous beliefs.

Migration in the contemporary era continues to create new cultural assemblages. For instance, the large-scale migration of South Asians to the United Kingdom has led to the emergence of British Asian culture, characterized by a fusion of South Asian and British cultural elements. This hybrid culture is reflected in various forms of expression, including music (e.g., Bhangra and Bollywood-inspired pop), cuisine (e.g., curry dishes adapted to British tastes), and fashion (e.g., the blending of traditional South Asian garments with Western styles).

Cultural hybridity, the process by which different cultural elements blend and interact, plays a significant role in identity formation. Individuals and communities navigate their identities within the context of multiple cultural influences, creating complex and multifaceted identities that reflect their diverse experiences and backgrounds. This hybridity challenges the notion of fixed and singular identities, emphasizing instead the fluid and dynamic nature of cultural identity.

For example, in multicultural societies, individuals often navigate multiple cultural identities, drawing on different cultural traditions to shape their sense of self. This process is particularly evident among second-generation immigrants, who may blend the cultural practices of their parents' homeland with those of their country of birth. This blending results in hybrid identities that reflect the interconnectedness of global cultures and the individual's unique experiences.

The impact of cultural hybridity on identity formation is also evident in the realm of popular culture. Artists, musicians, and writers often draw on multiple cultural influences to create works that resonate with diverse audiences. This blending of cultural elements not only enriches the cultural landscape but also provides individuals with a broader range of cultural resources to draw upon in shaping their identities.

A detailed case study of the influence of African, European, and Indigenous cultures in shaping Latin American music provides a compelling example of cultural assemblages in action. Latin American music is a rich and diverse tapestry that reflects the complex history and cultural interactions of the region. The blending of African, European, and Indigenous musical traditions has given rise to a wide array of genres and styles, each with its unique characteristics and influences.

The African influence on Latin American music is profound and can be traced back to the transatlantic slave trade. Enslaved Africans brought with them rich musical traditions, including rhythms, instruments, and vocal styles, which have significantly shaped the development of Latin American music. The use of percussion instruments, polyrhythms, call-and-response patterns, and improvisation in genres such as samba, rumba, and cumbia can be directly linked to African musical traditions.

European influence is also a key component of Latin American music. Spanish and Portuguese colonization introduced European musical forms, instruments, and harmonic structures to the region. European string instruments such as the guitar and violin became integral to many Latin American musical styles. Additionally, the European tradition of structured compositions and harmonic progressions influenced the development of genres such as tango and bossa nova.

Indigenous cultures in Latin America contributed their musical traditions to the cultural assemblage as well. Indigenous instruments such as pan flutes, drums, and ocarinas, along with vocal styles and ceremonial music, have been incorporated into various Latin American musical genres. The blending of Indigenous musical elements with African and European influences has created unique regional styles that reflect the cultural diversity of the region.

One of the most prominent examples of cultural assemblages in Latin American music is the genre of salsa. Salsa originated in the mid-20th century in New York City, where Puerto Rican and Cuban musicians blended elements of Afro-Cuban music with jazz, rock, and other popular music styles. The resulting genre incorporates African rhythms, European harmonic structures, and various Latin American musical elements, creating a dynamic and infectious dance music that has gained international popularity.

Another example is the genre of samba in Brazil. Samba's roots lie in the African musical traditions brought to Brazil by enslaved Africans. These traditions blended with European harmonic and melodic elements, as well as Indigenous Brazilian influences, to create a vibrant and rhythmically complex genre. Samba is characterized by its use of syncopated rhythms, call-and-response patterns, and a wide array of percussion instruments, reflecting the rich cultural assemblage that defines Brazilian music.

The tango, which originated in the late 19th century in the working-class neighborhoods of Buenos Aires, Argentina, is another genre that exemplifies cultural assemblages. Tango music and dance incorporate African rhythms, European (primarily Italian and Spanish) melodic and harmonic elements, and influences from the local criollo culture. The bandoneón, a type of accordion brought to Argentina by European immigrants, became a central instrument in tango music, symbolizing the blending of cultural influences that characterize the genre.

The impact of cultural hybridity on identity formation is evident in the way Latin American music reflects the diverse cultural heritage of the region. The blending of African, European, and Indigenous elements in music creates a sense of shared cultural identity that transcends individual ethnic or cultural backgrounds. This hybrid cultural identity is a source of pride and resilience for many Latin Americans, reflecting the region's rich history of cultural exchange and adaptation.

In conclusion, cultural assemblages represent the dynamic and fluid interactions between diverse cultural elements that give rise to new, hybrid forms of expression. Art, music, and literature are prime arenas where these assemblages manifest, as creators draw on multiple cultural traditions to innovate and create. Migration and diaspora play crucial roles in forming new cultural assemblages, as people bring their cultural practices into contact with new environments, leading to the blending and hybridization of cultures. Cultural hybridity significantly impacts identity formation, creating complex and multifaceted identities that reflect the interconnectedness of global cultures.

The case study of Latin American music illustrates the formation and impact of cultural assemblages, highlighting the profound influence of African, European, and Indigenous cultures in shaping the region's musical landscape. This blending of cultural elements not only enriches the cultural tapestry of Latin America but also reflects the broader processes of cultural exchange and adaptation that characterize human history. Understanding cultural assemblages provides valuable insights into the ways in which cultures interact, evolve, and create new forms of expression, enriching our appreciation of the diversity and complexity of human creativity.

25. ASSEMBLAGES IN FICTION

Assemblages in fiction represent a rich and dynamic exploration of how different elements come together to form complex, interconnected wholes. In literature and media, these assemblages are often depicted in genres like science fiction and fantasy, where the boundaries between worlds and beings are fluid and open to imaginative reconfiguration. This discussion will delve into how assemblages are represented in these genres, the narrative techniques used to portray their complexity, the thematic exploration of unity and multiplicity, and a detailed case study of the interstellar alliances in "Star Trek" as exemplars of diverse species and cultures forming intricate assemblages.

Science fiction and fantasy are genres particularly suited to depicting assemblages due to their inherent flexibility and imaginative scope. These genres frequently feature worlds that blend disparate elements, such as different species, technologies, and cultures, into cohesive but complex wholes. The ability to create entirely new settings and societies allows authors and creators to explore the dynamics of assemblages in ways that more realistic genres might not.

In science fiction, the depiction of interstellar civilizations often involves the assembly of diverse species, each with its own culture, technology, and social structure. These interstellar societies are rich in their diversity and complexity, reflecting the interconnectedness and interdependence of their components. The interactions between different species and cultures create a dynamic narrative space where themes of cooperation, conflict, and integration are explored.

Fantasy, on the other hand, often depicts assemblages of different magical creatures, realms, and mythologies. These assemblages bring together elements from various folklore and mythological traditions, creating rich tapestries of narrative and world-building. The blending of different magical systems, races, and histories within a single story provides a fertile ground for exploring the interplay between unity and multiplicity.

The narrative techniques used to portray complex assemblages in fiction are varied and innovative. One common technique is the use of multiple perspectives or point-of-view characters. By providing different characters' viewpoints, authors can illustrate the multifaceted nature of the assemblage, showing how different elements interact and influence one another. This technique allows readers to understand the assemblage from various angles, enhancing the depth and complexity of the narrative.

Another narrative technique is the incorporation of detailed world-building. Authors meticulously craft the histories, cultures, and technologies of the different elements within the assemblage, providing a rich context for the story. This world-building often involves the creation of intricate maps, languages, and customs, which help to ground the fantastical elements in a believable reality. By fleshing out the details of each component, authors can create a more immersive and coherent assemblage.

Interwoven plotlines and character arcs are also effective in portraying assemblages. By following multiple storylines that converge and diverge throughout the narrative, authors can highlight the interconnectedness and interdependence of the different elements. These interwoven plots often involve characters from diverse backgrounds and species coming together to achieve common goals, reflecting the themes of unity and multiplicity.

The thematic exploration of unity and multiplicity is central to the depiction of assemblages in fiction. These themes are often explored through the interactions between different elements, such as species, cultures, and technologies. Unity is portrayed through the cooperation and integration of these diverse elements, while multiplicity is depicted through the acknowledgment and celebration of their differences.

In many science fiction and fantasy narratives, the tension between unity and multiplicity drives the plot. Characters and societies must navigate the challenges of bringing together disparate elements while maintaining their distinct identities. This tension often leads to rich thematic explorations of identity, diversity, and the nature of cooperation.

A detailed case study of the interstellar alliances in "Star Trek" provides a compelling example of how assemblages of diverse species and cultures are depicted in fiction. "Star Trek," a seminal science fiction franchise created by Gene Roddenberry, is renowned for its depiction of a future where diverse species from across the galaxy come together to form complex interstellar alliances, most notably the United Federation of Planets.

The United Federation of Planets is an exemplary assemblage of diverse species and cultures. It is a political and social union of planetary governments that share common values and goals, such as peace, exploration, and mutual respect. The Federation is composed of various species, each bringing its unique culture, technology, and perspective to the alliance. This diversity is a source of strength, as it allows the Federation to draw on a wide range of resources and expertise.

The narrative techniques used in "Star Trek" to portray this complex assemblage include multiple perspectives, detailed world-building, and interwoven plotlines. The franchise features a wide array of characters from different species, each providing a unique viewpoint on the Federation and its challenges. By following the experiences of characters like Captain Kirk, Spock, and Captain Picard, the narrative illustrates how different species and cultures contribute to the Federation's mission.

Detailed world-building is a hallmark of "Star Trek." The franchise meticulously constructs the histories, cultures, and technologies of the various species within the Federation. From the logical and stoic

Vulcans to the honor-bound Klingons and the technologically advanced but socially conservative Andorians, each species is given a rich and distinct background. This detailed world-building provides a believable context for the interactions and conflicts within the Federation.

Interwoven plotlines are also central to "Star Trek's" portrayal of the Federation. The franchise's various series and films often feature multiple storylines that intersect and influence one another. These plotlines frequently involve characters from different species working together to solve problems, reflecting the themes of unity and multiplicity. For example, in "Star Trek: The Next Generation," the crew of the USS Enterprise-D includes humans, a Klingon, an android, and a Betazoid, among others. Their diverse backgrounds and perspectives are crucial in navigating the challenges they face.

The thematic exploration of unity and multiplicity is central to "Star Trek's" depiction of the Federation. The franchise emphasizes the importance of cooperation and mutual respect in achieving common goals. The Federation's motto, "Infinite Diversity in Infinite Combinations," encapsulates this theme, celebrating the idea that the union's strength lies in its diversity.

"Star Trek" frequently explores the tension between unity and multiplicity through its narratives. Episodes and films often depict conflicts arising from cultural differences and the challenges of integrating diverse species into the Federation. These conflicts provide opportunities to explore themes of identity, tolerance, and the value of diversity. For example, the character of Spock, who is half-human and half-Vulcan, embodies the tension between different cultural identities. His struggle to reconcile these identities reflects the broader challenges faced by the Federation in integrating diverse species.

The depiction of interstellar alliances in "Star Trek" highlights the complexities and benefits of cultural assemblages. The Federation's ability to harness the strengths of its diverse members allows it to navigate the challenges of exploration and diplomacy in a vast and often hostile galaxy. The franchise's optimistic vision of a future where diverse species work together for mutual benefit resonates with contemporary themes of multiculturalism and global cooperation.

In conclusion, assemblages in fiction offer a rich and dynamic exploration of how different elements come together to form complex, interconnected wholes. Science fiction and fantasy are particularly suited to depicting these assemblages, as they allow for the imaginative reconfiguration of worlds and beings. Narrative techniques such as multiple perspectives, detailed world-building, and interwoven plotlines are effective in portraying the complexity of assemblages.

The thematic exploration of unity and multiplicity is central to the depiction of assemblages in fiction. These themes are often explored through the interactions between different elements, such as species, cultures, and technologies. The tension between unity and multiplicity drives the plot and provides rich thematic material for exploring identity, diversity, and cooperation.

The case study of "Star Trek" illustrates how assemblages of diverse species and cultures are depicted in fiction. The United Federation of Planets exemplifies an assemblage where diverse elements come together to achieve common goals. The narrative techniques and thematic exploration in "Star Trek" highlight the complexities and benefits of cultural assemblages, offering an optimistic vision of a future where diversity is celebrated and harnessed for mutual benefit. Understanding these fictional assemblages provides valuable insights into the dynamics of cooperation and diversity, enriching our appreciation of the complexities of human and interstellar societies.

26. ASSEMBLAGES IN CONTEMPORARY ART

Assemblages in contemporary art represent a dynamic and innovative approach to creation, where artists combine found objects, materials, textures, and contexts to form new and meaningful works. This technique, known as assemblage art, has become a significant method in modern and contemporary art, allowing for rich expressions of political, social, and personal commentary. This discussion will explore the technique of assemblage art, the role of materials and textures, the impact of political and social commentary, and a detailed case study of works by artists like Robert Rauschenberg and Louise Nevelson.

Assemblage art is a technique that involves combining found objects and materials to create new, often three-dimensional, artworks. This method challenges traditional notions of artistic creation by emphasizing the use of everyday items, discarded objects, and materials that carry their own histories and meanings. Assemblage art emerged in the early 20th century, influenced by movements such as Dada and Surrealism, which sought to break away from conventional artistic practices and explore new forms of expression.

One of the defining features of assemblage art is its use of found objects, also known as "ready-mades." These objects are often chosen for their intrinsic qualities, such as their shapes, textures, colors, and the associations they evoke. By recontextualizing these items, artists create new narratives and meanings, inviting viewers to see the familiar in unfamiliar ways. The technique of assemblage allows for a tactile and visceral engagement with the artwork, as viewers are encouraged to consider the materiality and history of the objects used.

The role of materials, textures, and contexts in shaping artistic assemblages is crucial. Artists carefully select and arrange materials to create compositions that convey specific themes and emotions. The choice of materials can range from industrial debris, organic matter, and household items to more conventional art supplies. Each material brings its own texture and context, contributing to the overall impact of the artwork.

Textures play a significant role in assemblage art, as they add depth and complexity to the visual experience. Rough, smooth, soft, or hard textures can evoke different sensations and associations, enhancing the viewer's engagement with the piece. For example, the juxtaposition of rough, weathered metal with smooth, polished wood can create a striking contrast that highlights the interplay between natural and industrial elements.

The context in which materials are presented also shapes the meaning of an assemblage. By placing objects in new and unexpected settings, artists can challenge viewers' perceptions and encourage them to question established norms and assumptions. The recontextualization of materials allows for a layering of meanings, where the original function and symbolism of an object interact with its new artistic context.

Political and social commentary is a significant aspect of assemblage art. The use of found objects and everyday materials often carries inherent cultural and social connotations, making assemblage a powerful medium for addressing contemporary issues. Artists use assemblage to critique societal structures, explore identity, and comment on political events and social injustices.

For instance, the use of discarded materials and consumer goods in assemblage art can serve as a critique of consumer culture and environmental degradation. By repurposing waste and highlighting the material excesses of society, artists draw attention to the consequences of overconsumption and the need for sustainability. The incorporation of objects with historical and cultural significance can also provide commentary on issues such as colonialism, migration, and identity.

A detailed case study of the works of Robert Rauschenberg and Louise Nevelson exemplifies the impact and innovation of assemblage art. Both artists have made significant contributions to the development of this technique, using it to create compelling and thought-provoking works.

Robert Rauschenberg is renowned for his "Combines," a series of works created in the 1950s and 1960s that blend painting and sculpture through the use of found objects and materials. Rauschenberg's Combines challenge traditional distinctions between different artistic mediums, creating hybrid forms that defy easy categorization. His use of everyday objects, such as clothing, furniture, newspaper clippings, and taxidermy animals, reflects his interest in merging art with life and blurring the boundaries between art and reality.

One of Rauschenberg's most famous Combines, "Monogram" (1955-1959), features a stuffed goat encircled by a rubber tire, standing on a painted wooden platform. The goat, adorned with a painted face and a woolen scarf, becomes a focal point within the assemblage, evoking various interpretations and associations. The juxtaposition of the goat with disparate objects, such as the tire and the platform, creates a sense of playfulness and absurdity, while also prompting viewers to consider the relationships between art, life, and materiality.

Rauschenberg's use of found objects and everyday materials in his Combines also serves as a form of social commentary. By incorporating items from popular culture and daily life, he reflects the realities of post-war American society and critiques the commodification of art and culture. His works invite viewers to engage with the material world in new ways, encouraging them to see the artistic potential in the mundane and the discarded.

Louise Nevelson, another pioneering artist in the field of assemblage, is known for her monumental wooden sculptures, which she often painted in monochromatic colors. Nevelson's works are characterized by their intricate compositions and the use of found wooden objects, such as furniture parts, architectural elements, and industrial debris. Her assemblages create a sense of architectural space, where the interplay of light and shadow adds to the visual complexity and depth of her pieces.

One of Nevelson's most celebrated works, "Sky Cathedral" (1958), exemplifies her mastery of assemblage art. The sculpture is a large, wall-mounted piece composed of numerous wooden elements arranged in a grid-like structure. Painted entirely in black, "Sky Cathedral" creates a dramatic interplay of light and shadow, emphasizing the textures and shapes of the individual components. The work evokes a sense of grandeur and mystery, inviting viewers to explore its intricate details and ponder its meaning.

Nevelson's use of found wooden objects imbues her works with a sense of history and memory. The materials she chooses often bear the marks of their previous use, carrying with them the stories and associations of their past lives. By recontextualizing these objects within her assemblages, Nevelson transforms them into poetic and evocative compositions that speak to themes of time, memory, and transformation.

Nevelson's monochromatic color schemes also play a crucial role in her assemblages. By painting her works in a single color, she unifies the diverse elements and creates a cohesive visual experience. The choice of color, whether black, white, or gold, adds to the emotional and symbolic resonance of her pieces, enhancing their impact and significance.

Both Rauschenberg and Nevelson use assemblage art to explore and comment on contemporary social and political issues. Their works reflect the complexities and contradictions of modern life, challenging viewers to reconsider their perceptions of art, materiality, and society. Through their innovative use of found objects and materials, they create assemblages that are rich in meaning and open to multiple interpretations.

In conclusion, assemblages in contemporary art represent a dynamic and innovative approach to creation, where artists combine found objects, materials, textures, and contexts to form new and meaningful works. The technique of assemblage art challenges traditional notions of artistic creation by emphasizing the use of everyday items and discarded objects, recontextualizing them to create new narratives and meanings. The role of materials, textures, and contexts is crucial in shaping artistic assemblages, as each element brings its own qualities and associations to the work.

Political and social commentary is a significant aspect of assemblage art, as artists use found objects and everyday materials to address contemporary issues and critique societal structures. The works of Robert Rauschenberg and Louise Nevelson exemplify the impact and innovation of assemblage art, demonstrating how the technique can be used to create compelling and thought-provoking works that reflect the complexities of modern life.

Through their use of found objects, intricate compositions, and social commentary, Rauschenberg and Nevelson have made significant contributions to the development of assemblage art, challenging viewers to see the artistic potential in the mundane and the discarded. Their works invite viewers to engage with the material world in new ways, encouraging them to consider the relationships between art, life, and society. Understanding the role of assemblages in contemporary art provides valuable insights into the ways in which artists navigate and respond to the complexities of the modern world, enriching our appreciation of the diversity and innovation of artistic expression.

27. ASSEMBLAGES IN ORGANIZATIONAL THEORY

Applying the concept of assemblages to organizational theory offers a dynamic and flexible framework for understanding how organizations operate and evolve. Organizations can be viewed as assemblages of people, processes, technologies, and cultures, which interact in complex and often unpredictable ways. This perspective emphasizes the interconnectedness and interdependence of various elements within an organization, highlighting how they come together to form a functional whole. This discussion will explore organizations as assemblages, the dynamic nature of these assemblages in response to external pressures, strategies for managing and optimizing them in business contexts, and a detailed case study of the transformation of a traditional company into a networked organization.

Organizations as assemblages encompass a variety of elements, including individuals, teams, technologies, workflows, and cultural norms. These elements are not static; they continuously interact and adapt, creating a dynamic and evolving system. Viewing organizations through the lens of assemblages allows for a more holistic understanding of how these elements come together to achieve organizational goals and respond to changes in the external environment.

People are a core component of organizational assemblages. This includes employees at all levels, from front-line workers to senior management. Each individual brings unique skills, experiences, and perspectives to the organization, contributing to its overall functionality. Teams and departments within the organization represent sub-assemblages, where specific groups of individuals work together to achieve particular objectives. The interactions between these groups are crucial for the organization's success, as they facilitate collaboration, innovation, and problem-solving.

Processes within an organization are another critical element of assemblages. These include the formal procedures and workflows that guide how tasks are completed, as well as the informal practices that emerge through daily operations. Processes help to standardize activities, ensuring consistency and efficiency. However, they must also be flexible enough to adapt to changing circumstances. The interplay between formal and informal processes can create a dynamic organizational environment where innovation and adaptation are encouraged.

Technologies play a significant role in modern organizational assemblages. This encompasses a wide range of tools and systems, from basic office equipment to advanced information and communication technologies. Technologies facilitate communication, streamline operations, and enable data-driven decision-making. The integration of new technologies can significantly alter the organizational assemblage, creating new opportunities and challenges. For instance, the adoption of cloud computing and collaboration tools has transformed how teams work together, enabling greater flexibility and remote work capabilities.

Cultural norms and values are also fundamental to organizational assemblages. These encompass the shared beliefs, attitudes, and behaviors that characterize the organization. Culture shapes how individuals interact, make decisions, and approach their work. A strong organizational culture can foster a sense of belonging and motivation, while a misaligned culture can lead to conflicts and inefficiencies. The cultural dimension of assemblages is particularly important in managing organizational change, as cultural resistance can impede the successful implementation of new strategies or technologies.

The dynamic nature of organizational assemblages is evident in how they respond to external pressures. Organizations operate in complex and often turbulent environments, where they must continuously adapt to changes in the market, technology, regulation, and social expectations. This adaptability is a key characteristic of assemblages, as the interactions between their elements enable the organization to reconfigure itself in response to new challenges and opportunities.

For example, economic downturns or technological disruptions can prompt organizations to reassess their strategies and operations. This may involve restructuring teams, adopting new technologies, or changing processes to improve efficiency and competitiveness. The ability to quickly and effectively adapt to these changes is crucial for organizational resilience and long-term success.

External pressures can also drive innovation within organizational assemblages. The need to stay competitive in a rapidly changing market can encourage organizations to explore new ideas, develop new products or services, and experiment with different business models. Innovation often emerges from the interactions between diverse elements within the assemblage, as individuals from different backgrounds and areas of expertise collaborate to solve problems and create value.

Managing and optimizing organizational assemblages requires a strategic approach that considers the interconnectedness and interdependence of their elements. This involves several key strategies:

1. Fostering Collaboration and Communication: Effective communication and collaboration are essential for the smooth functioning of organizational assemblages. This involves creating channels for open and transparent communication, encouraging cross-functional teamwork, and leveraging collaboration tools and technologies. Leaders should promote a culture of trust and cooperation, where individuals feel empowered to share ideas and work together towards common goals.

2. Embracing Flexibility and Adaptability: Organizations must be flexible and adaptable to respond to changing circumstances. This involves fostering a culture of continuous improvement, where processes and practices are regularly reviewed and updated. Leaders should encourage experimentation and risk-taking, allowing teams to

explore new approaches and learn from their experiences. Flexibility also involves being open to new technologies and ways of working, such as remote work and agile methodologies.

3. Aligning Culture with Strategy: A strong and aligned organizational culture is crucial for the success of the assemblage. Leaders should actively shape and reinforce the desired culture through their actions and communication. This involves articulating clear values and expectations, recognizing and rewarding behaviors that align with the culture, and addressing behaviors that do not. Aligning culture with strategy ensures that individuals are motivated and committed to achieving organizational goals.

4. Leveraging Technology: Technology plays a pivotal role in modern organizational assemblages. Organizations should invest in technologies that enhance communication, collaboration, and data-driven decision-making. This includes adopting tools for project management, communication, and analytics. Leaders should also stay informed about emerging technologies and assess their potential impact on the organization, ensuring that they are leveraged effectively to drive innovation and efficiency.

5. Supporting Continuous Learning and Development: Organizations should invest in the continuous learning and development of their employees. This involves providing opportunities for training, skill development, and career growth. Leaders should encourage a culture of learning, where individuals are empowered to seek new knowledge and develop their capabilities. Continuous learning ensures that the assemblage remains dynamic and capable of adapting to new challenges and opportunities.

A detailed case study of the transformation of a traditional company into a networked organization illustrates the practical application of these strategies. Consider a traditional manufacturing company, "ManufactCo," which operates with a hierarchical structure, rigid processes, and limited use of modern technologies. Facing increasing competition and market pressures, the company decides to transform itself into a networked organization to enhance flexibility, innovation, and responsiveness.

Step 1: Fostering Collaboration and Communication

ManufactCo begins by breaking down silos and encouraging cross-functional collaboration. The company implements collaboration tools, such as Slack and Microsoft Teams, to facilitate communication across different departments. Regular cross-functional meetings and workshops are organized to foster teamwork and idea-sharing. Leaders promote a culture of open communication, where employees feel comfortable sharing their insights and suggestions.

Step 2: Embracing Flexibility and Adaptability

To enhance flexibility, ManufactCo adopts agile methodologies in its product development and project management processes. Teams are empowered to make decisions and experiment with new approaches, fostering a culture of innovation and continuous improvement. The company also introduces flexible work arrangements, allowing employees to work remotely or choose flexible hours. This flexibility enables the organization to quickly adapt to changing market conditions and customer needs.

Step 3: Aligning Culture with Strategy

ManufactCo's leadership articulates a clear vision and set of values that emphasize innovation, collaboration, and customer focus. These values are reinforced through regular communication, recognition programs, and leadership behavior. The company invests in cultural initiatives, such as team-building activities and diversity and inclusion programs, to strengthen the desired culture. Aligning culture with strategy ensures that employees are motivated and committed to the company's transformation goals.

Step 4: Leveraging Technology

ManufactCo invests in modern technologies to enhance its operations and decision-making processes. The company adopts cloud-based platforms for data storage and analytics, enabling real-time access to information and insights. Advanced manufacturing technologies, such as IoT and automation, are integrated into the production process to improve efficiency and reduce costs. The company also explores the use of artificial intelligence and machine learning to optimize supply chain management and predictive maintenance.

Step 5: Supporting Continuous Learning and Development

To ensure that employees are equipped with the necessary skills and knowledge, ManufactCo invests in continuous learning and development programs. The company offers training in new technologies, agile methodologies, and leadership development. Employees are encouraged to pursue certifications and attend industry conferences. A culture of learning is fostered through initiatives such as mentoring programs, knowledge-sharing sessions, and internal innovation challenges.

The transformation of ManufactCo into a networked organization exemplifies the dynamic and interconnected nature of organizational assemblages. By fostering collaboration, embracing flexibility, aligning culture with strategy, leveraging technology, and supporting continuous learning, the company successfully navigates the complexities of the modern business environment. The transformation enhances ManufactCo's ability to innovate, respond to market changes, and achieve sustainable growth.

In conclusion, applying the concept of assemblages to organizational theory offers a comprehensive framework for understanding how organizations operate and evolve. Organizations are assemblages of people, processes, technologies, and cultures, which interact in complex and dynamic ways. The dynamic nature of these assemblages allows organizations to adapt to external pressures and drive innovation. Managing and optimizing organizational assemblages requires a strategic approach that fosters collaboration, embraces flexibility, aligns culture with strategy, leverages technology, and supports continuous learning. The case study of ManufactCo's transformation illustrates the practical application of these strategies, demonstrating how organizations can thrive in a rapidly changing and interconnected world. Understanding organizational assemblages provides valuable insights into the complexities of modern business, enabling leaders to navigate challenges and seize opportunities for growth and success.

28. FUTURE IMPLICATIONS OF ASSEMBLAGES

Assemblage theory, as developed by Gilles Deleuze and Félix Guattari, offers a rich framework for understanding the complex, dynamic, and interconnected nature of various phenomena. As the world becomes increasingly interconnected, the concept of assemblages is likely to gain even more relevance. This discussion will speculate on the future developments and applications of assemblage theory, focusing on the potential for new forms of assemblages, the role of artificial intelligence (AI) and machine learning (ML) in forming new technological assemblages, predictions on the evolution of social, cultural, and organizational assemblages, and a detailed case study on the emergence of digital assemblages in virtual reality and the metaverse.

As our world becomes more interconnected through advances in technology and communication, the potential for new forms of assemblages is vast. The blending of digital and physical realities, the integration of AI and ML, and the increasing interdependence of global systems suggest that future assemblages will be more complex and multifaceted than ever before.

One area where new assemblages are likely to emerge is in the realm of smart cities. Smart cities represent a convergence of various technologies, including IoT, AI, big data, and cloud computing, to create urban environments that are more efficient, sustainable, and responsive to the needs of their inhabitants. In these smart cities, assemblages will form around interconnected infrastructures, such as transportation systems, energy grids, and public services, which will communicate and collaborate to optimize urban living.

The increasing use of AI and ML will also drive the formation of new technological assemblages. AI and ML algorithms are becoming integral to many aspects of life, from personal assistants like Siri and Alexa to complex systems in healthcare, finance, and security. These technologies will not only augment existing assemblages but also create entirely new ones. For example, autonomous vehicles represent an assemblage of sensors, data, and algorithms that interact to navigate and make decisions. As AI and ML become more sophisticated, they will enable more autonomous and adaptive systems, leading to the emergence of new technological assemblages that can learn, evolve, and interact in ways previously unimaginable.

The role of AI and ML in forming new technological assemblages cannot be overstated. These technologies are fundamentally changing how data is processed and utilized, allowing for more complex and responsive systems. In predictive maintenance, for instance, AI algorithms analyze data from machinery to predict when maintenance is needed, preventing breakdowns and optimizing performance. This forms an assemblage of machinery, sensors, data, and algorithms working together to maintain efficiency.

In healthcare, AI and ML are transforming diagnostics and treatment. AI-powered imaging systems can analyze medical scans with high accuracy, while predictive models can assess patient risk and recommend personalized treatments. These healthcare assemblages integrate medical devices, patient data, and AI algorithms, creating systems that enhance medical decision-making and patient care.

Social and cultural assemblages are also evolving rapidly due to technological advancements and increased global interconnectedness. Social media platforms are prime examples of digital assemblages, where users, algorithms, and content interact in complex ways to shape online communities and discourse. These platforms are continually evolving, driven by changes in technology, user behavior, and societal trends.

In the future, social assemblages may become even more intricate with the integration of augmented reality (AR) and virtual reality (VR). AR and VR technologies have the potential to create immersive social experiences that blend physical and digital interactions. Imagine social networks where users interact in virtual spaces, attending events, collaborating on projects, or simply socializing in a shared digital environment. These digital assemblages will combine human interactions, digital avatars, virtual environments, and AI-driven content moderation, creating new forms of socialization and community-building.

Cultural assemblages are also likely to see significant transformations. The blending of cultural elements across borders, facilitated by digital communication and global mobility, will continue to create new hybrid cultures. Cultural exchange will become more instantaneous and widespread, leading to the emergence of global cultural trends and movements. For instance, the popularity of K-pop worldwide illustrates how a local cultural phenomenon can become a global assemblage through digital media, fan communities, and cultural production.

Organizational assemblages will evolve to become more adaptive and resilient. The future of work is likely to be characterized by greater flexibility, remote collaboration, and the integration of AI and automation. Organizations will form assemblages that blend human talent, digital tools, and intelligent systems to create agile and innovative business models. These organizational assemblages will be capable of rapidly adapting to market changes, leveraging data-driven insights, and fostering continuous learning and development.

A detailed case study on the emergence of digital assemblages in virtual reality (VR) and the metaverse provides a compelling example of how assemblage theory can be applied to understand future developments. The metaverse, a collective virtual shared space created by the convergence of virtually enhanced physical reality and physically persistent virtual reality, represents a new frontier for digital assemblages.

In the metaverse, users interact with each other and the virtual environment through digital avatars. This creates an assemblage of individuals, digital identities, virtual objects, and AI-driven systems.

The metaverse is not a single platform but an interconnected network of virtual worlds and experiences, each contributing to the overall assemblage. These virtual spaces can include everything from social hubs and entertainment venues to educational institutions and workplaces.

The development of the metaverse involves the integration of various technologies, including VR, AR, blockchain, and AI. VR and AR provide the immersive experience, allowing users to interact with the virtual environment in a realistic manner. Blockchain technology enables secure and decentralized transactions within the metaverse, supporting digital currencies and ownership of virtual assets. AI enhances the user experience by powering intelligent avatars, personalized content recommendations, and dynamic virtual environments.

One of the key aspects of digital assemblages in the metaverse is the creation of virtual economies. Users can buy, sell, and trade virtual goods and services, creating a complex economic system. Virtual real estate, digital fashion, and in-game items are examples of virtual assets that hold real-world value. These economic activities form an assemblage of users, digital marketplaces, and financial systems, reflecting the interdependence of digital and physical economies.

Social interaction in the metaverse exemplifies the complexity of digital assemblages. Users can attend virtual events, collaborate on projects, and socialize in shared virtual spaces. These interactions are mediated by digital avatars, which can be customized to reflect the user's identity. AI-driven systems enhance social experiences by facilitating matchmaking, moderating content, and providing real-time language translation. The social assemblage in the metaverse thus combines human interactions, digital identities, and AI technologies, creating a rich and dynamic social environment.

The metaverse also has the potential to transform education and work. Virtual classrooms can offer immersive learning experiences, where students interact with each other and digital content in a shared virtual space. This creates an assemblage of learners, educators, digital tools, and educational content. Similarly, virtual workplaces can facilitate remote collaboration, allowing teams to work together in a virtual environment. This assemblage includes employees, digital collaboration tools, and organizational processes, enabling flexible and efficient work arrangements.

The emergence of the metaverse raises important questions about identity, privacy, and governance. As users create and interact with digital identities, issues of identity authenticity, data privacy, and digital rights become critical. The governance of the metaverse will require new frameworks and regulations to address these challenges, ensuring that the virtual environment is safe, inclusive, and equitable. This governance assemblage will involve policymakers, technology companies, users, and advocacy groups, reflecting the complexity of managing digital spaces.

In conclusion, the future implications of assemblage theory are vast and multifaceted. In an increasingly interconnected world, new forms of assemblages will emerge, driven by technological advancements and global interactions. AI and ML will play a crucial role in forming new technological assemblages, creating systems that are more autonomous and adaptive. Social, cultural, and organizational assemblages will continue to evolve, reflecting the dynamic interplay between human and technological elements.

The case study of digital assemblages in the metaverse illustrates how assemblage theory can be applied to understand the complexities of emerging digital spaces. The metaverse represents a new frontier for digital interaction, where users, technologies, and virtual environments come together to create immersive and interconnected experiences. Understanding these digital assemblages provides valuable insights into the future of socialization, work, education, and governance in a digital world.

As we look to the future, the concept of assemblages will remain a powerful framework for understanding the dynamic and interconnected nature of our world. By recognizing the complexity and interdependence of different elements, we can better navigate the challenges and opportunities of an increasingly interconnected and technologically advanced society.

29. REFERENCES

To provide a comprehensive understanding of assemblages and their future implications, it is essential to reference seminal works by Deleuze and Guattari as well as contributions from other scholars who have explored assemblage theory in various contexts. Below are some key references that can offer valuable insights into the concept of assemblages:

Works by Deleuze and Guattari

1. Deleuze, G., & Guattari, F. (1987). A Thousand Plateaus: Capitalism and Schizophrenia. Minneapolis: University of Minnesota Press.

This seminal text introduces the concept of assemblages, exploring how different elements come together to form complex, dynamic systems.

2. Deleuze, G., & Guattari, F. (1972). Anti-Oedipus: Capitalism and Schizophrenia. New York: Viking Press.

While primarily focused on psychoanalysis and capitalism, this book lays the groundwork for the ideas further developed in A Thousand Plateaus.

Books and Journal Articles on Assemblages

3. Bennett, J. (2010). Vibrant Matter: A Political Ecology of Things. Durham: Duke University Press.

Bennett explores the agency of non-human elements in assemblages, emphasizing the political and ecological implications of material interactions.

4. Marcus, G. E., & Saka, E. (2006). Assemblage. Theory, Culture & Society, 23(2-3), 101-106.

This article provides an overview of assemblage theory and its applications in social science, highlighting its relevance for contemporary cultural analysis.

5. DeLanda, M. (2006). A New Philosophy of Society: Assemblage Theory and Social Complexity. London: Continuum.

DeLanda extends Deleuze and Guattari's ideas, applying assemblage theory to social and economic systems and exploring how different elements interact within these assemblages.

6. Nail, T. (2017). What is an Assemblage? SubStance, 46(1), 21-37.

This article provides a clear and concise explanation of assemblage theory, outlining its key components and theoretical foundations.

7. Latour, B. (2005). Reassembling the Social: An Introduction to Actor-Network-Theory. Oxford: Oxford University Press.

Latour's work on actor-network theory is closely related to assemblage theory, emphasizing the interconnectedness of human and non-human actors in social networks.

8. Anderson, B., & McFarlane, C. (2011). Assemblage and Geography. Area, 43(2), 124-127.

This article explores the applications of assemblage theory in geography, discussing how it can be used to understand spatial and social dynamics.

9. Harman, G. (2009). Assemblage Theory and its Discontents: Interview with Manuel DeLanda. New Materialism: Interviews & Cartographies. Ann Arbor: Open Humanities Press.

This interview with DeLanda discusses the strengths and limitations of assemblage theory, providing insights into its theoretical development.

10. Law, J. (2004). After Method: Mess in Social Science Research. London: Routledge.

Law's work discusses the complexities and uncertainties in social science research, aligning with the principles of assemblage theory by acknowledging the messiness of real-world interactions.

CHAPTER 4: BODY WITHOUT ORGANS

154

30. INTRODUCTION TO THE BODY WITHOUT ORGANS

The concept of the Body without Organs (BwO) is a pivotal idea in the philosophical works of Gilles Deleuze and Félix Guattari, particularly in their influential text "A Thousand Plateaus: Capitalism and Schizophrenia" (1987). This notion originates from the surreal and provocative writings of the French dramatist and poet Antonin Artaud. The BwO represents a radical departure from traditional notions of the body, offering a framework for understanding the body as a fluid, dynamic, and unstructured entity. This exploration will define and introduce the BwO, trace its origins in Artaud's work, and examine its significance in Deleuze and Guattari's philosophy. Additionally, a case study will illustrate how Artaud's artistic vision inspired the development of the BwO concept.

Antonin Artaud, a groundbreaking figure in early 20th-century avant-garde theater, first introduced the idea of the Body without Organs. In his radio play "To Have Done with the Judgment of God" (1947), Artaud articulated a vision of the body freed from the constraints of organized structures and normative functions. He envisioned a body liberated from the hierarchical organization of organs and the rigid systems imposed by societal and medical norms. For Artaud, the Body without Organs was a site of potentiality and pure experience, unencumbered by the limitations of conventional bodily functions.

Artaud's vision of the Body without Organs was deeply rooted in his artistic and philosophical rebellion against the established order. He sought to dismantle the rigid structures that he believed constrained human potential and creativity. By advocating for a body liberated from its organs, Artaud aimed to explore new realms of experience and sensation, challenging the conventional understanding of human existence.

Deleuze and Guattari adopted and expanded upon Artaud's concept in their philosophical works, particularly in "A Thousand

Plateaus." They redefined the Body without Organs as a central component of their broader theoretical framework, which critiques traditional structures of thought and promotes a philosophy of becoming and multiplicity. For Deleuze and Guattari, the BwO represents a body in its most abstract and potential form, stripped of its structured functions and hierarchical organization. It is a site of pure possibility, where new connections and assemblages can emerge.

In "A Thousand Plateaus," Deleuze and Guattari describe the BwO as a body that exists outside the conventional organization of organs and functions. It is not a literal body without physical organs but rather a conceptual and philosophical body that rejects the imposed structures and categorizations. The BwO is a field of immanence, where the traditional boundaries and hierarchies that define bodies are dissolved, allowing for a fluid and dynamic interplay of forces and intensities.

The BwO is essential to Deleuze and Guattari's philosophy because it embodies their critique of hierarchical and fixed systems. They argue that traditional modes of thinking impose rigid structures on the body, constraining its potential and reducing it to a functional organism. In contrast, the BwO represents a body that resists these constraints, embracing a state of continuous becoming and transformation. It is a body open to experimentation, capable of forming new connections and assemblages that transcend established norms and functions.

The BwO is also linked to Deleuze and Guattari's broader critique of psychoanalysis, capitalism, and state control. They contend that these systems impose rigid structures on individuals, shaping their desires and bodies to fit predefined roles and functions. The BwO offers a way to resist these forces by reimagining the body as a site of freedom and potentiality, where new forms of life and desire can emerge.

A crucial aspect of the BwO is its relationship to desire. Deleuze and Guattari argue that desire is not a lack or a drive toward specific objects but a productive force that creates connections and assemblages. The BwO is the plane on which desire operates, free from the constraints of organized structures. It is a body in a state of continuous flux, where desire can manifest in myriad forms and intensities.

To further elucidate the concept of the BwO, it is helpful to examine how Antonin Artaud's artistic vision inspired its development. Artaud's work was marked by a relentless quest to transcend the boundaries of conventional theater and explore new forms of expression. His radical approach to art and life provided the impetus for Deleuze and Guattari to reconceptualize the body in their philosophical framework.

Artaud's "Theater of Cruelty" was a revolutionary theatrical movement that sought to break down the barriers between performers and audience, reality and illusion. He envisioned a theater that would engage the audience's senses and emotions at a visceral level, challenging their perceptions and preconceived notions. This approach was reflected in his idea of the Body without Organs, where the body is freed from its conventional roles and functions, becoming a site of raw, unmediated experience.

In "To Have Done with the Judgment of God," Artaud expressed his disdain for the ways in which society, religion, and medicine impose structures on the body. He called for a liberation of the body from these constraints, envisioning a state where the body could exist in its pure potentiality. Artaud's vision of the Body without Organs was deeply tied to his desire to explore new realms of sensation and experience, unencumbered by the limitations of organized structures.

Deleuze and Guattari drew upon Artaud's ideas to develop their concept of the BwO, incorporating it into their broader philosophical critique of hierarchical systems. They saw the BwO as a way to challenge the rigid structures imposed by psychoanalysis, capitalism, and the state, advocating for a body that exists in a state of continuous becoming. By embracing the BwO, they aimed to promote a philosophy of immanence and multiplicity, where new forms of life and desire could emerge.

The BwO has significant implications for various fields, including philosophy, psychoanalysis, political theory, and art. In philosophy, it challenges traditional notions of the body as a fixed and organized entity, promoting a view of the body as dynamic and fluid. In psychoanalysis, the BwO offers a critique of the ways in which desire is structured and controlled, advocating for a more expansive and productive understanding of desire. In political theory, the BwO provides a framework for resisting the rigid structures of state control and capitalist organization, promoting new forms of social and political organization. In art, the BwO inspires new approaches to creativity and expression, encouraging artists to explore the body's potential beyond its conventional roles and functions.

In conclusion, the concept of the Body without Organs (BwO) is a profound and influential idea in the philosophical works of Gilles Deleuze and Félix Guattari, rooted in the radical artistic vision of Antonin Artaud. The BwO represents a body in its most abstract and potential form, free from the constraints of structured functions and hierarchical organization. It embodies a philosophy of becoming and multiplicity, challenging traditional systems of thought and promoting new forms of life and desire. Artaud's artistic vision, particularly his "Theater of Cruelty" and his writings on the body, provided the inspiration for Deleuze and Guattari to develop this concept. The BwO has far-reaching implications across various fields, offering a framework for understanding the body as a site of continuous transformation and potentiality.

31. THEATRICAL FOUNDATIONS OF THE BODY WITHOUT ORGANS

The concept of the Body without Organs (BwO) is central to the philosophical work of Gilles Deleuze and Félix Guattari, particularly in their seminal text "A Thousand Plateaus: Capitalism and Schizophrenia" (1987). This concept, inspired by the radical ideas of the French dramatist and poet Antonin Artaud, challenges conventional understandings of the body, identity, and desire. By delving into the theoretical foundations of the BwO, we can gain a deeper appreciation of its significance and implications in Deleuze and Guattari's philosophy. This discussion will explore their work on the BwO in detail, elucidate the BwO as a state of pure potentiality and fluidity, distinguish between the organized body and the BwO, and compare the BwO with other philosophical concepts of the body and identity.

Deleuze and Guattari's concept of the BwO originates from Antonin Artaud's provocative and surreal vision of the body. Artaud introduced the idea in his radio play "To Have Done with the Judgment of God" (1947), where he depicted the body as a site of pure potential, free from the constraints of organized structures and societal norms. Artaud's BwO is a body stripped of its hierarchical organization, liberated from the imposed functions of organs and systems. It is a body that exists in a state of continuous becoming, open to new forms of experience and sensation.

Deleuze and Guattari adopted and expanded upon Artaud's idea, integrating it into their broader critique of psychoanalysis, capitalism, and state control. For them, the BwO represents a body in its most abstract and potential form, a body that defies the rigid structures and categorizations imposed by traditional thought. In "A Thousand Plateaus," they describe the BwO as a plane of immanence, a field where the conventional boundaries and hierarchies that define bodies are dissolved. It is a site where new connections and assemblages can emerge, unencumbered by the limitations of organized functions.

The BwO is characterized by its state of pure potentiality and fluidity. It is a body that is always in the process of becoming, never fixed or static. This state of becoming is central to Deleuze and Guattari's philosophy, which emphasizes the importance of continuous transformation and the rejection of fixed identities. The BwO embodies this philosophy by representing a body that is open to endless possibilities, capable of forming new relationships and connections.

In contrast to the BwO, the organized body is a body that has been structured and categorized according to specific functions and roles. It is a body that has been shaped by societal norms, medical classifications, and psychoanalytic theories. The organized body is subject to hierarchical organization, where each organ and function is assigned a specific place and purpose. This organization imposes limitations on the body's potential, reducing it to a functional organism that serves predefined roles.

Deleuze and Guattari argue that the organized body constrains desire by channeling it into fixed pathways and predetermined functions. In psychoanalytic theory, for example, desire is often understood as a lack or a drive toward specific objects, constrained by the structures of the Oedipus complex and other psychological frameworks. In contrast, Deleuze and Guattari view desire as a productive force that creates connections and assemblages. The BwO is the plane on which this productive desire operates, free from the constraints of organized structures.

The distinction between the BwO and the organized body is crucial for understanding Deleuze and Guattari's critique of traditional systems of thought. They argue that hierarchical structures, whether in psychoanalysis, capitalism, or the state, impose rigid classifications and roles that constrain the body's potential. The BwO offers a way to resist these constraints by envisioning a body that exists in a state of continuous flux and transformation. It is a body that can always become something new, forming new connections and assemblages that transcend established norms and functions.

To further elucidate the concept of the BwO, it is helpful to compare it with other philosophical concepts of the body and identity. One useful comparison is with the phenomenological concept of the lived body, as developed by philosophers like Maurice Merleau-Ponty. In phenomenology, the lived body is understood as the body experienced from the first-person perspective, the body as it is lived and perceived in everyday existence. This concept emphasizes the embodied nature of human experience, highlighting the ways in which the body is central to perception, action, and identity.

While the lived body in phenomenology shares some similarities with the BwO, such as the emphasis on the body's fluid and dynamic nature, there are important differences. The lived body is still understood within the context of its functions and roles in perception and action. It is a body that is always oriented toward the world and its tasks, shaped by its engagements and interactions. In contrast, the BwO represents a more radical departure from functional organization, envisioning a body that exists beyond the constraints of roles and functions.

Another useful comparison is with the post-structuralist concept of the fragmented body, as explored by theorists like Michel Foucault and Julia Kristeva. In post-structuralism, the body is understood as a site of multiple, often conflicting forces and identities. It is a body that is shaped by discourses, power relations, and cultural practices, fragmented and decentered. The fragmented body challenges the notion of a unified and stable identity, emphasizing the ways in which the body is always in the process of being constituted and reconstituted.

The BwO shares with the fragmented body the emphasis on multiplicity and fluidity. Both concepts reject the idea of a fixed and stable body, highlighting the ways in which the body is always open to new configurations and identities. However, the BwO goes further in its radical potentiality, envisioning a body that is not just fragmented but completely free from the constraints of any fixed organization. It is a body that can always become something new, forming connections and assemblages that are not limited by existing structures and categories.

In addition to these comparisons, the BwO can also be contrasted with more traditional philosophical concepts of the body, such as the Cartesian body-mind dualism. In Cartesian philosophy, the body is often understood as a machine, a collection of parts that function together according to mechanical principles. This understanding of the body as a machine imposes a rigid structure and hierarchy, where each part is assigned a specific role and function. The BwO challenges this mechanistic view by envisioning a body that is fluid, dynamic, and open to endless possibilities.

The BwO also contrasts with the Aristotelian concept of the body as a natural organism, where each part has a specific purpose and place within the whole. In Aristotelian philosophy, the body is understood in terms of its functions and roles, with each organ and system contributing to the overall functioning of the organism. The BwO rejects this teleological understanding of the body, envisioning a body that exists beyond the constraints of purpose and function.

In conclusion, the concept of the Body without Organs (BwO) is a profound and influential idea in the philosophical works of Gilles Deleuze and Félix Guattari. It represents a body in its most abstract and potential form, a body that defies the rigid structures and categorizations imposed by traditional thought. The BwO is characterized by its state of pure potentiality and fluidity, existing in a state of continuous becoming. It offers a radical critique of the organized body, which is constrained by hierarchical organization and fixed roles.

By comparing the BwO with other philosophical concepts of the body and identity, such as the phenomenological lived body, the post-structuralist fragmented body, and traditional Cartesian and Aristotelian notions, we can better understand its significance and implications. The BwO challenges conventional understandings of the body, promoting a philosophy of becoming and multiplicity, where new forms of life and desire can emerge. Understanding the theoretical foundations of the BwO provides valuable insights into Deleuze and Guattari's critique of hierarchical systems and their vision of a more fluid and dynamic world.

32. IMPLICATIONS OF THE BODY WITHOUT ORGANS IN CONTEMPORARY THOUGHT

The concept of the Body without Organs (BwO), developed by Gilles Deleuze and Félix Guattari, offers a radical rethinking of the body, identity, and subjectivity. By envisioning the body as a fluid, dynamic entity free from hierarchical organization, the BwO challenges traditional notions of identity and provides a framework for understanding the body in more complex and interconnected terms. This discussion will explore the broader implications of the BwO concept in contemporary thought, particularly its challenges to traditional identity and subjectivity, its application in postmodern and poststructuralist thought, and its influence on contemporary theories of embodiment and corporeality. A case study will also examine the BwO's impact on feminist and queer theories.

The BwO fundamentally challenges traditional notions of identity and subjectivity by proposing a body that is not constrained by fixed structures or predefined roles. Traditional Western philosophy has often conceptualized identity and subjectivity in terms of stable, coherent entities. For instance, Cartesian dualism posits a clear distinction between mind and body, with the mind as the seat of identity and the body as a machine-like entity. Similarly, psychoanalytic theories, such as those of Freud and Lacan, frame identity in terms of a structured psyche, with the body playing a secondary role.

In contrast, the BwO represents a body that is always in a state of becoming, open to new connections and assemblages. It is a body that defies the rigid classifications and hierarchical structures that typically define identity. This fluidity and openness suggest that identity is not a fixed essence but a dynamic process, constantly reconstituted through interactions and experiences. The BwO thus challenges the notion of a stable, unified self, proposing instead a multiplicity of selves that emerge through the body's interactions with the world.

This rethinking of identity and subjectivity aligns closely with postmodern and poststructuralist thought, which also critiques the idea of stable, coherent identities. Postmodern theorists, such as Jean-François Lyotard and Michel Foucault, argue that identities are constructed through discourse and power relations, rather than being inherent or fixed. They emphasize the fragmented and contingent nature of identity, reflecting the BwO's emphasis on fluidity and potentiality.

Poststructuralist thought, particularly as developed by thinkers like Jacques Derrida and Julia Kristeva, also resonates with the BwO concept. Derrida's notion of deconstruction, which involves the unraveling of fixed meanings and binary oppositions, parallels the BwO's challenge to hierarchical structures. Kristeva's exploration of abjection and the semiotic (the pre-linguistic, bodily dimension of experience) further aligns with the BwO's emphasis on the body's dynamic and disruptive potential.

The BwO's influence extends to contemporary theories of embodiment and corporeality, which seek to understand the body not as a passive object but as an active, dynamic agent. These theories challenge the traditional mind-body dualism and emphasize the body's role in shaping experience and identity. The BwO provides a framework for understanding the body as a site of continuous transformation, where new forms of embodiment can emerge.

For instance, phenomenological approaches to embodiment, as developed by thinkers like Maurice Merleau-Ponty, emphasize the body's central role in perception and action. Merleau-Ponty's notion of the lived body, which is experienced from a first-person perspective and engaged with the world, resonates with the BwO's emphasis on the body's potentiality and fluidity. However, while phenomenology tends to focus on the body's coherent and intentional engagement with the world, the BwO pushes this further by highlighting the body's capacity for disruption and transformation.

Contemporary feminist and queer theories have also drawn on the BwO to critique traditional understandings of gender and sexuality and to explore new forms of embodiment and identity. Feminist theorists like Elizabeth Grosz and Rosi Braidotti have used the BwO to challenge essentialist notions of the female body and to explore the potential for new, fluid forms of gender identity. Queer theorists like Judith Butler and José Esteban Muñoz have similarly engaged with the BwO to critique normative frameworks of sexuality and to imagine more expansive possibilities for queer existence.

In feminist theory, the BwO offers a way to think beyond the binary structures that typically define gender. Traditional gender norms impose rigid classifications and roles on bodies, constraining their potential for expression and transformation. The BwO's emphasis on fluidity and potentiality provides a framework for understanding gender as a dynamic process, open to continuous reconfiguration. This aligns with Butler's concept of gender performativity, which argues that gender is not a fixed identity but a series of acts and performances that constitute identity over time.

Braidotti's work on nomadic subjectivity also resonates with the BwO's emphasis on fluidity and becoming. Braidotti proposes a vision of subjectivity that is not fixed or stable but constantly in motion, adapting and transforming in response to changing conditions. This nomadic subjectivity aligns with the BwO's rejection of hierarchical structures and its embrace of continuous transformation.

Queer theory's engagement with the BwO similarly emphasizes the potential for new forms of identity and embodiment that resist normative constraints. Muñoz's concept of queer utopia, which imagines a future where queer identities and expressions can flourish without constraint, aligns with the BwO's vision of a body open to endless possibilities. The BwO provides a framework for imagining queer existence beyond the rigid binaries and normative frameworks that typically define sexuality.

A detailed case study of the BwO's impact on feminist and queer theories illustrates its profound influence on contemporary thought. Butler's work on gender performativity and Muñoz's exploration of queer utopia both draw on the BwO to critique traditional frameworks and to envision new possibilities for identity and embodiment.

Butler's concept of gender performativity argues that gender is not an inherent identity but a series of acts and performances that constitute identity over time. This aligns with the BwO's emphasis on the body's fluidity and potentiality, suggesting that gender is a dynamic process open to continuous reconfiguration. By rejecting the idea of a stable, essential gender identity, Butler's performativity theory resonates with the BwO's critique of hierarchical structures and its vision of continuous becoming.

Muñoz's concept of queer utopia similarly engages with the BwO to imagine a future where queer identities and expressions can flourish without constraint. Muñoz argues that queer existence is always oriented toward the future, seeking to create new possibilities and forms of life. This aligns with the BwO's emphasis on potentiality and transformation, suggesting that queer identities are always in the process of becoming, open to new connections and assemblages.

The BwO's influence on feminist and queer theories demonstrates its broader implications for contemporary thought. By challenging traditional notions of identity and subjectivity, the BwO provides a framework for understanding the body as a site of continuous transformation and potentiality. This has profound implications for how we understand gender, sexuality, and embodiment, offering new possibilities for identity and expression.

In conclusion, the concept of the Body without Organs (BwO) offers a radical rethinking of the body, identity, and subjectivity. By envisioning the body as a fluid, dynamic entity free from hierarchical organization, the BwO challenges traditional notions of identity and provides a framework for understanding the body in more complex and interconnected terms. Its application in postmodern and poststructuralist thought aligns closely with critiques of stable, coherent identities and emphasizes the fragmented, contingent nature of identity. The BwO's influence on contemporary theories of embodiment and corporeality highlights its significance in rethinking the body as an active, dynamic agent.

The BwO's impact on feminist and queer theories demonstrates its broader implications for contemporary thought. By challenging essentialist notions of gender and sexuality, the BwO provides a framework for exploring new forms of identity and embodiment that resist normative constraints. The case study of Butler's gender performativity and Muñoz's queer utopia illustrates the BwO's profound influence on these fields, offering new possibilities for understanding and expressing identity. Understanding the implications of the BwO provides valuable insights into contemporary critiques of identity and subjectivity, enriching our appreciation of the body's potential for transformation and becoming.

33. THE BODY WITHOUT ORGANS IN ART AND PERFORMANCE

The concept of the Body without Organs (BwO), as developed by Gilles Deleuze and Félix Guattari, has profoundly influenced various artistic and performance practices. This notion, which envisions the body as a fluid, dynamic entity free from hierarchical organization and fixed structures, offers a rich framework for understanding and creating art that challenges conventional forms and explores new realms of expression. This discussion will explore how the BwO is represented in experimental theater and performance art, its role in visual art focusing on abstraction and deconstruction, and examples of artists and performers who embody the BwO in their work. A detailed case study will analyze the works of performance artist Marina Abramović and her exploration of the body.

Experimental theater and performance art are particularly fertile grounds for the exploration of the BwO. These forms of art often seek to break down traditional boundaries between the performer and the audience, the body and its representation, and the physical and the conceptual. By doing so, they align closely with the BwO's emphasis on fluidity, potentiality, and the dismantling of hierarchical structures.

In experimental theater, the BwO can be seen in the work of practitioners who challenge conventional narrative structures, character development, and staging techniques. For instance, the Theater of Cruelty, developed by Antonin Artaud, who originally coined the term BwO, sought to create a visceral, immersive experience that disrupted the traditional separation between the audience and the performance. Artaud envisioned a theater that would engage the senses directly and powerfully, stripping away the layers of mediation that typically structure theatrical experiences. This approach aligns with the BwO's focus on immediate, unmediated experience and the breaking down of structured forms.

Performance art, which often involves the artist's body as the primary medium, provides a direct exploration of the BwO. Performance artists frequently engage in acts that challenge conventional uses and perceptions of the body, pushing the limits of endurance, sensation, and identity. These performances can be seen as attempts to actualize the BwO by exploring the body's potential beyond its conventional functions and constraints.

The BwO also plays a significant role in visual art, particularly in movements that emphasize abstraction and deconstruction. In abstract art, the traditional forms and representations are dissolved, giving way to compositions that explore pure form, color, and texture. This can be seen as an artistic parallel to the BwO's philosophical deconstruction of the body's organized structure. Abstract artists like Jackson Pollock and Mark Rothko, who focus on the interplay of forms and colors rather than figurative representation, create works that resonate with the BwO's emphasis on fluidity and potentiality.

Deconstruction in visual art involves breaking down and reconfiguring established forms and structures. Artists like Marcel Duchamp, with his readymades, and Pablo Picasso, with his Cubist explorations, challenged traditional notions of art and representation. By dismantling and reassembling visual elements, these artists created works that reflect the BwO's rejection of hierarchical organization and embrace of continuous transformation.

Several artists and performers have embodied the BwO in their work, creating pieces that explore the body's potential and challenge conventional forms. Performance artists like Chris Burden, Yoko Ono, and Marina Abramović have used their bodies to push the boundaries of endurance, sensation, and identity, creating works that resonate with the BwO's principles.

Chris Burden's early performance pieces, such as "Shoot" (1971), where he had himself shot in the arm, and "Trans-Fixed" (1974), where he had himself crucified to a Volkswagen Beetle, directly confront the body's limits and the societal structures that define and constrain it. These performances can be seen as attempts to actualize the BwO by exploring the body's potential for pain, endurance, and transformation.

Yoko Ono's "Cut Piece" (1964) is another seminal work that explores the BwO. In this performance, Ono sat on stage and invited the audience to cut pieces of her clothing with scissors, gradually exposing her body. The performance challenged the boundaries between the performer and the audience, the personal and the public, and the structured and the unstructured body. By inviting the audience to participate in the deconstruction of her body's representation, Ono created a powerful exploration of the BwO's principles.

Marina Abramović's work provides a particularly rich case study for examining the BwO in art and performance. Throughout her career, Abramović has used her body as both the subject and the medium of her art, exploring themes of endurance, vulnerability, and transformation. Her performances often push the limits of physical and psychological endurance, creating intense, visceral experiences that resonate with the BwO's emphasis on fluidity and potentiality.

In her performance "Rhythm 0" (1974), Abramović invited the audience to use 72 objects on her body in any way they desired, relinquishing control and allowing the audience to act upon her. Objects ranged from feathers and flowers to knives and a loaded gun. This performance highlighted the body's vulnerability and the fluid boundaries between the self and others, the structured and the unstructured. By surrendering control and allowing the audience to impose their actions upon her body, Abramović explored the BwO's principle of breaking down hierarchical structures and exposing the body's potential for transformation.

Another notable work, "The Artist is Present" (2010), involved Abramović sitting silently at a table in the Museum of Modern Art in New York, inviting visitors to sit across from her and engage in silent eye contact. This performance lasted for 736 hours and 30 minutes over the course of three months. By creating an open, unmediated space for interaction, Abramović explored the BwO's emphasis on immediate, direct experience. The performance dismantled traditional barriers between the artist and the audience, creating a space where new forms of connection and presence could emerge.

Abramović's work often involves elements of ritual and endurance, exploring the body's limits and its potential for transformation. In "The House with the Ocean View" (2002), she lived for 12 days in a constructed space in a gallery, with no food and limited interaction with the outside world. Visitors could observe her through the gallery windows, witnessing her daily rituals and endurance. This performance emphasized the body's potential for purification and transformation, aligning with the BwO's principles of fluidity and becoming.

In her collaboration with Ulay, such as in "Rest Energy" (1980), where the couple leaned backward holding a taut bow with an arrow pointed at Abramović's heart, they explored themes of trust, tension, and the limits of the body. These performances highlighted the relational aspects of the BwO, emphasizing the body's potential for connection and the dissolution of individual boundaries.

In visual art, the BwO has influenced a wide range of practices that emphasize abstraction, deconstruction, and the exploration of materiality. Artists like Eva Hesse, with her use of unconventional materials and organic forms, and Louise Bourgeois, with her exploration of bodily forms and emotional states, create works that resonate with the BwO's emphasis on fluidity and potentiality.

Eva Hesse's sculptures, often made from materials like latex, fiberglass, and resin, challenge traditional notions of form and structure. Her works, such as "Hang Up" (1966) and "Repetition Nineteen III" (1968), explore the tension between organic and industrial forms, creating pieces that seem to exist in a state of continuous transformation. This aligns with the BwO's rejection of fixed structures and its embrace of dynamic potentiality.

Louise Bourgeois's sculptures and installations, such as "Maman" (1999) and "The Destruction of the Father" (1974), explore themes of identity, memory, and the body. Her works often incorporate organic forms and evoke visceral, emotional responses, reflecting the BwO's emphasis on the body's fluidity and potential for transformation. Bourgeois's exploration of the body's interiority and emotional states aligns with the BwO's focus on breaking down hierarchical structures and revealing the body's potentiality.

In conclusion, the concept of the Body without Organs (BwO) has profoundly influenced art and performance, providing a framework for exploring the body's fluidity, potentiality, and resistance to hierarchical structures. In experimental theater and performance art, the BwO is represented through practices that challenge traditional boundaries and create immersive, visceral experiences. In visual art, the BwO influences movements that emphasize abstraction, deconstruction, and the exploration of materiality.

Artists and performers like Antonin Artaud, Chris Burden, Yoko Ono, and Marina Abramović embody the BwO in their work, creating pieces that challenge conventional forms and explore the body's potential for transformation. Abramović's performances, in particular, provide a rich case study for examining the BwO, as she uses her body to explore themes of endurance, vulnerability, and connection. Her work highlights the BwO's principles of fluidity, potentiality, and the dismantling of hierarchical structures, offering powerful explorations of the body's capacity for continuous becoming and transformation.

34. THE BODY WITHOUT ORGANS IN LITERATURE

The concept of the Body without Organs (BwO), formulated by Gilles Deleuze and Félix Guattari, offers a rich and provocative framework for exploring transformation, identity, and corporeality in literary narratives. In literature, the BwO can be employed as a metaphor for characters undergoing profound changes, challenging traditional notions of identity and fixed bodily forms. This discussion will examine the application of the BwO in literary narratives, focusing on how it serves as a metaphor for transformation, the narrative techniques that reflect its fluidity and potentiality, and the thematic exploration of identity and corporeality in fiction. A detailed case study will analyze William S. Burroughs' novels and his depiction of the BwO.

The BwO serves as a powerful metaphor in literature for characters experiencing transformation. Traditional narratives often depict characters with fixed identities and stable bodies, conforming to societal norms and biological determinism. However, the BwO challenges these conventions by envisioning characters whose bodies and identities are in constant flux, open to new possibilities and forms. This metaphor allows authors to explore themes of metamorphosis, identity crisis, and the dissolution of boundaries.

In Franz Kafka's "The Metamorphosis," the protagonist, Gregor Samsa, undergoes a dramatic physical transformation, waking up one morning to find himself turned into a giant insect. This transformation disrupts his previously stable identity and societal role, rendering him a being without a fixed form or function. Kafka's depiction of Gregor's metamorphosis echoes the BwO's rejection of hierarchical organization and fixed identities, highlighting the body's potential for radical change.

In Virginia Woolf's "Orlando," the protagonist undergoes a transformation in gender, living for centuries and changing from male to female. This fluidity in Orlando's identity and corporeality challenges the rigid binaries of gender and the notion of a fixed self. Woolf's narrative reflects the BwO's emphasis on the body's potential for transformation and the dissolution of conventional boundaries.

Narrative techniques that reflect the fluidity and potentiality of the BwO often involve fragmented structures, non-linear timelines, and multiple perspectives. These techniques disrupt traditional narrative coherence, mirroring the BwO's rejection of fixed forms and hierarchical organization.

In James Joyce's "Ulysses," the stream-of-consciousness technique captures the fluid and dynamic nature of human thought and experience. The narrative shifts between different characters' perspectives and inner monologues, creating a sense of multiplicity and continuous transformation. This technique reflects the BwO's emphasis on fluidity and the potential for new connections and assemblages.

In Samuel Beckett's "Molloy," the fragmented and disjointed narrative structure mirrors the BwO's rejection of linear progression and fixed identities. The protagonist, Molloy, experiences a dissolution of self and a blurring of boundaries between body and environment. Beckett's narrative technique, characterized by repetition, disorientation, and ambiguity, evokes the BwO's principles of fluidity and potentiality.

The thematic exploration of identity and corporeality in fiction often centers on the dissolution of fixed boundaries and the embrace of transformation. The BwO provides a framework for understanding characters and narratives that challenge traditional notions of the body and identity.

In Jeanette Winterson's "Written on the Body," the narrator's gender is never specified, creating a fluid and ambiguous identity that defies categorization. This narrative choice reflects the BwO's emphasis on the body's potential for continuous transformation and the rejection of fixed identities. Winterson's exploration of love, desire, and corporeality aligns with the BwO's principles, highlighting the body as a site of fluidity and potentiality.

In Octavia Butler's "Lilith's Brood" trilogy, the protagonist, Lilith, undergoes genetic modifications that transform her body and identity. The narrative explores themes of hybridity, adaptation, and the dissolution of boundaries between human and alien. Butler's depiction of Lilith's transformation reflects the BwO's emphasis on the body's potential for new connections and assemblages, challenging traditional notions of identity and corporeality.

William S. Burroughs' novels provide a compelling case study for examining the BwO in literature. Burroughs' work is characterized by a radical experimentation with narrative form, identity, and the body, reflecting the BwO's principles of fluidity and potentiality.

In "Naked Lunch," Burroughs presents a fragmented and non-linear narrative that defies traditional storytelling conventions. The novel's structure mirrors the BwO's rejection of fixed forms and hierarchical organization, creating a sense of disorientation and continuous transformation. Characters in "Naked Lunch" undergo extreme physical and psychological changes, reflecting the BwO's emphasis on the body's potential for metamorphosis.

The protagonist, William Lee, navigates a surreal and nightmarish landscape filled with grotesque and constantly shifting bodies. Burroughs' depiction of drug addiction, control, and the dissolution of identity aligns with the BwO's principles, challenging conventional notions of the self and the body. The novel's hallucinatory and chaotic narrative reflects the BwO's fluidity and potentiality, creating a literary exploration of the body without organs.

In "The Soft Machine," Burroughs continues to experiment with narrative form and the depiction of the body. The novel employs the cut-up technique, a method of cutting and rearranging text to create new and unexpected connections. This technique mirrors the BwO's emphasis on breaking down hierarchical structures and creating new assemblages. The fragmented and disjointed narrative reflects the BwO's rejection of linear progression and fixed identities, creating a sense of continuous transformation.

Characters in "The Soft Machine" undergo radical physical and psychological changes, often merging and dissolving in ways that challenge conventional notions of the body. Burroughs' depiction of shape-shifting, mutation, and the dissolution of boundaries between self and other reflects the BwO's principles, highlighting the body's potential for new forms and connections.

In "Nova Express," Burroughs explores themes of control, resistance, and the dissolution of identity. The novel's fragmented and non-linear narrative reflects the BwO's rejection of fixed forms and hierarchical organization. Characters in "Nova Express" are caught in a struggle against forces of control and manipulation, experiencing transformations that challenge conventional notions of the self and the body.

Burroughs' depiction of addiction, mind control, and the breakdown of identity aligns with the BwO's principles, emphasizing the body's potential for resistance and transformation. The novel's hallucinatory and surreal narrative creates a literary exploration of the body without organs, challenging traditional storytelling conventions and notions of corporeality.

In conclusion, the concept of the Body without Organs (BwO) offers a rich framework for exploring transformation, identity, and corporeality in literary narratives. The BwO serves as a powerful metaphor for characters undergoing profound changes, challenging traditional notions of fixed identities and stable bodies. Narrative techniques that reflect the fluidity and potentiality of the BwO often involve fragmented structures, non-linear timelines, and multiple perspectives, mirroring the BwO's rejection of hierarchical organization.

Thematic exploration of identity and corporeality in fiction often centers on the dissolution of fixed boundaries and the embrace of transformation. The BwO provides a framework for understanding characters and narratives that challenge traditional notions of the body and identity, highlighting the body's potential for continuous becoming and new connections.

William S. Burroughs' novels provide a compelling case study for examining the BwO in literature. Burroughs' radical experimentation with narrative form, identity, and the body reflects the BwO's principles of fluidity and potentiality. His fragmented and hallucinatory narratives, filled with characters undergoing extreme transformations, create a literary exploration of the body without organs, challenging conventional storytelling conventions and notions of corporeality. Through the lens of the BwO, Burroughs' work highlights the body's potential for resistance, transformation, and continuous becoming.

35. THE BODY WITHOUT ORGANS IN FILM AND MEDIA

The concept of the Body without Organs (BwO), introduced by Gilles Deleuze and Félix Guattari, has found profound and dynamic expressions in film and media. By envisioning the body as a fluid, dynamic entity free from hierarchical organization and fixed structures, the BwO challenges conventional representations of the body and identity. This discussion explores how the BwO is represented in film and media, focusing on cinematic techniques that evoke the BwO, examples of films and media that challenge conventional representations of the body, the role of special effects and digital technology in creating BwO-like imagery, and a detailed case study of the portrayal of the BwO in David Cronenberg's films, such as "Videodrome" and "eXistenZ."

Cinematic techniques that evoke the BwO often involve visual and narrative strategies that disrupt conventional representations of the body and identity. These techniques emphasize fluidity, transformation, and the dissolution of boundaries, mirroring the BwO's rejection of fixed forms and hierarchical organization.

One such technique is the use of fragmented and disjointed narratives that disrupt linear storytelling and challenge the coherence of identity. Films like David Lynch's "Mulholland Drive" and Christopher Nolan's "Memento" use non-linear structures and fragmented timelines to reflect the fluid and dynamic nature of identity. These films create a sense of disorientation and continuous transformation, aligning with the BwO's emphasis on the body's potential for new connections and assemblages.

Another technique is the use of surreal and dreamlike imagery to depict the body in states of metamorphosis and fluidity. Films by directors such as Federico Fellini and Luis Buñuel often employ surreal visual elements to challenge conventional representations of the body and identity. Fellini's "8½" and Buñuel's "Un Chien Andalou" use dream sequences and surreal imagery to explore the body's potential for transformation, reflecting the BwO's principles.

Special effects and digital technology play a crucial role in creating BwO-like imagery in contemporary cinema. Advances in CGI (computer-generated imagery) and practical effects allow filmmakers to depict the body in ways that were previously impossible, emphasizing its fluidity and potential for transformation.

In films like "The Matrix" and "Inception," digital technology is used to create visual representations of the body that challenge conventional notions of identity and reality. "The Matrix" uses CGI to depict characters' bodies in virtual environments, where the boundaries between physical and digital realities are blurred. This visual representation of the body as a site of continuous transformation and potentiality aligns with the BwO's principles.

"Avatar," directed by James Cameron, uses advanced motion capture and CGI to create the Na'vi, a fictional race whose bodies are depicted with a high degree of fluidity and adaptability. The film's visual effects emphasize the interconnectedness of the Na'vi with their environment, reflecting the BwO's emphasis on the body's potential for new connections and assemblages.

Films and media that challenge conventional representations of the body often explore themes of transformation, hybridity, and the dissolution of boundaries. These works align with the BwO's principles by depicting the body as a site of continuous becoming and potentiality.

David Cronenberg's films provide a compelling case study for examining the BwO in cinema. Cronenberg's work is characterized by a fascination with the body's potential for transformation and the dissolution of boundaries between the self and the other, the human and the machine. His films often depict extreme physical and psychological changes, reflecting the BwO's emphasis on fluidity and potentiality.

In "Videodrome" (1983), Cronenberg explores themes of media influence, bodily transformation, and the dissolution of reality. The protagonist, Max Renn, experiences a series of hallucinations and physical changes after being exposed to a mysterious broadcast signal. His body undergoes radical transformations, including the development of a vaginal-like opening in his abdomen that can receive videotapes. These transformations challenge conventional representations of the body, depicting it as a fluid and dynamic entity. The film's use of practical effects and surreal imagery creates a visual representation of the BwO, emphasizing the body's potential for new connections and assemblages.

"eXistenZ" (1999) continues Cronenberg's exploration of the BwO through themes of virtual reality, identity, and bodily transformation. The film's protagonists, Allegra Geller and Ted Pikul, navigate a virtual reality game that blurs the boundaries between the real and the virtual. Their bodies are depicted as sites of continuous transformation, with bio-ports implanted in their spines to connect to the game and organic game consoles that resemble mutated living organisms. The film's visual effects and narrative structure emphasize the fluidity and potentiality of the body, reflecting the BwO's principles.

In "The Fly" (1986), Cronenberg depicts the gradual transformation of scientist Seth Brundle into a human-fly hybrid after a teleportation experiment goes wrong. Brundle's body undergoes a series of grotesque changes, challenging conventional representations of human identity and corporeality. The film's use of practical effects and makeup creates a visceral depiction of the body in a state of continuous becoming, reflecting the BwO's emphasis on transformation and potentiality.

Cronenberg's "Crash" (1996) explores themes of bodily transformation, desire, and the dissolution of boundaries between the human and the mechanical. The film's characters are sexually aroused by car crashes and the physical injuries they sustain, blurring the boundaries between pleasure and pain, the organic and the mechanical. The film's depiction of bodies modified by technology and desire aligns with the BwO's principles, emphasizing the body's potential for new forms and connections.

Other filmmakers and media creators have also explored the BwO through their work, using cinematic techniques and digital technology to challenge conventional representations of the body. In Ridley Scott's "Blade Runner" (1982) and its sequel "Blade Runner 2049" (2017), the depiction of replicants—artificial beings with human-like bodies—explores themes of identity, transformation, and the dissolution of boundaries between the human and the artificial. The films' visual effects and narrative structures reflect the BwO's principles, emphasizing the fluidity and potentiality of the body.

In Jonathan Glazer's "Under the Skin" (2013), the protagonist, an alien played by Scarlett Johansson, undergoes a series of transformations that challenge conventional representations of the body and identity. The film's use of surreal and abstract imagery, combined with its fragmented narrative structure, creates a sense of continuous becoming and potentiality, aligning with the BwO's principles.

The television series "Westworld," created by Jonathan Nolan and Lisa Joy, explores themes of bodily transformation, identity, and the dissolution of boundaries between the human and the artificial. The show's depiction of hosts—androids with human-like bodies that can be reprogrammed and modified—reflects the BwO's emphasis on fluidity and potentiality. The series' use of advanced visual effects and narrative techniques challenges conventional representations of the body, creating a complex exploration of the BwO.

In conclusion, the concept of the Body without Organs (BwO) has found profound and dynamic expressions in film and media. Cinematic techniques that evoke the BwO often involve visual and narrative strategies that disrupt conventional representations of the body and identity, emphasizing fluidity, transformation, and the dissolution of boundaries. Special effects and digital technology play a crucial role in creating BwO-like imagery, allowing filmmakers to depict the body in ways that emphasize its potential for new connections and assemblages.

Films and media that challenge conventional representations of the body often explore themes of transformation, hybridity, and the dissolution of boundaries, aligning with the BwO's principles. David Cronenberg's films, such as "Videodrome," "eXistenZ," "The Fly," and "Crash," provide a compelling case study for examining the BwO in cinema. Cronenberg's work is characterized by a fascination with the body's potential for transformation and the dissolution of boundaries, using practical effects, digital technology, and narrative techniques to create visual representations of the BwO.

Other filmmakers and media creators, such as Ridley Scott, Jonathan Glazer, and the creators of "Westworld," have also explored the BwO through their work, using cinematic techniques and digital technology to challenge conventional representations of the body and identity. By reflecting the BwO's principles of fluidity, potentiality, and the dismantling of hierarchical structures, these films and media provide powerful explorations of the body without organs in contemporary visual culture.

36. THE BODY WITHOUT ORGANS IN TECHNOLOGY AND CYBERCULTURE

The concept of the Body without Organs (BwO), introduced by Gilles Deleuze and Félix Guattari, provides a rich framework for understanding the evolving relationship between the body and technology in contemporary cyberculture. By envisioning the body as a fluid, dynamic entity free from hierarchical organization and fixed structures, the BwO challenges traditional notions of corporeality and identity. This exploration will analyze the implications of the BwO in the context of technology and cyberculture, focusing on virtual bodies and avatars in digital spaces, the intersection of BwO with transhumanism and posthumanism, and the impact of biohacking and cyborg cultures on the perception of the body. A detailed case study will examine the role of the BwO in the online gaming community and virtual reality environments.

The BwO's relationship to virtual bodies and avatars in digital spaces is a fundamental aspect of its application in cyberculture. In virtual worlds, such as those found in online games and social media platforms, users create and manipulate avatars that represent their presence in these environments. These avatars are often customizable, allowing users to experiment with different forms and identities. This flexibility aligns with the BwO's principle of fluidity and potentiality, as avatars can be continuously transformed and adapted to suit the user's desires.

Virtual bodies in digital spaces challenge the fixed and hierarchical structures traditionally associated with physical bodies. In virtual environments, the boundaries between self and other, human and non-human, and physical and digital become blurred. Users can adopt multiple avatars, explore different genders and species, and engage in activities that defy the limitations of the physical world. This multiplicity and fluidity resonate with the BwO's rejection of fixed identities and its emphasis on continuous becoming.

The BwO's principles are evident in the ways users interact with their avatars. For instance, in virtual worlds like "Second Life" or "World of Warcraft," users can create avatars that transcend their physical limitations, exploring new forms of identity and expression. These virtual bodies are not constrained by the same rules and norms that govern physical bodies, allowing for a more expansive exploration of the self. The fluid and dynamic nature of these avatars reflects the BwO's emphasis on the potential for new connections and assemblages.

The intersection of the BwO with concepts of transhumanism and posthumanism further expands its implications in cyberculture. Transhumanism advocates for the use of technology to enhance human capabilities and transcend biological limitations. This movement envisions a future where humans can augment their bodies with advanced technologies, such as brain-computer interfaces, genetic modifications, and artificial organs. The BwO aligns with transhumanism's emphasis on breaking down the boundaries between human and machine, exploring the body's potential for continuous transformation.

Posthumanism, on the other hand, critiques the anthropocentric focus of traditional humanism and emphasizes the interconnectedness of humans with technology, animals, and the environment. Posthumanist thought challenges the notion of a stable, unified human identity, instead highlighting the fluid and dynamic nature of existence. The BwO's rejection of fixed structures and its embrace of multiplicity resonate with posthumanist principles, suggesting that the body is a site of ongoing negotiation and transformation.

The impact of biohacking and cyborg cultures on the perception of the body illustrates the BwO's relevance in contemporary technological practices. Biohacking involves the modification of the body using DIY biology and technology, often outside traditional medical and scientific institutions. Biohackers may implant RFID chips, experiment with genetic modifications, or use nootropics to enhance cognitive function. These practices challenge conventional understandings of the body, aligning with the BwO's emphasis on fluidity and potentiality.

Cyborg culture, which embraces the integration of technology with the human body, also reflects the BwO's principles. Cyborgs, or cybernetic organisms, combine biological and technological components, blurring the boundaries between organic and inorganic, human and machine. Pioneering figures like Neil Harbisson, who has an antenna implanted in his skull that allows him to perceive colors as sound, exemplify the cyborg ethos. Harbisson's body is a site of continuous transformation, embodying the BwO's rejection of fixed structures and its embrace of new connections and assemblages.

A detailed case study of the BwO in the online gaming community and virtual reality environments highlights its practical implications in digital culture. Online gaming communities and virtual reality (VR) environments provide immersive experiences that challenge traditional notions of the body and identity, reflecting the BwO's principles of fluidity and potentiality.

In online gaming, players create and control avatars that represent them within the game world. These avatars are highly customizable, allowing players to experiment with different appearances, abilities, and identities. Games like "World of Warcraft," "Final Fantasy XIV," and "The Elder Scrolls Online" offer expansive character creation systems, enabling players to design avatars that reflect their desires and imaginations. This customization process embodies the BwO's emphasis on the body's potential for continuous transformation.

The immersive nature of online games allows players to explore new forms of identity and expression. Players can adopt different genders, species, and roles, experiencing the game world from multiple perspectives. This multiplicity of identities challenges traditional notions of a stable, unified self, aligning with the BwO's rejection of fixed structures. In multiplayer games, the social interactions between players further emphasize the fluidity of identity, as players form connections and alliances that transcend their physical identities.

Virtual reality environments take this immersion to another level, creating digital spaces where users can interact with their surroundings and each other in real-time. VR platforms like "Oculus Rift," "HTC Vive," and "PlayStation VR" enable users to enter virtual worlds where the boundaries between the physical and digital become increasingly porous. In VR, users can manipulate their virtual bodies with a high degree of precision, exploring new forms of movement and interaction that defy the limitations of the physical body.

The use of haptic feedback and motion tracking in VR further enhances the sense of embodiment, allowing users to feel as though they are truly present in the virtual environment. This sense of presence aligns with the BwO's emphasis on immediate, unmediated experience, as users engage with their virtual bodies in ways that challenge conventional representations of corporeality.

The portrayal of the BwO in VR environments often involves the use of special effects and digital technology to create fluid, dynamic representations of the body. In VR experiences like "The Void" or "Half-Life: Alyx," users encounter virtual bodies and environments that transform and adapt in response to their actions. These transformations emphasize the potential for new connections and assemblages, reflecting the BwO's principles.

Moreover, the social aspects of online gaming and VR communities highlight the BwO's relevance in digital culture. Players and users form connections and alliances that transcend physical boundaries, creating virtual communities that are dynamic and fluid. These social interactions challenge traditional notions of identity and community, aligning with the BwO's emphasis on the dissolution of hierarchical structures.

In conclusion, the concept of the Body without Organs (BwO) provides a powerful framework for understanding the evolving relationship between the body and technology in contemporary cyberculture. The BwO's principles of fluidity, potentiality, and the rejection of fixed structures resonate with the ways virtual bodies and avatars are represented in digital spaces. The intersection of the BwO with transhumanism and posthumanism further expands its implications, highlighting the body's potential for continuous transformation and interconnectedness.

Biohacking and cyborg cultures illustrate the BwO's impact on the perception of the body, as individuals modify their bodies to enhance their capabilities and explore new forms of identity. The detailed case study of the BwO in the online gaming community and virtual reality environments underscores its practical relevance in digital culture. Online gaming and VR provide immersive experiences that challenge traditional notions of the body and identity, reflecting the BwO's principles through customizable avatars, immersive interactions, and the dissolution of boundaries between the physical and digital.

By embracing the BwO, technology and cyberculture offer new possibilities for understanding and experiencing the body, identity, and community, enriching our appreciation of the body's potential for continuous becoming and transformation.

37. THE BODY WITHOUT ORGANS IN CONTEMPORARY PHILOSOPHY

The concept of the Body without Organs (BwO), introduced by Gilles Deleuze and Félix Guattari in their seminal work "A Thousand Plateaus," remains a vital and provocative idea in contemporary philosophy. By envisioning the body as a fluid, dynamic entity free from hierarchical organization and fixed structures, the BwO challenges traditional notions of corporeality and identity. This exploration will delve into the ongoing relevance of the BwO in current philosophical debates, its connections with other philosophical movements such as object-oriented ontology and new materialism, and the critiques and expansions of the BwO concept in recent scholarship. A detailed case study will examine contemporary philosophers like Rosi Braidotti and Manuel DeLanda who engage with the BwO in their work.

The ongoing relevance of the BwO in contemporary philosophical debates is evident in its application across various fields, including metaphysics, ethics, political theory, and aesthetics. The BwO's emphasis on fluidity, potentiality, and the rejection of fixed structures resonates with current discussions on identity, embodiment, and the nature of being. As philosophers continue to grapple with the complexities of human existence in an increasingly interconnected and technologically advanced world, the BwO offers a framework for understanding the body and identity as dynamic and ever-evolving.

In metaphysics, the BwO challenges traditional dualistic thinking by emphasizing the body's continuous process of becoming. This perspective aligns with contemporary efforts to move beyond rigid categorizations and embrace a more holistic understanding of reality. The BwO's rejection of fixed structures also has ethical implications, as it encourages a more inclusive and flexible approach to identity and difference. By viewing identity as fluid and open to transformation, the

BwO promotes an ethic of openness and adaptability, which is crucial in addressing issues of diversity and inclusion.

The BwO's relevance in political theory is reflected in its critique of hierarchical systems and its advocacy for more decentralized and flexible forms of organization. In an era marked by increasing political polarization and the rise of authoritarianism, the BwO offers a vision of social and political structures that are more adaptive and responsive to change. This perspective is particularly relevant in discussions on grassroots movements, networked forms of governance, and the role of technology in shaping political engagement.

The BwO's connections with other philosophical movements, such as object-oriented ontology (OOO) and new materialism, further underscore its significance in contemporary thought. Object-oriented ontology, as developed by thinkers like Graham Harman and Timothy Morton, emphasizes the autonomy and agency of objects, challenging the anthropocentric focus of traditional philosophy. This perspective resonates with the BwO's rejection of hierarchical structures and its emphasis on the body's potential for new connections and assemblages.

In OOO, objects are seen as having their own intrinsic properties and capacities, independent of human perception and interaction. This view aligns with the BwO's emphasis on the body's dynamic and fluid nature, as both perspectives challenge the idea of a fixed and stable identity. By highlighting the agency and interconnectedness of objects, OOO offers a framework for understanding the body as a site of continuous transformation and potentiality.

New materialism, as articulated by scholars like Jane Bennett and Rosi Braidotti, emphasizes the vitality and agency of matter, challenging the traditional distinction between the organic and the inorganic. This perspective resonates with the BwO's emphasis on the body's potential for new connections and assemblages, as it views matter as dynamic and interconnected. New materialism's focus on the entanglement of human and non-human actors aligns with the BwO's rejection of fixed structures and its embrace of multiplicity.

Critiques and expansions of the BwO concept in recent scholarship highlight its continued relevance and the ongoing efforts to refine and develop its implications. Some critics argue that the BwO's emphasis on fluidity and potentiality can lead to a neglect of the material and embodied aspects of existence. They caution against an overly abstract or idealized view of the body, emphasizing the importance of grounding the BwO in concrete, lived experiences.

In response to these critiques, contemporary philosophers have sought to expand the BwO concept by incorporating insights from feminist theory, queer theory, and disability studies. These perspectives emphasize the importance of considering the material, embodied, and situated aspects of the body, highlighting the ways in which power, oppression, and resistance shape bodily experiences. By integrating these insights, scholars aim to develop a more nuanced and grounded understanding of the BwO that remains attentive to the complexities of lived experience.

Rosi Braidotti and Manuel DeLanda are two contemporary philosophers who have engaged deeply with the BwO concept, offering valuable expansions and interpretations that reflect its ongoing relevance in contemporary thought.

Rosi Braidotti, a prominent feminist philosopher, has drawn on the BwO to develop her concept of nomadic subjectivity. In her work, Braidotti emphasizes the fluid and dynamic nature of identity, challenging traditional notions of a stable, unified self. She argues that subjectivity is a process of continuous becoming, shaped by multiple and intersecting forces. This perspective aligns closely with the BwO's rejection of fixed structures and its embrace of multiplicity.

Braidotti's nomadic subjectivity is deeply influenced by the BwO's emphasis on potentiality and transformation. She envisions the nomadic subject as a body in motion, constantly adapting and responding to changing conditions. This perspective highlights the importance of flexibility and resilience in navigating the complexities of contemporary existence. By drawing on the BwO, Braidotti offers a vision of subjectivity that is open to new connections and assemblages, challenging the rigid boundaries that traditionally define identity.

Manuel DeLanda, a philosopher known for his work on assemblage theory, has also engaged extensively with the BwO concept. In his book "A New Philosophy of Society," DeLanda expands on Deleuze and Guattari's ideas to develop a framework for understanding social and material systems as dynamic assemblages. He argues that both social structures and material entities are composed of heterogeneous elements that interact and evolve over time.

DeLanda's assemblage theory aligns closely with the BwO's emphasis on fluidity and potentiality. He emphasizes the importance of considering the dynamic and interconnected nature of entities, challenging the notion of fixed and stable structures. By viewing social and material systems as assemblages, DeLanda offers a perspective that highlights the potential for transformation and innovation. This approach resonates with the BwO's rejection of hierarchical organization and its embrace of continuous becoming.

In addition to Braidotti and DeLanda, other contemporary philosophers have engaged with the BwO to develop new insights and perspectives. Elizabeth Grosz, for example, has drawn on the BwO to explore the intersections of bodies, space, and time. She emphasizes the importance of considering the spatial and temporal dimensions of bodily existence, highlighting the ways in which bodies are shaped by their environments and histories. This perspective aligns with the BwO's emphasis on the body's potential for new connections and assemblages, offering a more nuanced understanding of the ways in which bodies interact with their surroundings.

Jasbir Puar, a scholar in queer theory and disability studies, has also engaged with the BwO to critique normative frameworks of embodiment and identity. In her work, Puar emphasizes the importance of considering the ways in which power and oppression shape bodily experiences, highlighting the intersections of race, gender, sexuality, and disability. By drawing on the BwO, Puar offers a perspective that challenges the rigid boundaries that traditionally define bodies and identities, emphasizing the importance of flexibility and adaptability in navigating the complexities of contemporary existence.

In conclusion, the concept of the Body without Organs (BwO) remains a vital and provocative idea in contemporary philosophy, offering a framework for understanding the body and identity as dynamic and ever-evolving. The BwO's ongoing relevance in current philosophical debates is evident in its application across various fields, including metaphysics, ethics, political theory, and aesthetics. Its connections with other philosophical movements, such as object-oriented ontology and new materialism, further underscore its significance in contemporary thought.

Critiques and expansions of the BwO concept in recent scholarship highlight its continued relevance and the ongoing efforts to refine and develop its implications. By incorporating insights from feminist theory, queer theory, and disability studies, contemporary philosophers aim to develop a more nuanced and grounded understanding of the BwO that remains attentive to the complexities of lived experience.

The work of contemporary philosophers like Rosi Braidotti and Manuel DeLanda illustrates the BwO's ongoing impact and relevance. Braidotti's concept of nomadic subjectivity and DeLanda's assemblage theory both draw on the BwO to offer new perspectives on identity, subjectivity, and social systems. These engagements highlight the BwO's potential to inform and enrich contemporary philosophical thought, offering valuable insights into the fluid, dynamic, and interconnected nature of existence.

38. PRACTICAL APPLICATIONS OF THE BODY WITHOUT ORGANS

The concept of the Body without Organs (BwO), introduced by Gilles Deleuze and Félix Guattari, provides a rich and versatile framework for understanding the body and identity as fluid, dynamic, and interconnected entities. This theoretical construct, which envisions the body free from hierarchical organization and fixed structures, has found practical applications in various fields, including therapeutic practices, organizational theory, management, and education. This discussion will explore these practical applications, focusing on the BwO in therapeutic practices and mental health, its application in organizational theory and management practices, and its role in educational and pedagogical contexts. A detailed case study will examine the use of BwO principles in innovative therapy approaches, such as art therapy and somatic practices.

The BwO's emphasis on fluidity, potentiality, and the rejection of fixed structures resonates strongly with contemporary therapeutic practices and mental health approaches. In therapeutic settings, the BwO offers a framework for understanding and addressing the complex, multifaceted nature of human experience, encouraging more holistic and adaptable interventions.

In mental health, the BwO can be applied to challenge and deconstruct rigid diagnostic categories and treatment protocols. Traditional mental health practices often rely on fixed diagnostic criteria and standardized treatments, which can inadvertently constrain the understanding of an individual's unique experiences and needs. By embracing the BwO, mental health practitioners can adopt a more flexible and person-centered approach, recognizing the fluidity of mental states and the potential for continuous transformation.

Therapeutic practices that incorporate the BwO emphasize the importance of creating spaces where individuals can explore their identities and experiences without the constraints of rigid structures.

This approach is particularly relevant in trauma therapy, where the emphasis is on helping individuals reclaim agency over their bodies and experiences. The BwO's focus on potentiality and transformation aligns with trauma-informed practices that seek to empower individuals and promote healing through personal agency and resilience.

Art therapy is a notable example of a therapeutic practice that aligns with the BwO principles. In art therapy, individuals use creative expression to explore and communicate their emotions, experiences, and identities. This process allows for the dissolution of rigid boundaries between self and other, conscious and unconscious, and mind and body. By engaging in creative activities, individuals can access new forms of self-expression and transformation, reflecting the BwO's emphasis on fluidity and potentiality.

Somatic practices, which focus on the body's role in healing and personal development, also resonate with the BwO. Somatic therapies, such as somatic experiencing, body-oriented psychotherapy, and dance/movement therapy, emphasize the interconnectedness of body and mind and the importance of bodily awareness in promoting mental health. These practices align with the BwO's emphasis on the body's potential for transformation and the importance of addressing embodied experiences in therapeutic work.

In organizational theory and management practices, the BwO offers a framework for understanding organizations as dynamic and interconnected assemblages, rather than fixed and hierarchical structures. This perspective encourages more flexible and adaptive approaches to management, fostering innovation and resilience in the face of change.

The BwO's emphasis on fluidity and potentiality aligns with contemporary organizational theories that challenge traditional top-down management structures. Approaches such as agile management, holacracy, and networked organizations emphasize the importance of adaptability, collaboration, and decentralized decision-making. These practices reflect the BwO's rejection of rigid hierarchies and its embrace of continuous transformation.

Agile management, for instance, promotes iterative development, cross-functional teams, and responsiveness to change. This approach encourages organizations to remain flexible and adaptive, continuously evolving in response to new information and changing conditions. By viewing organizations as dynamic assemblages, agile management aligns with the BwO's principles of fluidity and potentiality, fostering a culture of innovation and continuous improvement.

Holacracy, a system of decentralized management and organizational governance, also reflects the BwO's principles. In holacracy, traditional managerial roles and hierarchies are replaced by distributed authority and self-organizing teams. This approach encourages individuals to take on multiple roles and responsibilities, fostering a sense of agency and collaboration. By dismantling rigid structures and promoting adaptability, holacracy aligns with the BwO's emphasis on continuous transformation and interconnectedness.

In educational and pedagogical contexts, the BwO offers a framework for rethinking traditional approaches to teaching and learning. The BwO's emphasis on potentiality, transformation, and the rejection of fixed structures resonates with contemporary educational theories that prioritize student-centered learning, creativity, and critical thinking.

The BwO challenges traditional hierarchical models of education, where knowledge is transmitted from teacher to student in a top-down manner. Instead, it promotes more dynamic and interactive approaches to learning, where students and teachers engage in a collaborative process of knowledge creation and exploration. This perspective aligns with constructivist and experiential learning theories, which emphasize the importance of active, hands-on learning and the co-construction of knowledge.

Incorporating BwO principles into educational practices encourages educators to create learning environments that are flexible, adaptive, and responsive to students' needs and interests. This approach promotes a culture of inquiry and exploration, where students are encouraged to take risks, ask questions, and engage in creative problem-solving. By fostering a sense of agency and autonomy, BwO-informed pedagogy supports the development of critical thinking skills and lifelong learning.

Project-based learning (PBL) is an educational approach that aligns with the BwO's principles. In PBL, students engage in complex, real-world projects that require collaboration, creativity, and critical thinking. This approach emphasizes the importance of interdisciplinary learning and the integration of multiple perspectives, reflecting the BwO's emphasis on interconnectedness and fluidity. By engaging in meaningful projects, students can explore their interests and develop new skills, embodying the BwO's potential for continuous transformation.

A detailed case study of the use of BwO principles in innovative therapy approaches, such as art therapy and somatic practices, highlights the practical applications of the BwO in therapeutic contexts.

Art therapy, which involves the use of creative expression to explore emotions and experiences, aligns closely with the BwO's emphasis on fluidity and potentiality. In art therapy, individuals are encouraged to engage in artistic activities, such as drawing, painting, sculpture, and collage, to express their thoughts and feelings. This process allows for the dissolution of rigid boundaries between self and other, conscious and unconscious, and mind and body.

By engaging in creative expression, individuals can access new forms of self-expression and transformation, reflecting the BwO's principles. Art therapy provides a safe and supportive space for individuals to explore their identities and experiences, promoting healing and personal growth. This approach is particularly effective in trauma therapy, where the emphasis is on helping individuals reclaim agency over their bodies and experiences.

Somatic practices, which focus on the body's role in healing and personal development, also resonate with the BwO. Somatic therapies, such as somatic experiencing, body-oriented psychotherapy, and dance/movement therapy, emphasize the interconnectedness of body and mind and the importance of bodily awareness in promoting mental health.

Somatic experiencing, developed by Peter Levine, is a therapeutic approach that focuses on resolving trauma by addressing the physiological effects of stress and trauma on the body. This approach emphasizes the importance of bodily awareness and the release of stored tension and energy, reflecting the BwO's emphasis on the body's potential for transformation and healing.

Body-oriented psychotherapy, such as the methods developed by Wilhelm Reich and Alexander Lowen, also aligns with the BwO's principles. These approaches emphasize the importance of addressing embodied experiences and releasing physical tension to promote mental and emotional well-being. By focusing on the body's role in healing, body-oriented psychotherapy reflects the BwO's emphasis on the interconnectedness of body and mind.

Dance/movement therapy, which involves the use of movement and dance to promote emotional, cognitive, and physical integration, also resonates with the BwO. This approach emphasizes the importance of bodily expression and the release of stored emotions through movement, reflecting the BwO's emphasis on fluidity and potentiality. By engaging in creative and expressive movement, individuals can explore new forms of self-expression and transformation, promoting healing and personal growth.

In conclusion, the concept of the Body without Organs (BwO) provides a versatile and impactful framework for practical applications in various fields, including therapeutic practices, organizational theory and management, and education. The BwO's emphasis on fluidity, potentiality, and the rejection of fixed structures offers valuable insights for rethinking traditional approaches and fostering more dynamic, flexible, and adaptive practices.

In therapeutic practices, the BwO encourages a more holistic and person-centered approach, emphasizing the importance of creating spaces where individuals can explore their identities and experiences without the constraints of rigid structures. Art therapy and somatic practices, such as somatic experiencing, body-oriented psychotherapy, and dance/movement therapy, exemplify the practical application of BwO principles in promoting healing and personal growth.

In organizational theory and management, the BwO offers a framework for understanding organizations as dynamic and interconnected assemblages, encouraging more flexible and adaptive approaches to management. Approaches such as agile management and holacracy reflect the BwO's principles, fostering innovation and resilience in the face of change.

In educational and pedagogical contexts, the BwO challenges traditional hierarchical models of education, promoting more dynamic and interactive approaches to learning. By creating flexible, adaptive, and responsive learning environments, educators can foster a culture of inquiry, creativity, and critical thinking, supporting the development of critical thinking skills and lifelong learning.

Through its practical applications, the BwO provides valuable insights for rethinking traditional approaches and fostering more dynamic, flexible, and adaptive practices across various fields. By embracing the BwO, practitioners in therapy, management, and education can promote healing, innovation, and personal growth, enriching our understanding of the body's potential for continuous becoming and transformation.

39. FUTURE DIRECTIONS FOR THE BODY WITHOUT ORGANS

The concept of the Body without Organs (BwO), as introduced by Gilles Deleuze and Félix Guattari, continues to be a provocative and influential idea in contemporary thought. As we look to the future, the BwO's emphasis on fluidity, potentiality, and the rejection of fixed structures offers valuable insights for understanding and navigating emerging technologies, scientific advancements, and social and cultural transformations. This discussion will speculate on the future implications and developments of the BwO concept, exploring its potential evolution in light of new technologies, its role in future social and cultural changes, and its continuing influence on art, literature, and philosophy. A detailed case study will provide a speculative exploration of the BwO in the context of artificial intelligence (AI) and biotechnology.

The potential evolution of the BwO concept in light of emerging technologies and scientific advancements is vast. As new technologies continue to reshape our understanding of the body, identity, and reality, the BwO offers a framework for exploring these changes. Technologies such as AI, virtual reality (VR), augmented reality (AR), and biotechnology are pushing the boundaries of what it means to be human, creating new possibilities for identity and embodiment that align with the BwO's principles of fluidity and transformation.

AI, for instance, is revolutionizing how we interact with technology and with each other. As AI systems become more advanced, they offer new ways of augmenting human capabilities and expanding our understanding of the body and mind. AI-powered personal assistants, for example, can enhance our cognitive abilities by providing real-time information and insights, effectively extending the capabilities of our minds. This augmentation aligns with the BwO's emphasis on potentiality, as AI technologies create new assemblages that transform our cognitive and sensory experiences.

In the realm of VR and AR, the BwO's principles are particularly relevant. These technologies create immersive digital environments where the boundaries between physical and virtual realities become increasingly porous. In VR, users can inhabit avatars that transcend the limitations of their physical bodies, exploring new forms of identity and interaction. This experience reflects the BwO's emphasis on fluidity and potentiality, as users can continuously transform their virtual bodies and environments. AR, which overlays digital information onto the physical world, similarly challenges conventional notions of reality and embodiment, creating new possibilities for interaction and perception.

Biotechnology is another area where the BwO's principles are highly applicable. Advances in genetic engineering, synthetic biology, and biohacking are enabling unprecedented modifications to the human body, challenging traditional boundaries between the natural and the artificial. Genetic engineering techniques, such as CRISPR, allow for precise modifications to DNA, potentially eliminating genetic diseases and enhancing physical and cognitive abilities. These capabilities align with the BwO's rejection of fixed structures, as they enable continuous transformation and adaptation of the body.

The BwO's role in future social and cultural transformations is also significant. As societies become increasingly interconnected through digital technologies and global communication networks, the BwO offers a framework for understanding the fluid and dynamic nature of social and cultural identities. In a world where traditional boundaries of nation, ethnicity, and culture are constantly being renegotiated, the BwO's emphasis on potentiality and transformation provides valuable insights for navigating these changes.

One potential future direction for the BwO is its application in understanding and addressing issues of identity and diversity in a globalized world. The BwO's rejection of fixed identities and its embrace of multiplicity can inform efforts to promote inclusivity and adaptability in diverse societies. By viewing identity as fluid and open to continuous transformation, the BwO encourages a more flexible and responsive approach to social and cultural differences.

Additionally, the BwO can play a role in shaping future political and economic systems. As traditional hierarchical structures are increasingly challenged by networked and decentralized forms of organization, the BwO's principles of fluidity and potentiality offer a framework for understanding and navigating these changes. The rise of digital currencies, blockchain technologies, and peer-to-peer networks exemplifies this shift towards more flexible and adaptive systems. The BwO's emphasis on continuous transformation can inform efforts to create more resilient and responsive political and economic structures.

Predictions on how the BwO will continue to influence art, literature, and philosophy suggest that its impact will remain significant. In art, the BwO's principles of fluidity and potentiality will continue to inspire new forms of creative expression that challenge conventional boundaries and explore new possibilities for identity and embodiment. Artists will likely continue to experiment with digital technologies, such as VR and AI, to create immersive and interactive experiences that reflect the BwO's emphasis on transformation and interconnectedness.

In literature, the BwO will inspire new narrative forms that challenge traditional structures and explore the fluid nature of identity and reality. Writers will continue to experiment with non-linear narratives, fragmented structures, and multiple perspectives, creating works that reflect the BwO's principles of continuous becoming. Themes of transformation, hybridity, and the dissolution of boundaries will remain central to literary explorations of the BwO.

In philosophy, the BwO will continue to inform and challenge contemporary debates on identity, embodiment, and the nature of being. Philosophers will likely engage with the BwO to explore the implications of emerging technologies and scientific advancements, as well as to address ongoing social and cultural transformations. The BwO's principles of fluidity and potentiality will provide a valuable framework for understanding the complexities of contemporary existence and for envisioning new possibilities for human life.

A detailed case study of the BwO in the context of artificial intelligence and biotechnology highlights its potential future applications and implications.

AI and biotechnology are two fields where the BwO's principles are particularly relevant. AI technologies, such as machine learning and neural networks, are transforming our understanding of cognition and intelligence, creating new possibilities for human-machine interaction. Biotechnology, including genetic engineering and synthetic biology, is enabling unprecedented modifications to the human body, challenging traditional boundaries between the natural and the artificial.

In the context of AI, the BwO's emphasis on fluidity and potentiality can inform efforts to develop more adaptive and responsive AI systems. For example, AI algorithms that learn and evolve continuously, rather than being fixed and deterministic, reflect the BwO's principles of continuous becoming. These adaptive AI systems can create new assemblages that enhance human capabilities and expand our understanding of the body and mind.

One speculative application of the BwO in AI is the development of AI-powered exoskeletons that enhance human physical abilities. These exoskeletons could be designed to adapt to the user's movements and needs, continuously evolving to optimize performance. By integrating AI algorithms that learn from the user's behavior and environment, these exoskeletons can create a dynamic and responsive interface between the human body and the machine. This application reflects the BwO's emphasis on fluidity and potentiality, as the exoskeleton and the human body form a continuously evolving assemblage.

In biotechnology, the BwO's principles can inform efforts to create more flexible and adaptable modifications to the human body. Genetic engineering techniques, such as CRISPR, allow for precise modifications to DNA, potentially enabling continuous adaptation and enhancement of physical and cognitive abilities. By embracing the BwO's emphasis on potentiality, genetic engineers can explore new possibilities for modifying the human body in ways that promote resilience and adaptability.

One speculative application of the BwO in biotechnology is the development of dynamic, self-regulating genetic modifications that respond to environmental changes. For example, genetically engineered organisms could be designed to adapt to different environmental conditions, such as changes in temperature or nutrient availability. These dynamic modifications would enable organisms to continuously evolve and adapt, reflecting the BwO's principles of fluidity and potentiality.

In conclusion, the concept of the Body without Organs (BwO) remains a vital and influential idea in contemporary thought, offering valuable insights for understanding and navigating emerging technologies, scientific advancements, and social and cultural transformations. The BwO's principles of fluidity, potentiality, and the rejection of fixed structures provide a framework for exploring new possibilities for identity and embodiment in the context of AI, VR, AR, and biotechnology.

The BwO's role in future social and cultural transformations is significant, as it offers a framework for understanding the fluid and dynamic nature of social and cultural identities in a globalized world. By embracing the BwO's principles, societies can promote inclusivity and adaptability, creating more resilient and responsive political and economic structures.

Predictions on how the BwO will continue to influence art, literature, and philosophy suggest that its impact will remain significant. Artists, writers, and philosophers will continue to draw on the BwO to challenge conventional boundaries and explore new possibilities for identity and embodiment, creating works that reflect the BwO's principles of continuous becoming.

A speculative exploration of the BwO in the context of AI and biotechnology highlights its potential future applications and implications. By embracing the BwO's principles of fluidity and potentiality, AI and biotechnology can create new assemblages that enhance human capabilities and expand our understanding of the body and mind. Through its practical applications, the BwO provides valuable insights for rethinking traditional approaches and fostering more dynamic, flexible, and adaptive practices across various fields, enriching our understanding of the body's potential for continuous becoming and transformation.

40. REFERENCES

To provide a comprehensive understanding of the Body without Organs (BwO) and its applications, the following references include seminal works by Deleuze and Guattari as well as contributions from other scholars who have explored the BwO in various contexts:

Works by Deleuze and Guattari

1. Deleuze, G., & Guattari, F. (1987). A Thousand Plateaus: Capitalism and Schizophrenia. Minneapolis: University of Minnesota Press.

This seminal text introduces the concept of the BwO, exploring how different elements come together to form complex, dynamic systems.

2. Deleuze, G., & Guattari, F. (1972). Anti-Oedipus: Capitalism and Schizophrenia. New York: Viking Press.

While primarily focused on psychoanalysis and capitalism, this book lays the groundwork for the ideas further developed in A Thousand Plateaus.

Books and Journal Articles on the Body without Organs

3. Bogue, R. (2003). Deleuze on Music, Painting, and the Arts. New York: Routledge.

This book discusses Deleuze's ideas on the arts, including the application of the BwO concept in various artistic practices.

4. Braidotti, R. (2011). Nomadic Subjects: Embodiment and Sexual Difference in Contemporary Feminist Theory. New York: Columbia University Press.

Braidotti explores the implications of the BwO for feminist theory and the concept of nomadic subjectivity.

5. DeLanda, M. (2006). A New Philosophy of Society: Assemblage Theory and Social Complexity. London: Continuum.

DeLanda expands on Deleuze and Guattari's ideas, applying the BwO and assemblage theory to social and economic systems.

6. Grosz, E. (1994). Volatile Bodies: Toward a Corporeal Feminism. Bloomington: Indiana University Press.

Grosz engages with Deleuze and Guattari's concept of the BwO to develop a feminist theory of the body.

7. Massumi, B. (1992). A User's Guide to Capitalism and Schizophrenia: Deviations from Deleuze and Guattari. Cambridge: MIT Press.

This book provides an accessible introduction to Deleuze and Guattari's concepts, including the BwO, and explores their implications for various fields.

8. Nail, T. (2017). What is an Assemblage? SubStance, 46(1), 21-37.

This article provides a clear and concise explanation of assemblage theory, outlining its key components and theoretical foundations, which include the BwO.

9. Puar, J. K. (2007). Terrorist Assemblages: Homonationalism in Queer Times. Durham: Duke University Press.

Puar explores the concept of assemblages, including the BwO, in the context of queer theory and geopolitics.

10. Smith, D. W. (2003). Deleuze on Bacon: Three Conceptual Trajectories in The Logic of Sensation. Journal of Visual Culture, 2(2), 229-237.

This article explores Deleuze's interpretation of Francis Bacon's artwork through the lens of the BwO.

Additional References on Future Implications and Applications

11. Bennett, J. (2010). Vibrant Matter: A Political Ecology of Things. Durham: Duke University Press.

Bennett discusses the agency of non-human elements in assemblages, emphasizing the political and ecological implications of material interactions, related to the BwO.

12. Dolphijn, R., & van der Tuin, I. (2012). New Materialism: Interviews & Cartographies. Ann Arbor: Open Humanities Press.

This book includes interviews and discussions that link new materialism to Deleuze and Guattari's concepts, including the BwO.

13. Grosz, E. (2008). Chaos, Territory, Art: Deleuze and the Framing of the Earth. New York: Columbia University Press.

Grosz engages with the BwO to explore the intersections of art, space, and territory.

14. Hickey-Moody, A., & Malins, P. (2007). Deleuzian Encounters: Studies in Contemporary Social Issues. New York: Palgrave Macmillan.

This collection of essays explores contemporary social issues through the lens of Deleuze and Guattari's concepts, including the BwO.

15. Patton, P. (2000). Deleuze and the Political. New York: Routledge.

Patton examines the political implications of Deleuze and Guattari's work, including the concept of the BwO.

16. Protevi, J. (2009). Political Affect: Connecting the Social and the Somatic. Minneapolis: University of Minnesota Press.

Protevi explores the connections between social and bodily experiences, drawing on the concept of the BwO.

These references provide a robust theoretical foundation for understanding the Body without Organs and its applications across various fields. They offer insights into the concept's implications for contemporary philosophy, art, literature, social theory, and beyond, highlighting the ongoing relevance and potential of the BwO in addressing complex issues of identity, embodiment, and social transformation.

CHAPTER 5: SCHIZOANALYSIS

41. INTRODUCTION TO SCHIZOANALYSIS

Schizoanalysis is a revolutionary concept developed by the French philosophers Gilles Deleuze and Félix Guattari, introduced in their seminal work "Anti-Oedipus: Capitalism and Schizophrenia" (1972). This framework emerged as a radical alternative to traditional psychoanalysis, challenging established norms and offering a new lens through which to analyze social, cultural, and psychological phenomena. By rejecting the rigid structures of psychoanalysis, Deleuze and Guattari proposed schizoanalysis as a method for understanding the complexities of human desire, social organization, and the production of subjectivity. This discussion will define and introduce the concept of schizoanalysis, explore its key concepts, and provide an overview of the historical and philosophical context in which it emerged.

Schizoanalysis was born out of Deleuze and Guattari's critique of psychoanalysis, particularly the work of Sigmund Freud and Jacques Lacan. Traditional psychoanalysis, with its focus on the Oedipus complex and the centrality of familial relationships in the development of the psyche, was seen by Deleuze and Guattari as overly reductive and repressive. They argued that psychoanalysis imposed a rigid framework on the understanding of human desire and subjectivity, limiting the potential for understanding the full complexity of human experience.

In contrast, schizoanalysis seeks to liberate desire from these constraints, viewing it as a productive force that operates across various social, cultural, and psychological dimensions. Schizoanalysis does not pathologize desire but rather celebrates its creative and generative capacities. By examining the flows and assemblages of desire, schizoanalysis aims to uncover the ways in which desire interacts with and shapes social and cultural formations.

At its core, schizoanalysis is concerned with desiring-production, a key concept introduced by Deleuze and Guattari. Desiring-production refers to the idea that desire is not a lack or a deficiency, as traditional psychoanalysis suggests, but a productive force that drives the creation and transformation of reality. This concept challenges the notion that desire is always oriented towards something that is missing or unattainable. Instead, desire is seen as a generative process that continuously produces new connections, assemblages, and realities.

The body without organs (BwO) is another central concept in schizoanalysis. The BwO represents a state of pure potentiality and fluidity, free from the hierarchical organization and fixed structures that typically define bodies and identities. It is a site where new forms of desiring-production can emerge, unencumbered by the constraints of traditional psychoanalytic and social frameworks. The BwO challenges the idea of a stable, coherent self, emphasizing instead the multiplicity and continuous becoming that characterize human existence.

Deterritorialization is a third key concept in schizoanalysis. Deterritorialization refers to the process by which established structures and territories are disrupted or dismantled, allowing for new forms of organization and connection to emerge. This concept is closely related to the idea of the BwO, as both emphasize the fluid and dynamic nature of social and psychological realities. Deterritorialization challenges the fixed boundaries and categorizations that typically define social and cultural life, promoting instead a view of reality as constantly shifting and evolving.

The historical and philosophical context in which schizoanalysis emerged is crucial for understanding its development and significance. Schizoanalysis was born in the late 1960s and early 1970s, a period marked by significant social and political upheaval. The student and worker protests of May 1968 in France, the rise of anti-psychiatry movements, and the broader cultural revolutions of the time all contributed to the intellectual environment in which Deleuze and Guattari were working.

May 1968, in particular, had a profound impact on the development of schizoanalysis. The protests, which began as a student movement and quickly spread to include workers and other social groups, challenged the established social and political order in France. The events of May 1968 exposed the limitations and repressive nature of traditional social structures, highlighting the need for new ways of thinking about social organization and individual subjectivity.

Deleuze and Guattari were deeply influenced by the spirit of May 1968, and schizoanalysis can be seen as a theoretical response to the demands for liberation and transformation that characterized the protests. Schizoanalysis aims to break down the rigid structures that limit human potential, promoting instead a view of reality as fluid, dynamic, and open to continuous change.

Philosophically, schizoanalysis draws on a wide range of influences, including Marxism, structuralism, and post-structuralism. Deleuze and Guattari were influenced by the work of Karl Marx, particularly his analysis of capitalism and the ways in which economic systems shape social and individual life. Schizoanalysis incorporates a Marxist critique of capitalism, viewing it as a system that channels and constrains desiring-production, limiting human potential and creativity.

Structuralism, particularly the work of Claude Lévi-Strauss and Ferdinand de Saussure, also influenced schizoanalysis. Structuralism emphasizes the underlying structures that shape human culture and language, viewing these structures as essential for understanding social and individual life. Deleuze and Guattari, however, critiqued structuralism for its emphasis on fixed and stable structures, arguing instead for a more dynamic and fluid understanding of reality.

Post-structuralism, particularly the work of Michel Foucault and Jacques Derrida, provided further inspiration for schizoanalysis. Post-structuralism challenges the idea of fixed meanings and stable identities, emphasizing instead the fluid and contingent nature of reality. Deleuze and Guattari incorporated these ideas into schizoanalysis, emphasizing the importance of understanding the ways in which desire and power operate across various social and cultural dimensions.

The case study of the historical and philosophical context in which schizoanalysis emerged highlights the significance of this framework for understanding contemporary social, cultural, and psychological phenomena. Schizoanalysis provides a powerful tool for analyzing the complexities of human desire and the ways in which it shapes and is shaped by social and cultural formations.

One of the key contributions of schizoanalysis is its critique of the Oedipus complex, a central concept in traditional psychoanalysis. Deleuze and Guattari argue that the Oedipus complex imposes a rigid framework on the understanding of desire, limiting its potential and constraining individual and social life. By rejecting the Oedipus complex, schizoanalysis opens up new possibilities for understanding the ways in which desire operates and interacts with various social and cultural dimensions.

Schizoanalysis also offers a critique of the repressive nature of traditional psychoanalytic practices. Deleuze and Guattari argue that psychoanalysis often reinforces existing power structures, pathologizing and constraining desire rather than liberating it. Schizoanalysis, in contrast, seeks to free desire from these constraints, viewing it as a productive and generative force that can drive social and individual transformation.

In addition to its critiques, schizoanalysis offers a positive vision for understanding and engaging with desire. By emphasizing desiring-production, the BwO, and deterritorialization, schizoanalysis provides a framework for understanding the dynamic and fluid nature of reality. This perspective encourages a more flexible and adaptable approach to social, cultural, and psychological life, promoting creativity, innovation, and continuous transformation.

Schizoanalysis has also influenced a wide range of fields beyond philosophy, including literature, art, and political theory. In literature, schizoanalysis has inspired new forms of narrative and character development that challenge traditional structures and explore the fluid nature of identity and desire. In art, schizoanalysis has influenced various movements and practices that emphasize the dynamic and interconnected nature of artistic production. In political theory, schizoanalysis has informed critiques of traditional power structures and inspired new forms of social and political organization.

In conclusion, schizoanalysis is a revolutionary concept developed by Gilles Deleuze and Félix Guattari that offers a powerful framework for analyzing social, cultural, and psychological phenomena. By emphasizing desiring-production, the body without organs, and deterritorialization, schizoanalysis challenges traditional psychoanalytic practices and offers a more dynamic and fluid understanding of reality. The historical and philosophical context in which schizoanalysis emerged highlights its significance for understanding contemporary social and cultural transformations, and its influence continues to be felt across various fields. Through its critiques and positive vision, schizoanalysis provides valuable insights for understanding and engaging with the complexities of human desire and the dynamic nature of social and individual life.

42. THEORETICAL FOUNDATIONS OF SCHIZOANALYSIS

Schizoanalysis, developed by Gilles Deleuze and Félix Guattari in their seminal works "Anti-Oedipus: Capitalism and Schizophrenia" (1972) and "A Thousand Plateaus" (1987), presents a radical departure from traditional psychoanalysis. It offers a comprehensive framework for understanding the complexities of human desires, social structures, and cultural phenomena. This exploration delves into the theoretical foundations of schizoanalysis, contrasts it with Freud's psychoanalysis, particularly the Oedipus complex, and examines the roles of capitalism and schizophrenia in shaping human desires and social structures. A case study will compare schizoanalysis with psychoanalytic and other critical theories to highlight its unique contributions and implications.

Deleuze and Guattari's work on schizoanalysis emerged as a critique and expansion of psychoanalytic theories, particularly those of Sigmund Freud and Jacques Lacan. Traditional psychoanalysis, according to Freud, centers around the concept of the unconscious and the resolution of internal conflicts primarily through the framework of the Oedipus complex. Freud posited that the Oedipus complex—a child's unconscious desire for the opposite-sex parent and rivalry with the same-sex parent—was a universal stage in human development and the root of many psychological issues. Lacan further developed these ideas, emphasizing language and symbolic structures in shaping the unconscious.

Deleuze and Guattari rejected the universality and centrality of the Oedipus complex, arguing that it imposed a restrictive framework on human desire. They contended that the Oedipus complex limited the understanding of desire to familial and neurotic dimensions, ignoring broader social, cultural, and economic factors. Instead, they proposed that desire is a productive force that operates beyond the confines of the familial structure, continually creating new realities and assemblages.

In "Anti-Oedipus," Deleuze and Guattari introduce the concept of desiring-production, which posits that desire is not a lack or deficiency (as Freud suggested) but a positive, productive force inherent in all human activity. Desiring-production is the process through which desire creates connections and assemblages, generating new social, cultural, and psychological realities. This concept contrasts sharply with the Freudian view of desire as something to be controlled or sublimated.

Central to schizoanalysis is the idea of the Body without Organs (BwO), which represents a state of pure potentiality and fluidity, free from the hierarchical organization of the traditional body. The BwO is a key element in understanding desiring-production, as it embodies the continuous process of becoming and transformation that characterizes human existence. In contrast to the organized, stratified body posited by psychoanalysis, the BwO is a plane of immanence where desires flow freely and new connections are constantly formed.

Another foundational concept in schizoanalysis is deterritorialization. This refers to the process by which established structures, norms, and territories are disrupted, allowing for the emergence of new forms of organization and meaning. Deterritorialization challenges the fixed boundaries and categorizations imposed by traditional psychoanalytic and social frameworks, promoting a view of reality as dynamic and continuously evolving.

Deleuze and Guattari also critique the repressive function of psychoanalysis, arguing that it often serves to reinforce existing power structures by pathologizing desire and limiting its creative potential. Schizoanalysis, in contrast, seeks to liberate desire from these constraints, viewing it as a force for social and individual transformation.

The role of capitalism and schizophrenia in shaping human desires and social structures is another crucial aspect of schizoanalysis. Deleuze and Guattari argue that capitalism operates as a vast machine that channels and manipulates desires, integrating them into its mechanisms of production and consumption. Capitalism, they suggest, perpetually decodes and recodes desires, creating a cycle of deterritorialization and reterritorialization that keeps the system dynamic and adaptable.

Schizophrenia, in this context, is not merely a mental illness but a metaphor for the process of continuous transformation and disruption that characterizes both individual subjectivity and social structures under capitalism. Schizophrenic processes, according to Deleuze and Guattari, reveal the underlying dynamics of desiring-production, highlighting the fluid and contingent nature of reality. Schizoanalysis thus seeks to harness the positive, creative aspects of schizophrenia, viewing it as a model for understanding the potential for radical social and personal change.

The contrast between schizoanalysis and Freud's psychoanalysis is stark. Freud's focus on the Oedipus complex and the resolution of internal conflicts through family dynamics is replaced by Deleuze and Guattari's broader examination of social, cultural, and economic factors. While Freud viewed desire as something to be controlled and sublimated within the boundaries of societal norms, schizoanalysis celebrates desire as a productive force that continuously generates new possibilities and assemblages.

Deleuze and Guattari also critique the role of psychoanalysis in reinforcing capitalist structures. They argue that traditional psychoanalysis often pathologizes deviations from normative behavior, thus maintaining social order and control. Schizoanalysis, in contrast, seeks to uncover the ways in which desire is manipulated and constrained by these structures, advocating for a more liberated and expansive understanding of human potential.

A case study comparing schizoanalysis with psychoanalytic and other critical theories reveals its unique contributions and implications.

For instance, while psychoanalysis focuses on individual pathology and familial structures, schizoanalysis emphasizes the broader social, cultural, and economic contexts that shape human desires. This broader perspective aligns schizoanalysis with other critical theories, such as Marxism, post-structuralism, and feminist theory, which also critique the ways in which power and ideology shape individual and collective experiences.

Marxism, with its focus on the economic and material conditions of life, shares common ground with schizoanalysis in its critique of capitalism. Both theories highlight the ways in which capitalist systems manipulate and constrain human potential, though schizoanalysis extends this critique to the realm of desire and subjectivity. By examining the intersections of economic, social, and psychological factors, schizoanalysis provides a more comprehensive framework for understanding the complexities of human existence.

Post-structuralism, particularly the work of Michel Foucault, also resonates with schizoanalysis. Foucault's analysis of power, knowledge, and discourse parallels Deleuze and Guattari's examination of the ways in which desire is shaped and constrained by social and cultural structures. Both approaches reject the idea of fixed identities and stable meanings, emphasizing instead the fluid and contingent nature of reality.

Feminist theory, too, finds affinities with schizoanalysis, particularly in its critique of traditional psychoanalytic concepts and its emphasis on the embodied, lived experiences of individuals. Feminist scholars such as Rosi Braidotti and Elizabeth Grosz have drawn on schizoanalysis to develop new frameworks for understanding gender, sexuality, and the body. By emphasizing the fluidity and potentiality of desire, schizoanalysis aligns with feminist efforts to challenge normative structures and promote more inclusive and flexible understandings of identity.

One notable comparison is between schizoanalysis and Lacanian psychoanalysis. While both approaches critique the limitations of traditional Freudian psychoanalysis, they diverge significantly in their theoretical orientations. Lacan's emphasis on language and the symbolic order highlights the ways in which subjectivity is constructed through linguistic and cultural frameworks. Schizoanalysis, in contrast, focuses on the productive, material aspects of desire, emphasizing the ways in which it generates new realities and assemblages.

Schizoanalysis also offers a more dynamic and process-oriented view of subjectivity compared to Lacanian psychoanalysis. While Lacan's focus on the symbolic and imaginary orders provides valuable insights into the formation of identity, schizoanalysis emphasizes the continuous process of becoming and transformation that characterizes human existence. This perspective aligns with contemporary efforts to understand the fluid and contingent nature of identity in a rapidly changing world.

In summary, schizoanalysis, developed by Gilles Deleuze and Félix Guattari, presents a radical departure from traditional psychoanalysis by emphasizing the productive, generative aspects of desire and the dynamic, fluid nature of reality. By rejecting the Oedipus complex and critiquing the repressive functions of psychoanalysis, schizoanalysis offers a more expansive framework for understanding social, cultural, and psychological phenomena.

The role of capitalism and schizophrenia in shaping human desires and social structures is central to schizoanalysis, highlighting the ways in which desire is manipulated and constrained by capitalist systems. Schizoanalysis seeks to uncover the creative potential of desire, advocating for a more liberated and transformative understanding of human existence.

Comparing schizoanalysis with psychoanalytic and other critical theories reveals its unique contributions and implications. By integrating insights from Marxism, post-structuralism, and feminist theory, schizoanalysis provides a comprehensive framework for understanding the complexities of human desire and the ways in which it interacts with broader social and cultural contexts. Through its emphasis on desiring-production, the Body without Organs, and deterritorialization, schizoanalysis offers valuable insights for understanding and engaging with the dynamic, interconnected nature of contemporary life.

43. CORE CONCEPTS IN SCHIZOANALYSIS

Schizoanalysis, a radical theoretical framework developed by Gilles Deleuze and Félix Guattari, offers a novel approach to understanding the complexities of human desire, social structures, and cultural phenomena. At its core, schizoanalysis revolves around several key concepts: desiring-production, the Body without Organs (BwO), and assemblages. These concepts provide a foundation for analyzing and interpreting the dynamic and interconnected nature of social and cultural realities. This discussion will explain and illustrate these core concepts, providing a detailed analysis of how they are applied to social and cultural phenomena.

Desiring-production is a central concept in schizoanalysis, introduced by Deleuze and Guattari to challenge traditional psychoanalytic notions of desire. In contrast to Freud's view of desire as a lack or deficiency, desiring-production posits that desire is a productive force that continuously generates new realities, connections, and assemblages. Rather than being oriented towards something that is missing, desire is seen as inherently creative and generative.

Desiring-production operates on multiple levels, from individual psychological processes to broader social and cultural dynamics. It encompasses the ways in which desires flow through various systems, creating new forms of social organization and cultural expression. This concept highlights the dynamic and fluid nature of desire, emphasizing its role in shaping and transforming reality.

One way to understand desiring-production is to consider its role in artistic and creative processes. Artists, writers, and musicians often describe their creative work as being driven by a kind of productive desire—a force that compels them to create and innovate. This creative drive can be seen as an example of desiring-production, as it generates new forms of expression and meaning.

Desiring-production also plays a crucial role in social and economic systems. In capitalism, for instance, desires are continuously produced, manipulated, and channeled to drive consumption and economic growth. Advertisements, media, and consumer culture all contribute to the production and flow of desires, shaping individuals' behaviors and social dynamics. Schizoanalysis seeks to uncover these processes and understand how they influence and shape human experience.

The Body without Organs (BwO) is another foundational concept in schizoanalysis, representing a state of potentiality and fluidity that opposes structured, hierarchical organization. The BwO is not a literal body but a conceptual and philosophical idea that challenges the fixed and stratified nature of traditional understandings of the body and identity.

The BwO embodies the idea of pure potentiality, where desires can flow freely and new connections and assemblages can emerge. It represents a state of continuous becoming, where the body is not constrained by predefined roles, functions, or structures. In this sense, the BwO stands in opposition to the organized body, which is shaped by social, cultural, and biological hierarchies.

To illustrate the BwO, consider the experience of improvisational dance. In improvisational dance, the dancer's movements are not pre-planned or choreographed but are instead created spontaneously in response to the music, environment, and internal impulses. This fluid and dynamic state of movement reflects the BwO, as the dancer's body is free to explore new possibilities and connections without the constraints of a fixed structure.

The BwO also has significant implications for understanding identity and subjectivity. Traditional views of identity often emphasize stability and coherence, where individuals are defined by fixed characteristics and roles. The BwO, however, challenges this notion by emphasizing the fluid and dynamic nature of identity. It suggests that identity is not a fixed essence but a continuous process of becoming, shaped by the flow of desires and the interactions of various elements.

Assemblages are another key concept in schizoanalysis, referring to the interaction of diverse elements that come together to form functional wholes. An assemblage is a dynamic and heterogeneous collection of components that interact and influence each other, creating new forms and structures. Assemblages can encompass a wide range of elements, including individuals, objects, technologies, ideas, and social practices.

The concept of assemblages highlights the interconnected and relational nature of reality. It emphasizes that entities and phenomena are not isolated or static but are constantly interacting and evolving through their relationships with other elements. Assemblages are characterized by their fluidity and adaptability, as they can change and transform in response to new connections and influences.

An example of an assemblage can be seen in a city. A city is not just a collection of buildings and infrastructure but a complex and dynamic assemblage of people, technologies, social practices, economic activities, and cultural expressions. These elements interact and influence each other, creating the unique character and dynamics of the city. The concept of assemblages allows us to understand the city as a living, evolving entity rather than a static structure.

Assemblages also play a crucial role in understanding social and cultural phenomena. Social movements, for instance, can be seen as assemblages of individuals, ideas, practices, and technologies that come together to create collective action and change. The interactions and connections within these assemblages shape the movement's dynamics and outcomes, highlighting the importance of relationality and fluidity in social and cultural processes.

To illustrate the application of these core concepts to social and cultural phenomena, let's consider the example of the Occupy Wall Street movement. This social movement, which emerged in 2011, sought to address issues of economic inequality and corporate influence in politics. The movement provides a rich case study for understanding how desiring-production, the BwO, and assemblages operate in social and cultural contexts.

The Occupy Wall Street movement can be understood as a manifestation of desiring-production. The movement was driven by a collective desire for economic justice, social change, and the creation of alternative forms of organization. This productive desire generated new forms of social and political action, as individuals and groups came together to articulate their demands and create spaces for dialogue and activism.

The movement's slogans, such as "We are the 99%," encapsulated the collective desires of the participants, highlighting their shared goals and aspirations. These slogans and messages were not just expressions of discontent but productive forces that generated new connections and mobilized people to take action. The creative and generative nature of desiring-production was evident in the movement's ability to inspire and sustain collective action.

The concept of the BwO is also relevant to understanding the Occupy Wall Street movement. The movement's encampments, such as the one in Zuccotti Park in New York City, can be seen as spaces where traditional hierarchical structures were challenged and new forms of organization emerged. These encampments represented a state of potentiality and fluidity, where participants could experiment with new ways of living, organizing, and relating to each other.

In the encampments, participants created communal kitchens, libraries, medical tents, and spaces for open discussion and decision-making. These practices reflected the BwO's emphasis on breaking down rigid structures and exploring new possibilities. The movement's commitment to horizontal decision-making and consensus-based processes further embodied the principles of the

BwO, as it sought to create non-hierarchical and inclusive forms of organization.

The Occupy Wall Street movement can also be understood as an assemblage. The movement brought together a diverse array of individuals, groups, ideas, and practices, creating a dynamic and heterogeneous collective. This assemblage included activists, students, workers, artists, and various advocacy groups, each contributing their perspectives and resources to the movement.

The interactions and connections within this assemblage shaped the movement's dynamics and outcomes. The use of social media and digital technologies, for example, played a crucial role in organizing and mobilizing participants, facilitating communication, and spreading the movement's messages. The physical spaces of the encampments, the cultural practices of protest and resistance, and the ideological frameworks of economic justice and democracy all interacted to create the unique character of the movement.

The concept of assemblages highlights the interconnected and relational nature of the Occupy Wall Street movement. It emphasizes that the movement was not a monolithic entity but a fluid and evolving collective shaped by the interactions of its diverse components. This perspective allows us to understand the movement's complexity and the ways in which it adapted and transformed in response to new challenges and opportunities.

Schizoanalysis, with its core concepts of desiring-production, the Body without Organs, and assemblages, offers a powerful framework for understanding the dynamic and interconnected nature of social and cultural phenomena. Desiring-production emphasizes the productive and generative nature of desire, challenging traditional psychoanalytic notions of lack and deficiency. The BwO represents a state of potentiality and fluidity, opposing structured and hierarchical organization. Assemblages highlight the relational and interconnected nature of reality, emphasizing the interactions and connections that shape social and cultural dynamics.

The application of these concepts to the Occupy Wall Street movement illustrates their relevance and explanatory power. The movement's collective desires, experimental organizational practices, and dynamic interactions exemplify the principles of schizoanalysis, providing valuable insights into the ways in which social and cultural phenomena are produced and transformed. Through its emphasis on fluidity, potentiality, and interconnectedness, schizoanalysis offers a rich and nuanced understanding of the complexities of human experience and social reality.

44. SCHIZOANALYSIS IN SOCIAL AND CULTURAL CRITIQUE

Schizoanalysis, developed by Gilles Deleuze and Félix Guattari in their works "Anti-Oedipus" and "A Thousand Plateaus," offers a revolutionary framework for social and cultural critique. This approach emphasizes the productive nature of desire, the fluidity of identity, and the dynamic interplay between social forces and individual subjectivities. Schizoanalysis provides powerful tools for critiquing institutions, power structures, and cultural norms, with a focus on processes of deterritorialization and reterritorialization in social change. This discussion will explore these applications, provide examples of schizoanalytic critique in contemporary social movements, and analyze the countercultural movements of the 1960s and 1970s through the lens of schizoanalysis.

Schizoanalysis critiques institutions, power structures, and cultural norms by uncovering the ways in which desire is manipulated and constrained within society. Traditional psychoanalysis tends to focus on individual pathologies and familial structures, often reinforcing existing social norms. In contrast, schizoanalysis broadens the scope to include the social, political, and economic dimensions of desire, highlighting the ways in which institutions and power structures shape and are shaped by desiring-production.

Institutions, such as schools, prisons, and hospitals, can be critiqued through schizoanalysis by examining how they regulate and control desire. For example, the education system often channels desire into conformist and productive behaviors, promoting certain forms of knowledge and excluding others. By imposing rigid structures and hierarchies, educational institutions can limit the potential for creative and critical thinking. Schizoanalysis seeks to uncover these mechanisms of control and explore alternative forms of education that foster experimentation and the free flow of desire.

Power structures, including governments and corporations, also manipulate desire to maintain control and perpetuate their dominance. Capitalism, as analyzed by Deleuze and Guattari, operates by decoding and recoding desires, creating a continuous cycle of consumption and production. Advertising, media, and consumer culture play crucial roles in this process, shaping individuals' desires and behaviors to align with market interests. Schizoanalysis critiques these power structures by revealing the underlying dynamics of desiring-production and exploring ways to subvert and transform them.

Cultural norms and values, often taken for granted, are also subject to schizoanalytic critique. Norms related to gender, sexuality, race, and class are constructed and maintained through various social practices and institutions. These norms can constrain individuals' identities and behaviors, limiting the potential for diverse and fluid expressions of desire. Schizoanalysis challenges these norms by emphasizing the multiplicity and fluidity of identity, promoting a more inclusive and flexible understanding of human experience.

The processes of deterritorialization and reterritorialization are central to schizoanalysis and its application to social change. Deterritorialization involves the disruption or dismantling of established structures, norms, and territories, allowing for new forms of organization and meaning to emerge. This process is dynamic and ongoing, reflecting the fluid and contingent nature of social reality. Reterritorialization, on the other hand, refers to the re-establishment of new structures and territories following deterritorialization. These new formations can either reinforce existing power structures or create alternative and transformative possibilities.

Deterritorialization and reterritorialization are evident in various forms of social change, from revolutionary movements to everyday acts of resistance. For example, the civil rights movement in the United States involved the deterritorialization of racial segregation and discrimination, challenging the established social order and advocating for new forms of equality and justice. The subsequent reterritorialization involved the establishment of new laws, policies, and social norms aimed at promoting civil rights, though these new formations were also subject to ongoing struggles and contestations.

Contemporary social movements, such as Black Lives Matter (BLM), provide examples of schizoanalytic critique in action. BLM critiques institutionalized racism, police violence, and systemic inequality, challenging established power structures and cultural norms. The movement involves processes of deterritorialization, as it disrupts the existing social order and demands accountability and change. At the same time, BLM engages in reterritorialization by advocating for new policies, practices, and cultural understandings that promote racial justice and equity.

Another example is the environmental justice movement, which critiques the ways in which environmental degradation and climate change disproportionately affect marginalized communities. This movement involves deterritorialization by challenging the established economic and political systems that prioritize profit over environmental and social well-being. The reterritorialization aspect includes advocating for sustainable practices, equitable policies, and a reimagining of the relationship between humans and the environment.

A detailed case study of the countercultural movements of the 1960s and 1970s illustrates the application of schizoanalysis in social and cultural critique. These movements, which included the civil rights movement, the anti-war movement, the feminist movement, and the sexual liberation movement, sought to challenge and transform established social norms, institutions, and power structures.

The countercultural movements of the 1960s and 1970s can be understood as processes of deterritorialization. These movements disrupted the dominant cultural and political order, challenging norms related to race, gender, sexuality, and authority. For example, the civil rights movement sought to dismantle the structures of racial segregation and discrimination, advocating for civil rights and social justice. The feminist movement challenged patriarchal norms and structures, advocating for gender equality and women's rights.

The sexual liberation movement critiqued traditional norms related to sexuality, advocating for sexual freedom and the decriminalization of homosexuality. These movements involved the deterritorialization of established norms and institutions, creating spaces for new forms of expression, identity, and social organization.

Reterritorialization occurred as these movements achieved certain goals and established new norms, practices, and institutions. For example, the civil rights movement led to the passage of landmark legislation, such as the Civil Rights Act of 1964 and the Voting Rights Act of 1965, which aimed to promote racial equality and justice. The feminist movement achieved significant legal and social reforms, including changes in laws related to reproductive rights, workplace equality, and gender-based violence.

However, the process of reterritorialization is not linear or unidirectional. The new formations established by these movements were subject to ongoing struggles, contestations, and adaptations. For example, the gains of the civil rights movement were met with resistance and backlash, leading to continued efforts to address racial injustice. Similarly, the feminist movement has faced ongoing challenges in achieving gender equality, with new waves of activism emerging to address issues such as intersectionality, gender identity, and systemic discrimination.

The countercultural movements of the 1960s and 1970s also involved the creation of alternative spaces and practices that embodied the principles of schizoanalysis. For example, the establishment of communes, free schools, and alternative media provided spaces for experimentation with new forms of social organization, education, and communication. These spaces reflected the principles of desiring-production, the BwO, and assemblages, as they sought to create new connections and possibilities beyond the constraints of established norms and structures.

In conclusion, schizoanalysis offers a powerful framework for social and cultural critique, emphasizing the productive nature of desire, the fluidity of identity, and the dynamic interplay between social forces and individual subjectivities. By critiquing institutions, power structures, and cultural norms, schizoanalysis reveals the ways in which desire is manipulated and constrained within society, while also highlighting the potential for alternative forms of organization and expression.

The processes of deterritorialization and reterritorialization are central to understanding social change, as they involve the disruption of established structures and the creation of new formations. Contemporary social movements, such as Black Lives Matter and the environmental justice movement, exemplify the application of schizoanalytic critique in challenging and transforming established power structures and norms.

The countercultural movements of the 1960s and 1970s provide a rich case study for understanding the application of schizoanalysis in social and cultural critique. These movements involved processes of deterritorialization and reterritorialization, challenging established norms and institutions and creating new possibilities for social organization and expression. Through its emphasis on desiring-production, the BwO, and assemblages, schizoanalysis offers valuable insights for understanding and engaging with the complexities of social and cultural phenomena, promoting a more inclusive, fluid, and dynamic vision of human experience and social reality.

45. PRACTICAL APPLICATIONS OF SCHIZOANALYSIS IN THERAPY

Schizoanalysis, developed by Gilles Deleuze and Félix Guattari in their works "Anti-Oedipus" and "A Thousand Plateaus," offers a radical departure from traditional psychoanalysis, providing a novel framework for understanding and addressing psychological and emotional issues. In therapeutic settings, schizoanalysis can be applied to explore the complexities of human desire, identity, and social relationships in ways that differ significantly from traditional psychoanalytic approaches. This discussion will explore the practical applications of schizoanalysis in therapy, highlighting the differences between schizoanalytic therapy and traditional psychoanalysis, the unique techniques and practices of schizoanalytic therapy, and the potential benefits and challenges of applying this approach in mental health. A case study will illustrate the use of schizoanalysis in therapeutic practice.

Schizoanalytic therapy differs fundamentally from traditional psychoanalysis, particularly in its approach to desire, identity, and the unconscious. Traditional psychoanalysis, rooted in the work of Sigmund Freud and later developed by figures such as Jacques Lacan, focuses on uncovering and interpreting unconscious conflicts, typically centered around the Oedipus complex. This approach views desire as a lack or deficiency, something to be managed or sublimated within the constraints of societal norms.

In contrast, schizoanalysis views desire as a positive, productive force that continuously generates new connections, assemblages, and realities. Rather than seeing desire as something to be controlled or sublimated, schizoanalysis emphasizes its creative and generative capacities. This shift in perspective leads to a different therapeutic approach, one that seeks to liberate desire from repressive structures and explore its potential for transformation and growth.

Traditional psychoanalysis often focuses on interpreting the patient's unconscious through techniques such as free association, dream analysis, and transference. These methods aim to uncover hidden conflicts and resolve them within the framework of the individual's familial and social relationships. Schizoanalytic therapy, on the other hand, is less concerned with interpretation and more focused on facilitating the flow of desire and exploring new possibilities for connection and expression.

Techniques and practices unique to schizoanalytic therapy reflect its emphasis on fluidity, potentiality, and the breaking down of rigid structures. These techniques often involve creative and experimental approaches that encourage patients to explore their desires, identities, and relationships in new and transformative ways.

One technique used in schizoanalytic therapy is the creation of "desiring-machines." This concept, introduced by Deleuze and Guattari, refers to the ways in which desire operates through connections and assemblages. In therapy, patients might be encouraged to identify and explore their own desiring-machines, mapping out the various connections and flows of desire in their lives. This process can help patients understand how their desires are shaped by and interact with social, cultural, and personal factors.

Another technique involves the use of creative expression, such as art, music, or writing, to explore and express desires. By engaging in creative activities, patients can tap into the productive and generative aspects of desire, discovering new forms of self-expression and connection. This approach aligns with the schizoanalytic emphasis on desiring-production and the Body without Organs (BwO), providing a space for patients to experiment with new identities and assemblages.

Schizoanalytic therapy also emphasizes the importance of bodily awareness and movement. Techniques such as dance, somatic practices, and bodywork can help patients connect with their bodies and explore the ways in which desire flows through physical sensations and movements. This focus on the body aligns with the concept of the BwO, encouraging patients to experience their bodies as dynamic and fluid entities rather than fixed and hierarchical structures.

The potential benefits of applying schizoanalysis in mental health include its emphasis on creativity, fluidity, and transformation. By viewing desire as a productive force and encouraging patients to explore new possibilities for connection and expression, schizoanalytic therapy can foster a sense of agency and empowerment. Patients may discover new ways of understanding and relating to themselves and others, breaking free from restrictive patterns and developing more flexible and adaptive approaches to life's challenges.

Schizoanalytic therapy can also be particularly beneficial for individuals who feel constrained by traditional psychoanalytic frameworks or who struggle with issues related to identity and social norms. By emphasizing the fluid and dynamic nature of identity, schizoanalysis offers a more inclusive and flexible approach to understanding and addressing these issues. This can be especially valuable for individuals dealing with experiences of marginalization or those who feel alienated from dominant cultural norms.

However, there are also challenges associated with applying schizoanalysis in therapeutic settings. One challenge is the complexity and abstract nature of some of the concepts involved. Ideas such as desiring-production, the BwO, and assemblages can be difficult to grasp and apply in practical therapy. Therapists need to find ways to translate these concepts into concrete practices that are accessible and meaningful to patients.

Another challenge is the potential resistance to the unconventional and experimental nature of schizoanalytic therapy. Patients who are accustomed to more traditional therapeutic approaches may find it difficult to engage with the creative and fluid methods of schizoanalysis. Therapists need to be sensitive to these concerns and provide appropriate support and guidance to help patients navigate the process.

Additionally, the emphasis on fluidity and transformation in schizoanalysis can sometimes lead to a sense of instability or uncertainty. For patients who are seeking stability and coherence in their lives, the focus on continuous becoming and change can be challenging. Therapists need to balance the emphasis on transformation with the need for grounding and stability, helping patients find a sense of equilibrium amidst the process of exploration and change.

To illustrate the practical applications of schizoanalysis in therapy, consider the case of a patient named Sarah. Sarah is a 35-year-old woman who has been struggling with anxiety, depression, and a sense of disconnection from her life and relationships. Traditional therapy has provided some relief, but Sarah feels that it hasn't fully addressed her deeper sense of dissatisfaction and longing for something more.

In schizoanalytic therapy, Sarah begins by exploring her desiring-machines. She identifies various aspects of her life where desire seems to be blocked or constrained, such as her job, her relationships, and her creative pursuits. Through discussions and creative exercises, Sarah maps out the connections and flows of desire in these areas, gaining insight into how her desires are shaped by social expectations and personal fears.

Sarah is encouraged to engage in creative expression as a way of exploring and expressing her desires. She begins to write poetry and paint, activities she had abandoned years ago. Through these creative practices, Sarah taps into the productive and generative aspects of her desire, discovering new forms of self-expression and connection. This process helps her to see herself and her life in new ways, opening up possibilities for change and growth.

Bodily awareness and movement are also integrated into Sarah's therapy. She participates in dance and somatic practices, exploring how desire flows through her body and how physical sensations and movements can connect with her emotions and thoughts. This focus on the body helps Sarah to experience her body as a dynamic and fluid entity, challenging the fixed and hierarchical ways she had previously understood herself.

As Sarah continues with schizoanalytic therapy, she begins to experience a sense of empowerment and agency. She discovers new ways of relating to herself and others, breaking free from restrictive patterns and developing more flexible and adaptive approaches to life's challenges. The creative and experimental nature of schizoanalytic therapy allows Sarah to explore new possibilities for connection and expression, fostering a sense of curiosity and openness.

However, Sarah also faces challenges in her therapeutic journey. The abstract nature of some of the schizoanalytic concepts can be difficult to grasp, and she sometimes feels uncertain about how to apply them to her life. Her therapist provides support and guidance, helping Sarah to translate these concepts into concrete practices that are meaningful and accessible.

Sarah also experiences moments of instability and uncertainty as she navigates the process of continuous becoming and change. Her therapist helps her to balance the emphasis on transformation with the need for grounding and stability, providing a sense of equilibrium amidst the process of exploration and change.

Through her journey in schizoanalytic therapy, Sarah gains a deeper understanding of her desires, identity, and relationships. She learns to see herself as a dynamic and fluid entity, capable of continuous transformation and growth. This new perspective fosters a sense of empowerment and agency, enabling Sarah to navigate life's challenges with greater resilience and creativity.

In conclusion, schizoanalysis offers a radical and innovative approach to therapy, emphasizing the productive nature of desire, the fluidity of identity, and the dynamic interplay between social forces and individual subjectivities. Schizoanalytic therapy differs fundamentally from traditional psychoanalysis, focusing on the liberation of desire and the exploration of new possibilities for connection and expression. Unique techniques and practices, such as the creation of desiring-machines, creative expression, and bodily awareness, reflect the core principles of schizoanalysis and provide powerful tools for therapeutic transformation.

The potential benefits of schizoanalytic therapy include fostering a sense of agency and empowerment, promoting creativity and fluidity, and providing a more inclusive and flexible approach to understanding identity and social norms. However, there are also challenges, such as the complexity of the concepts and the potential resistance to unconventional methods. Therapists need to provide appropriate support and guidance to help patients navigate these challenges and translate schizoanalytic concepts into meaningful practices.

The case study of Sarah illustrates the practical applications of schizoanalysis in therapy, highlighting the transformative potential of this approach. Through her journey in schizoanalytic therapy, Sarah gains a deeper understanding of her desires and identity, discovering new forms of self-expression and connection. This new perspective fosters a sense of empowerment and resilience, enabling Sarah to navigate life's challenges with greater creativity and openness. Through its emphasis on fluidity, potentiality, and interconnectedness, schizoanalysis offers a rich and nuanced framework for therapeutic practice, promoting a more dynamic and inclusive vision of human experience and mental health.

46. SCHIZOANALYSIS IN LITERATURE

Schizoanalysis, a radical theoretical framework developed by Gilles Deleuze and Félix Guattari, has found significant applications in the realm of literary criticism. This approach offers novel ways to interpret texts and characters, identify desiring-machines and flows within literary works, and explore themes of schizophrenia and fragmented identities. By applying schizoanalysis to literature, critics can uncover the complex interplay of desires, identities, and social structures that shape literary narratives. This discussion will examine the application of schizoanalysis in literary criticism, providing a detailed analysis of James Joyce's "Ulysses" and William S. Burroughs' "Naked Lunch" through a schizoanalytic lens.

The use of schizoanalysis to interpret texts and characters involves viewing literary works as dynamic and fluid assemblages of desires, identities, and social relations. Unlike traditional psychoanalytic approaches, which often focus on uncovering hidden meanings and resolving unconscious conflicts, schizoanalysis emphasizes the productive and generative aspects of desire, exploring how it flows through and shapes literary narratives.

In schizoanalytic literary criticism, characters are not seen as fixed and coherent entities but as dynamic processes of becoming. This perspective allows critics to explore the multiplicity and fluidity of characters' identities, highlighting how they are shaped by various social, cultural, and personal forces. Schizoanalysis also encourages a focus on the connections and interactions between characters, rather than isolating them within individual psychologies.

To interpret texts schizoanalytically, critics identify the desiring-machines and flows within literary works. Desiring-machines refer to the mechanisms through which desire operates, creating connections and assemblages that generate new forms of meaning and expression. Flows, on the other hand, represent the continuous movement and transformation of desire as it interacts with various elements of the text.

In literature, desiring-machines can take many forms, from the relationships between characters to the symbolic structures that shape the narrative. Identifying these desiring-machines involves mapping out the ways in which desire flows through the text, uncovering the dynamic and interconnected processes that drive the narrative forward.

The thematic exploration of schizophrenia and fragmented identities is another key aspect of schizoanalysis in literature. Schizophrenia, in this context, is not merely a clinical diagnosis but a metaphor for the process of continuous transformation and disruption that characterizes both individual subjectivity and social structures. Literary works that explore themes of schizophrenia and fragmented identities often challenge traditional notions of coherence and stability, highlighting the fluid and contingent nature of identity.

By examining these themes, schizoanalysis reveals the ways in which literary texts engage with broader social and cultural dynamics, challenging normative structures and exploring alternative possibilities for identity and desire. This approach allows critics to uncover the radical potential of literature to question and transform existing social realities.

James Joyce's "Ulysses" and William S. Burroughs' "Naked Lunch" are two literary works that lend themselves particularly well to schizoanalytic interpretation. Both texts explore themes of desire, identity, and social fragmentation, employing innovative narrative techniques that reflect the dynamic and fluid nature of human experience.

"Ulysses," published in 1922, is a modernist masterpiece that follows the experiences of Leopold Bloom over the course of a single day in Dublin. The novel's stream-of-consciousness narrative style, fragmented structure, and multiplicity of voices make it an ideal text for schizoanalytic interpretation.

In "Ulysses," desiring-machines are evident in the complex relationships between characters, as well as in the symbolic and narrative structures that shape the text. For example, the relationship between Bloom and his wife, Molly, can be seen as a desiring-machine that generates multiple flows of desire and meaning. Bloom's desire for connection and understanding is juxtaposed with Molly's infidelity and independence, creating a dynamic interplay of desires that drives the narrative forward.

The novel's stream-of-consciousness technique allows readers to experience the continuous flow of Bloom's thoughts and desires, revealing the fluid and interconnected nature of his identity. This narrative style breaks down the boundaries between internal and external realities, highlighting the ways in which Bloom's desires are shaped by his interactions with the world around him.

The theme of schizophrenia and fragmented identities is also central to "Ulysses." The novel's fragmented structure, with its shifts in narrative perspective and style, reflects the multiplicity and fluidity of the characters' identities. Each chapter presents a different facet of Bloom's identity, revealing the ways in which his sense of self is continuously transformed by his experiences and interactions.

The city of Dublin itself can be seen as an assemblage of desiring-machines and flows, with its diverse inhabitants and social structures creating a dynamic and interconnected network of desires. By mapping out these flows and interactions, schizoanalysis reveals the ways in which the city shapes and is shaped by the desires of its inhabitants.

"Naked Lunch," published in 1959, is a groundbreaking work of experimental fiction that explores themes of addiction, control, and the breakdown of social and psychological boundaries. The novel's fragmented narrative structure, surreal imagery, and exploration of altered states of consciousness make it a rich text for schizoanalytic interpretation.

In "Naked Lunch," desiring-machines are evident in the novel's depiction of addiction and the ways in which desire is manipulated and controlled by various forces. The protagonist, William Lee, navigates a nightmarish landscape of drug addiction, government surveillance, and social decay, encountering a series of desiring-machines that shape his experiences and identity.

The novel's fragmented structure reflects the fluid and dynamic nature of Lee's identity, as he shifts between different personas and realities. This narrative style breaks down the boundaries between self and other, internal and external, highlighting the ways in which Lee's desires are continuously transformed by his interactions with the world around him.

The theme of schizophrenia and fragmented identities is central to "Naked Lunch," as the novel explores the ways in which desire is manipulated and controlled by social and political forces. The characters in the novel often experience a sense of dislocation and fragmentation, as their identities are shaped by the oppressive structures of addiction and control.

The novel's depiction of the Interzone, a surreal and chaotic cityscape, can be seen as an assemblage of desiring-machines and flows. The Interzone is a space where traditional social and psychological boundaries break down, revealing the fluid and interconnected nature of desire. By mapping out these flows and interactions, schizoanalysis uncovers the ways in which the Interzone shapes and is shaped by the desires of its inhabitants.

Both "Ulysses" and "Naked Lunch" illustrate the application of schizoanalysis in literary criticism, highlighting the ways in which desire, identity, and social structures interact and transform within literary texts. By focusing on desiring-machines and flows, schizoanalysis reveals the dynamic and interconnected processes that drive these narratives, uncovering the radical potential of literature to question and transform existing social realities.

In conclusion, schizoanalysis offers a powerful framework for literary criticism, providing novel ways to interpret texts and characters, identify desiring-machines and flows, and explore themes of schizophrenia and fragmented identities. By applying schizoanalysis to literature, critics can uncover the complex interplay of desires, identities, and social structures that shape literary narratives, revealing the radical potential of literature to question and transform existing social realities.

Through the detailed analysis of James Joyce's "Ulysses" and William S. Burroughs' "Naked Lunch," this discussion has illustrated the practical applications of schizoanalysis in literary criticism. These texts, with their innovative narrative techniques and exploration of desire and identity, provide rich material for schizoanalytic interpretation, highlighting the ways in which literature can engage with and challenge broader social and cultural dynamics.

By emphasizing the productive and generative aspects of desire, the fluidity of identity, and the dynamic interplay of social forces, schizoanalysis offers valuable insights for understanding and engaging with the complexities of literary texts. This approach encourages critics to explore the multiplicity and fluidity of characters and narratives, uncovering the radical potential of literature to inspire new ways of thinking and being. Through its emphasis on desiring-machines, flows, and the theme of schizophrenia, schizoanalysis provides a rich and nuanced framework for literary criticism, promoting a more inclusive, fluid, and dynamic vision of human experience and social reality.

47. SCHIZOANALYSIS IN FILM AND MEDIA

Schizoanalysis, the theoretical framework developed by Gilles Deleuze and Félix Guattari, provides a unique lens through which to analyze film and media. This approach offers novel ways to understand how cinematic techniques evoke schizoanalytic concepts, how certain films and media challenge conventional narratives and representations, and how the fragmentation and fluidity of identity are portrayed. This discussion will delve into these aspects, with a particular focus on the portrayal of schizoanalytic themes in David Lynch's films, such as "Mulholland Drive."

Cinematic techniques that evoke schizoanalytic concepts often involve the disruption of linear narratives, the use of fragmented storytelling, and the exploration of multiple perspectives and realities. These techniques mirror the schizoanalytic emphasis on fluidity, multiplicity, and the dynamic interplay of desires and identities. By employing these methods, filmmakers can create a cinematic experience that reflects the continuous becoming and transformation that characterize schizoanalysis.

One such technique is the use of non-linear narratives. Films that employ this technique often disrupt the traditional sequence of events, presenting the story in a fragmented or non-chronological order. This approach challenges the viewer's perception of time and causality, creating a sense of disorientation and fluidity. This narrative style can be seen in films like Quentin Tarantino's "Pulp Fiction," where the story is told out of sequence, forcing the audience to piece together the narrative from different perspectives and timelines.

Another technique is the use of multiple perspectives and voices within the narrative. This can involve shifting the point of view between different characters, presenting the same events from various angles, or blending subjective and objective realities. This multiplicity of perspectives reflects the schizoanalytic notion of the fragmented self and the fluid nature of identity. An example of this can be found in

Akira Kurosawa's "Rashomon," where the same incident is recounted by different characters, each with their own version of the truth, highlighting the subjective nature of reality and memory.

Surreal and dreamlike imagery is another cinematic technique that aligns with schizoanalytic concepts. By incorporating surreal elements and blending reality with fantasy, filmmakers can evoke the fluid and dynamic nature of desire and identity. These elements can create a sense of the uncanny and challenge the viewer's perception of reality. David Lynch's films are renowned for their use of surreal and dreamlike imagery, often blurring the lines between reality and hallucination.

Films and media that challenge conventional narratives and representations often do so by questioning established norms and structures, exploring alternative realities, and presenting complex and multifaceted characters. These works align with schizoanalysis by emphasizing the multiplicity and fluidity of identity, the dynamic interplay of desires, and the potential for transformation and change.

An example of this is the film "Fight Club," directed by David Fincher. The film explores themes of identity, consumerism, and rebellion through the story of an unnamed narrator who creates an alter ego, Tyler Durden. The film's narrative structure, which includes unreliable narration, fragmented storytelling, and the blurring of reality and fantasy, reflects the schizoanalytic emphasis on the fluidity of identity and the interplay of desires. The protagonist's struggle with his fragmented self and his desire to break free from societal constraints embodies the schizoanalytic exploration of desiring-production and the Body without Organs.

Another example is Charlie Kaufman's "Eternal Sunshine of the Spotless Mind," directed by Michel Gondry. The film explores memory, identity, and the nature of relationships through a non-linear narrative that moves between past and present, reality and memory. The use of surreal imagery and fragmented storytelling creates a sense of fluidity and multiplicity, aligning with schizoanalytic concepts. The characters' journey through their memories and the reconfiguration of their identities highlight the dynamic and transformative nature of desire and identity.

The role of schizoanalysis in understanding the fragmentation and fluidity of identity in media is particularly significant. Media representations often shape and reflect our understanding of identity, influencing how we perceive ourselves and others. Schizoanalysis provides a framework for exploring these representations, revealing the ways in which identity is constructed, deconstructed, and reconstructed within media narratives.

In the context of schizoanalysis, identity is not seen as a fixed and coherent entity but as a dynamic and fluid process of becoming. This perspective allows for the exploration of multiple and shifting identities, highlighting the ways in which desire, social structures, and cultural norms shape and transform the self. Media representations that embrace this fluidity can challenge traditional notions of identity and promote a more inclusive and flexible understanding of the self.

David Lynch's films, particularly "Mulholland Drive," provide a rich case study for examining the application of schizoanalysis in film and media. Lynch's work is characterized by its surreal and dreamlike imagery, fragmented narratives, and exploration of multiple realities and identities. These elements align closely with schizoanalytic concepts, making Lynch's films an ideal subject for this analysis.

"Mulholland Drive," released in 2001, is a neo-noir mystery that explores themes of identity, desire, and the nature of reality. The film's complex and fragmented narrative structure, along with its surreal and dreamlike imagery, creates a sense of disorientation and fluidity, challenging the viewer's perception of reality and identity.

The film begins with the story of Rita, an amnesiac woman who survives a car accident on Mulholland Drive and takes refuge in an apartment belonging to Betty, an aspiring actress. As the two women try to uncover Rita's identity, the narrative becomes increasingly fragmented and surreal, blending dreams, memories, and reality. This narrative style reflects the schizoanalytic emphasis on the fluidity and multiplicity of identity, as the characters' sense of self is continuously transformed by their desires and interactions.

One of the key schizoanalytic themes in "Mulholland Drive" is the concept of desiring-production. The film explores how the characters' desires shape and are shaped by their relationships and experiences. Betty's desire for success and recognition in Hollywood, Rita's search for her identity, and the complex interplay of their desires create a dynamic and fluid narrative that continuously generates new connections and meanings.

The Body without Organs (BwO) is another central theme in the film. The characters' identities are not fixed but are in a state of continuous becoming, reflecting the potentiality and fluidity of the BwO. This is particularly evident in the film's dream sequences, where the boundaries between reality and fantasy blur, and the characters' identities become fragmented and fluid. The use of surreal and dreamlike imagery in these sequences evokes the BwO, creating a space where new connections and assemblages can emerge.

The theme of schizophrenia and fragmented identities is also central to "Mulholland Drive." The film's narrative structure, with its shifts between different realities and perspectives, creates a sense of dislocation and fragmentation. The characters' identities are not stable but are continuously reconfigured by their desires and experiences. This reflects the schizoanalytic exploration of the fragmented self and the fluid nature of identity.

The portrayal of multiple realities and identities in "Mulholland Drive" aligns with the schizoanalytic emphasis on the dynamic interplay of desires and the potential for transformation. The film's ending, which defies conventional narrative resolution and leaves many questions unanswered, further emphasizes the fluidity and multiplicity of identity. This open-endedness invites the viewer to engage with the film's themes on a deeper level, reflecting the schizoanalytic focus on continuous becoming and transformation.

David Lynch's use of cinematic techniques, such as non-linear narratives, multiple perspectives, and surreal imagery, creates a cinematic experience that evokes schizoanalytic concepts. These techniques challenge traditional notions of coherence and stability, creating a sense of fluidity and multiplicity that aligns with the schizoanalytic exploration of desire and identity.

In conclusion, schizoanalysis provides a powerful framework for analyzing film and media, offering novel ways to understand cinematic techniques, narrative structures, and the representation of identity. By focusing on desiring-production, the Body without Organs, and the fluidity of identity, schizoanalysis reveals the dynamic and interconnected processes that drive film narratives, uncovering the radical potential of media to question and transform existing social realities.

The application of schizoanalysis to films like "Mulholland Drive" highlights the ways in which cinematic techniques can evoke schizoanalytic concepts, creating a sense of fluidity and multiplicity that challenges conventional narratives and representations. Through its emphasis on the fragmentation and fluidity of identity, schizoanalysis provides valuable insights for understanding and engaging with the complexities of film and media, promoting a more inclusive, dynamic, and transformative vision of human experience and social reality. David Lynch's films, with their innovative narrative techniques and exploration of desire and identity, provide rich material for schizoanalytic interpretation, illustrating the profound potential of this approach in film and media analysis.

48. SCHIZOANALYSIS IN ART

Schizoanalysis, the theoretical framework developed by Gilles Deleuze and Félix Guattari, has significantly influenced contemporary art, both in terms of creation and interpretation. This approach offers novel ways to understand how art can express complex desires, identities, and social dynamics. Schizoanalysis emphasizes the productive nature of desire, the fluidity of identity, and the dynamic interplay of social forces, all of which resonate deeply with the practices and interpretations of contemporary art. This discussion explores the influence of schizoanalysis on art, focusing on how it informs artistic creation and interpretation, the roles of assemblages, deterritorialization, and desiring-production in artistic practices, and examples of artists whose work embodies schizoanalytic principles. A detailed case study examines the works of Jean-Michel Basquiat and their relation to schizoanalytic concepts.

Schizoanalysis informs the creation and interpretation of art by encouraging artists and viewers to explore the dynamic and fluid nature of desire and identity. Unlike traditional approaches that often seek to categorize and interpret art within fixed frameworks, schizoanalysis emphasizes the multiplicity and interconnectedness of artistic expression. This perspective allows for a more expansive and inclusive understanding of art, highlighting its potential to challenge and transform established norms and structures.

In the creation of art, schizoanalysis encourages artists to engage with their desires and explore new possibilities for expression and connection. This approach emphasizes the productive and generative aspects of desire, viewing art as a form of desiring-production that continuously generates new meanings and connections. Artists are encouraged to break free from conventional forms and techniques, experimenting with new materials, styles, and processes that reflect the fluid and dynamic nature of desire.

In the interpretation of art, schizoanalysis shifts the focus from uncovering hidden meanings to exploring the multiple and interconnected flows of desire that shape the artwork. This approach recognizes that art is not a static object but a dynamic assemblage of elements that interact and transform each other. By examining these interactions and flows, viewers can gain a deeper understanding of the complex desires and social forces that inform the artwork.

Assemblages, deterritorialization, and desiring-production are central concepts in schizoanalysis that play crucial roles in artistic practices. Assemblages refer to the interaction of diverse elements that come together to form functional wholes. In art, assemblages can encompass a wide range of elements, including materials, techniques, ideas, and cultural references. By viewing art as an assemblage, artists and viewers can explore the dynamic and interconnected relationships that shape the artwork.

Deterritorialization involves the disruption or dismantling of established structures, norms, and territories, allowing for new forms of organization and meaning to emerge. In artistic practices, deterritorialization can take the form of challenging conventional techniques, styles, and genres, creating space for new and innovative forms of expression. This process reflects the fluid and dynamic nature of art, highlighting its potential to transform and reconfigure existing social and cultural landscapes.

Desiring-production emphasizes the productive nature of desire, viewing it as a force that continuously generates new connections and meanings. In art, desiring-production can be seen in the ways that artists engage with their desires to create new forms of expression and connection. This process highlights the generative potential of art, emphasizing its role in shaping and transforming social and cultural realities.

Several contemporary artists embody schizoanalytic principles in their work, challenging conventional forms and exploring the dynamic interplay of desire and identity. One notable example is Jean-Michel Basquiat, whose works reflect the influence of schizoanalysis in both their creation and interpretation.

Jean-Michel Basquiat's art embodies the principles of schizoanalysis through its dynamic and fluid nature, its exploration of multiple identities, and its engagement with social and cultural dynamics. Basquiat's works are characterized by their use of diverse materials, styles, and cultural references, creating complex assemblages that reflect the interconnected and multifaceted nature of desire and identity.

Basquiat's use of assemblages is evident in his incorporation of various elements, such as text, symbols, and imagery, drawn from a wide range of cultural sources, including African American culture, African art, graffiti, and popular culture. These elements interact and transform each other within the artwork, creating a dynamic and interconnected network of meanings and associations. By viewing Basquiat's art as an assemblage, viewers can explore the complex relationships and flows of desire that inform his work.

Deterritorialization is also a key aspect of Basquiat's artistic practice. His works often challenge conventional techniques and styles, blending different artistic traditions and genres in innovative ways. For example, Basquiat's use of graffiti and street art techniques within the context of fine art disrupts traditional boundaries between high and low art, creating space for new forms of expression. This process of deterritorialization reflects the fluid and dynamic nature of Basquiat's art, highlighting its potential to transform and reconfigure existing cultural landscapes.

Desiring-production is central to Basquiat's work, as his art continuously generates new connections and meanings through the interplay of desire and identity. Basquiat's exploration of multiple identities, including his own experiences as a Black artist in a predominantly white art world, reflects the productive nature of desire and its role in shaping and transforming identity. His works often address themes of race, identity, and social justice, engaging with the complex desires and social forces that inform these issues.

One notable example of Basquiat's work that embodies schizoanalytic principles is his painting "Horn Players" (1983). This work features a dynamic and fragmented composition, incorporating text, symbols, and imagery drawn from various cultural sources. The painting depicts two jazz musicians, Charlie Parker and Dizzy Gillespie, whose images are surrounded by a chaotic assemblage of words, symbols, and abstract forms.

In "Horn Players," Basquiat's use of assemblages is evident in the interaction of diverse elements within the composition. The fragmented and layered imagery creates a complex network of meanings and associations, reflecting the interconnected nature of desire and identity. The incorporation of text and symbols drawn from African American culture and jazz music highlights the cultural and social dynamics that inform the work, creating a rich and multifaceted assemblage.

The process of deterritorialization is also evident in "Horn Players," as Basquiat challenges conventional artistic techniques and styles. The painting's fragmented composition and use of graffiti-like text disrupt traditional notions of coherence and stability, creating a sense of fluidity and multiplicity. This approach reflects the dynamic and transformative nature of Basquiat's art, highlighting its potential to reconfigure existing cultural landscapes.

Desiring-production is central to "Horn Players," as the painting continuously generates new connections and meanings through the interplay of desire and identity. Basquiat's exploration of jazz musicians and African American culture reflects his engagement with the complex desires and social forces that shape these identities. The dynamic and fluid nature of the painting highlights the productive and generative aspects of desire, emphasizing its role in shaping and transforming identity and culture.

Another example of Basquiat's work that embodies schizoanalytic principles is "Untitled" (1981), often referred to as "Skull." This painting features a large, fragmented skull surrounded by a chaotic assemblage of text, symbols, and abstract forms. The skull's distorted and layered imagery creates a sense of dislocation and fragmentation, reflecting the fluid and dynamic nature of identity.

In "Untitled (Skull)," Basquiat's use of assemblages is evident in the interaction of diverse elements within the composition. The fragmented and layered imagery creates a complex network of meanings and associations, reflecting the interconnected nature of desire and identity. The incorporation of text and symbols drawn from various cultural sources highlights the cultural and social dynamics that inform the work, creating a rich and multifaceted assemblage.

The process of deterritorialization is also evident in "Untitled (Skull)," as Basquiat challenges conventional artistic techniques and styles. The painting's fragmented composition and use of graffiti-like text disrupt traditional notions of coherence and stability, creating a sense of fluidity and multiplicity. This approach reflects the dynamic and transformative nature of Basquiat's art, highlighting its potential to reconfigure existing cultural landscapes.

Desiring-production is central to "Untitled (Skull)," as the painting continuously generates new connections and meanings through the interplay of desire and identity. Basquiat's exploration of the skull as a symbol of mortality and identity reflects his engagement with the complex desires and social forces that shape these themes. The dynamic and fluid nature of the painting highlights the productive and generative aspects of desire, emphasizing its role in shaping and transforming identity and culture.

In conclusion, schizoanalysis offers a powerful framework for understanding the influence of contemporary art, both in terms of creation and interpretation. By emphasizing the productive nature of desire, the fluidity of identity, and the dynamic interplay of social forces, schizoanalysis provides novel ways to explore the complexities of artistic expression. Concepts such as assemblages, deterritorialization, and desiring-production play crucial roles in artistic practices, highlighting the interconnected and transformative nature of art.

The works of Jean-Michel Basquiat exemplify the principles of schizoanalysis, reflecting the dynamic and fluid nature of desire and identity. Basquiat's use of assemblages, his challenge to conventional techniques and styles, and his engagement with social and cultural dynamics embody the core concepts of schizoanalysis. Through his innovative and transformative approach to art, Basquiat's work highlights the radical potential of schizoanalysis to inspire new ways of thinking and being.

By applying schizoanalysis to contemporary art, critics and viewers can gain a deeper understanding of the complex desires and social forces that inform artistic expression. This approach encourages a more expansive and inclusive vision of art, promoting a dynamic and transformative engagement with the world. Through its emphasis on the fluidity and multiplicity of identity, schizoanalysis offers valuable insights for understanding and appreciating the richness and diversity of contemporary art.

49. SCHIZOANALYSIS AND POLITICAL THEORY

Schizoanalysis, as formulated by Gilles Deleuze and Félix Guattari, offers a radical rethinking of traditional political theory and activism. By focusing on the productive nature of desire, the fluidity of identity, and the dynamic interplay of social forces, schizoanalysis provides a unique framework for critiquing established political structures and ideologies, understanding the formation and operation of political movements, and informing contemporary political activism. This discussion will explore these aspects and provide a detailed case study on the application of schizoanalysis in analyzing and critiquing neoliberal capitalism.

Schizoanalysis fundamentally critiques traditional political structures and ideologies by challenging the fixed, hierarchical, and often repressive nature of these systems. Traditional political theory often relies on static categories and clear boundaries—between state and citizen, public and private, economic and political—that constrain our understanding of power and social organization. Schizoanalysis, in contrast, views these categories as fluid and interconnected, shaped by the continuous flow and production of desire.

In traditional political structures, power is typically seen as a top-down process, where decisions and control emanate from centralized authorities. Schizoanalysis disrupts this view by emphasizing the multiplicity and decentralization of power. Power, in the schizoanalytic framework, is not merely a tool wielded by those at the top but is dispersed throughout the social body, manifested in various forms of social, economic, and cultural interactions. This perspective aligns with Michel Foucault's idea of power as pervasive and productive, rather than simply repressive.

Desiring-production is a core concept in schizoanalysis that plays a crucial role in shaping political movements. Desiring-production refers to the idea that desire is a generative force that continuously produces new realities, connections, and social formations. In the context of political theory, desiring-production can help explain how political movements arise, evolve, and gain momentum.

Political movements can be seen as assemblages of desires, where individuals and groups come together to express and actualize their collective desires for change. These movements are dynamic and fluid, continually reshaped by the interactions and flows of desire among their participants. This view contrasts with traditional political theories that often see movements as rigid entities with clear hierarchies and fixed goals.

Assemblages, another key concept in schizoanalysis, refer to the dynamic and interconnected collection of elements that come together to form functional wholes. In political contexts, assemblages can include a wide range of elements, such as individuals, organizations, ideologies, technologies, and practices. Understanding political movements as assemblages allows for a more nuanced analysis of how these movements operate, adapt, and interact with broader social and political contexts.

Schizoanalysis also emphasizes the processes of deterritorialization and reterritorialization in political movements. Deterritorialization involves the disruption or dismantling of established structures and norms, creating space for new forms of organization and meaning. Reterritorialization, on the other hand, involves the re-establishment of new structures and norms following deterritorialization. These processes are dynamic and ongoing, reflecting the fluid nature of political movements and social change.

Deterritorialization can be seen in political movements that challenge and disrupt existing power structures and social norms. For example, the civil rights movement in the United States involved the deterritorialization of racial segregation and discrimination, challenging the established social order and advocating for new forms of equality and justice. The subsequent reterritorialization involved the establishment of new laws, policies, and social norms aimed at promoting civil rights, though these new formations were also subject to ongoing struggles and contestations.

Contemporary political activism can benefit from the insights provided by schizoanalysis. By emphasizing the productive nature of desire and the fluidity of identity, schizoanalysis encourages activists to embrace creativity, flexibility, and adaptability in their strategies and tactics. This approach can help movements remain resilient and responsive to changing circumstances, fostering a culture of continuous innovation and transformation.

For instance, the Occupy Wall Street movement, which emerged in 2011, exemplifies the application of schizoanalytic principles in contemporary activism. The movement's emphasis on horizontal decision-making, consensus-building, and the creation of autonomous spaces reflects the schizoanalytic focus on decentralization and fluidity. Occupy Wall Street challenged traditional power structures and social norms by creating a space for collective expression and experimentation, embodying the processes of deterritorialization and reterritorialization.

The Black Lives Matter (BLM) movement also illustrates how schizoanalysis can inform contemporary activism. BLM critiques institutionalized racism, police violence, and systemic inequality, challenging established power structures and cultural norms. The movement's emphasis on intersectionality, decentralized organization, and the use of social media to mobilize and connect participants reflects the schizoanalytic focus on the multiplicity and interconnectedness of desires and identities.

The application of schizoanalysis in analyzing and critiquing neoliberal capitalism provides a compelling case study. Neoliberal capitalism, characterized by the deregulation of markets, privatization of public goods, and the emphasis on individual entrepreneurialism, has profoundly shaped contemporary social and economic life. Schizoanalysis offers a unique framework for understanding the dynamics of neoliberal capitalism and exploring potential avenues for resistance and transformation.

One of the key critiques of neoliberal capitalism through a schizoanalytic lens is its manipulation and exploitation of desire. Neoliberal capitalism operates by decoding and recoding desires, channeling them into the consumption of goods and services. Advertising, media, and consumer culture play crucial roles in this process, shaping individuals' desires and behaviors to align with market interests. Schizoanalysis reveals how neoliberal capitalism perpetuates a cycle of desire and consumption, where the continuous production of desire fuels economic growth and maintains social control.

Desiring-production in the context of neoliberal capitalism can be seen in the ways that desires are commodified and turned into profit. For example, the desire for social connection and community is commodified through social media platforms, where users' interactions and personal data are monetized. The desire for health and well-being is commodified through the wellness industry, where products and services promise to fulfill these desires in exchange for financial gain. Schizoanalysis exposes these dynamics, highlighting the ways in which neoliberal capitalism exploits and manipulates desire for economic and political ends.

Assemblages within neoliberal capitalism involve the complex interplay of economic, social, and cultural elements that sustain the system. These assemblages include corporations, financial institutions, government policies, media, and cultural practices. By understanding neoliberal capitalism as an assemblage, schizoanalysis provides a framework for analyzing the interconnected and dynamic nature of the system, revealing the multiple points of interaction and influence that shape its operation.

Deterritorialization and reterritorialization are also central to understanding neoliberal capitalism. The process of deterritorialization involves the dismantling of traditional social and economic structures, such as labor unions, welfare states, and public institutions, creating space for the expansion of market logic. Reterritorialization involves the establishment of new forms of organization and control that align with neoliberal principles, such as the gig economy, financialization, and the commodification of public goods.

For example, the shift from stable, long-term employment to precarious gig work reflects the deterritorialization of traditional labor structures and the reterritorialization of work within the framework of neoliberal capitalism. This shift creates new forms of exploitation and control, as workers navigate a fragmented and insecure labor market. Schizoanalysis reveals the ways in which these processes shape and are shaped by the flows of desire, highlighting the need for new forms of resistance and solidarity.

Contemporary political activism can draw on schizoanalysis to critique and resist neoliberal capitalism. By emphasizing the productive nature of desire and the fluidity of identity, schizoanalysis encourages activists to develop creative and flexible strategies that challenge the system's manipulation and exploitation of desire. This approach can help movements remain resilient and adaptive, fostering a culture of continuous innovation and transformation.

For instance, movements advocating for economic justice and the rights of precarious workers can benefit from the insights provided by schizoanalysis. By highlighting the ways in which neoliberal capitalism exploits and commodifies desire, activists can develop strategies that challenge these dynamics and promote alternative forms of economic organization. This might include advocating for universal basic income, cooperative ownership models, and the decommodification of essential goods and services.

Environmental justice movements can also draw on schizoanalysis to critique the exploitation of natural resources and the commodification of the environment under neoliberal capitalism. By emphasizing the interconnectedness of social, economic, and ecological systems, schizoanalysis provides a framework for understanding the complex dynamics of environmental degradation and climate change. Activists can develop strategies that challenge the exploitation of the environment and promote sustainable and equitable forms of ecological organization.

In conclusion, schizoanalysis offers a powerful framework for political theory and activism, providing novel ways to critique traditional political structures and ideologies, understand the formation and operation of political movements, and inform contemporary activism. By emphasizing the productive nature of desire, the fluidity of identity, and the dynamic interplay of social forces, schizoanalysis reveals the complex dynamics of power and resistance in contemporary society.

The application of schizoanalysis in analyzing and critiquing neoliberal capitalism provides valuable insights into the ways in which desire is manipulated and exploited within the system. By understanding neoliberal capitalism as an assemblage shaped by processes of deterritorialization and reterritorialization, schizoanalysis uncovers the multiple points of interaction and influence that sustain the system. Contemporary political activism can draw on these insights to develop creative and flexible strategies that challenge neoliberal capitalism and promote alternative forms of economic and social organization.

Through its emphasis on fluidity, multiplicity, and interconnectedness, schizoanalysis offers a rich and nuanced framework for political theory and activism, promoting a more inclusive, dynamic, and transformative vision of social and political change.

50. FUTURE DIRECTIONS FOR SCHIZOANALYSIS

Schizoanalysis, a revolutionary theoretical framework developed by Gilles Deleuze and Félix Guattari, provides profound insights into the complexities of desire, identity, and social dynamics. As we move further into the 21st century, the relevance and application of schizoanalysis are likely to expand, addressing emerging social and technological changes, contemporary issues such as digital culture, environmental crises, and global capitalism. This discussion will explore the future directions for schizoanalysis, speculating on its evolution and potential applications, and provide a case study on its speculative application in the context of artificial intelligence (AI) and virtual reality (VR).

The potential evolution of schizoanalysis in light of emerging social and technological changes is vast and multifaceted. As societies become increasingly interconnected and digitized, the dynamics of desire, identity, and social interaction are also transforming. Schizoanalysis, with its emphasis on fluidity, multiplicity, and desiring-production, is uniquely positioned to address these transformations.

One significant area where schizoanalysis could evolve is in the analysis of digital culture. The rise of social media, digital communication, and virtual communities has fundamentally altered the ways in which people interact, form identities, and express desires. Schizoanalysis can provide valuable insights into the flows of desire within digital spaces, the formation of digital assemblages, and the processes of deterritorialization and reterritorialization that shape online identities and communities.

For instance, social media platforms operate as complex assemblages where users' desires for connection, recognition, and self-expression are continuously produced and manipulated. These platforms create new forms of social interaction and identity formation, but they also commodify and exploit users' desires for profit. Schizoanalysis can help unravel these dynamics, highlighting the interplay between individual desires and the structural forces that shape digital culture.

Another area where schizoanalysis can evolve is in addressing environmental crises. The Anthropocene epoch, characterized by significant human impact on the Earth's ecosystems, presents urgent challenges that require innovative theoretical and practical approaches. Schizoanalysis, with its emphasis on interconnectedness and the fluidity of assemblages, offers a framework for understanding the complex relationships between human societies and natural environments.

Environmental crises can be viewed through the lens of desiring-production and deterritorialization. The exploitation of natural resources, driven by capitalist desires for growth and profit, can be seen as a form of deterritorialization that disrupts ecological systems. Schizoanalysis can provide insights into how these destructive flows of desire can be redirected towards more sustainable and regenerative practices, fostering a reterritorialization that promotes ecological balance and resilience.

Global capitalism, with its pervasive influence on social, economic, and cultural life, remains a critical area for schizoanalytic critique and intervention. As capitalism continues to evolve, incorporating new technologies and expanding its reach, schizoanalysis can offer valuable tools for understanding and challenging its dynamics. By focusing on the flows of desire and the formation of capitalist assemblages, schizoanalysis can reveal the ways in which capitalism manipulates and exploits desires, creating new forms of control and inequality.

For example, the gig economy, characterized by flexible, precarious work arrangements, represents a new form of capitalist assemblage that exploits workers' desires for autonomy and flexibility. Schizoanalysis can help unpack the ways in which these desires are commodified and manipulated, highlighting the potential for alternative economic arrangements that prioritize workers' well-being and agency.

Looking ahead, schizoanalysis is likely to continue influencing theory, practice, and cultural production in diverse and innovative ways. In academic theory, schizoanalysis can provide new perspectives on contemporary issues such as identity politics, migration, and social justice. By emphasizing the fluidity and multiplicity of identity, schizoanalysis can offer more inclusive and dynamic frameworks for understanding and addressing these issues.

In practice, schizoanalysis can inform various fields, including psychotherapy, education, and community organizing. By emphasizing the productive nature of desire and the potential for continuous transformation, schizoanalysis can inspire new approaches that prioritize creativity, flexibility, and adaptability. For example, in psychotherapy, schizoanalysis can help practitioners develop techniques that encourage clients to explore their desires and identities in innovative and transformative ways.

In cultural production, schizoanalysis can inspire artists, writers, and creators to experiment with new forms and styles that reflect the fluid and interconnected nature of desire and identity. By embracing multiplicity and breaking down conventional boundaries, cultural producers can create works that challenge and transform existing social and cultural norms.

The speculative application of schizoanalysis in the context of artificial intelligence (AI) and virtual reality (VR) provides a fascinating case study. Both AI and VR represent significant technological advancements that are transforming various aspects of human experience, from communication and entertainment to work and social interaction. Schizoanalysis can offer valuable insights into the dynamics of desire, identity, and social assemblages within these emerging technologies.

AI, with its capabilities for machine learning, data analysis, and autonomous decision-making, is increasingly integrated into various aspects of daily life. From personal assistants like Siri and Alexa to complex algorithms that shape social media feeds and financial markets, AI systems are reshaping how desires are produced and managed. Schizoanalysis can help unpack the ways in which AI systems manipulate and channel desires, creating new forms of control and commodification.

For example, AI-driven recommendation systems on platforms like Netflix or Spotify analyze users' preferences and behaviors to suggest content that aligns with their desires. These systems operate as desiring-machines that continuously produce and shape users' desires, creating a feedback loop that reinforces certain patterns of consumption. Schizoanalysis can reveal the underlying dynamics of these systems, highlighting the potential for more user-centric and ethical approaches to AI design.

VR, on the other hand, offers immersive experiences that blur the boundaries between reality and virtuality. By creating fully realized virtual environments, VR technologies allow users to explore new identities, interactions, and experiences in ways that were previously unimaginable. Schizoanalysis can provide a framework for understanding the fluidity and multiplicity of identities within VR, exploring how virtual experiences can expand and transform users' sense of self.

In VR environments, users can create and inhabit avatars that reflect different aspects of their identity, engaging in experiences that may be constrained in physical reality. This fluid and dynamic exploration of identity aligns with the schizoanalytic emphasis on continuous becoming and the Body without Organs (BwO). VR can be seen as a space of deterritorialization where traditional social and physical boundaries are disrupted, allowing for new forms of expression and connection to emerge.

A speculative exploration of AI and VR through a schizoanalytic lens might consider the potential for these technologies to foster new forms of social organization and collective desire. For example, AI could be used to facilitate decentralized decision-making processes in political movements, enabling more inclusive and participatory forms of governance. VR could create virtual commons where users collaborate on creative projects, share knowledge, and build communities that transcend geographical and social boundaries.

However, the integration of AI and VR also raises important ethical and social questions that schizoanalysis can help address. The potential for surveillance, data exploitation, and loss of privacy in AI-driven systems is a significant concern. Schizoanalysis can critique these dynamics, advocating for technologies that prioritize users' autonomy and well-being. In VR, the blurring of reality and virtuality can lead to issues of addiction, escapism, and the commodification of experiences. Schizoanalysis can provide a framework for exploring these risks and developing strategies to mitigate them, promoting a more balanced and ethical approach to VR.

In conclusion, the future directions for schizoanalysis are vast and promising, offering valuable insights and applications across various domains. As societies and technologies continue to evolve, schizoanalysis can provide a dynamic and flexible framework for understanding and addressing the complexities of desire, identity, and social interaction. By emphasizing the productive nature of desire, the fluidity of identity, and the interconnectedness of social assemblages, schizoanalysis can inspire innovative approaches to contemporary issues such as digital culture, environmental crises, and global capitalism.

The speculative application of schizoanalysis in the context of artificial intelligence and virtual reality highlights the potential for these technologies to transform human experience in profound ways. By offering a framework for understanding the dynamics of desire and identity within these emerging technologies, schizoanalysis can help shape their development and integration in ways that prioritize creativity, inclusivity, and ethical considerations. As we move further into the 21st century, the relevance and influence of schizoanalysis are likely to expand, providing valuable tools for navigating the complexities of an increasingly interconnected and digitized world.

51. REFERENCES

To provide a comprehensive understanding of schizoanalysis and its applications, the following references include seminal works by Deleuze and Guattari, as well as contributions from other scholars who have explored schizoanalysis in various contexts.

Works by Deleuze and Guattari

1. Deleuze, G., & Guattari, F. (1972). Anti-Oedipus: Capitalism and Schizophrenia. New York: Viking Press.

This foundational text introduces the concept of schizoanalysis, critiquing traditional psychoanalytic models and exploring the intersections of desire, capitalism, and schizophrenia.

2. Deleuze, G., & Guattari, F. (1987). A Thousand Plateaus: Capitalism and Schizophrenia. Minneapolis: University of Minnesota Press.

This continuation of their earlier work further develops the concepts of schizoanalysis, including desiring-production, the Body without Organs, assemblages, and deterritorialization.

Books and Journal Articles on Schizoanalysis

3. Holland, E. W. (1999). Deleuze and Guattari's Anti-Oedipus: Introduction to Schizoanalysis. London: Routledge.

Holland provides an accessible introduction to the key concepts of schizoanalysis and their implications for various fields, including political theory and cultural studies.

4. Bogue, R. (1989). Deleuze and Guattari. London: Routledge.

This book offers a detailed analysis of Deleuze and Guattari's collaborative work, including their development of schizoanalysis and its application to different areas of thought.

5. Genosko, G. (2002). Félix Guattari: An Aberrant Introduction. London: Continuum.

Genosko explores the life and work of Félix Guattari, providing insights into the development of schizoanalysis and its practical applications.

6. Massumi, B. (1992). A User's Guide to Capitalism and Schizophrenia: Deviations from Deleuze and Guattari. Cambridge: MIT Press.

Massumi offers a detailed and accessible interpretation of Deleuze and Guattari's concepts, including schizoanalysis, and explores their implications for contemporary theory and practice.

7. O'Sullivan, S. (2006). Art Encounters Deleuze and Guattari: Thought Beyond Representation. London: Palgrave Macmillan.

O'Sullivan examines the intersection of art and schizoanalysis, exploring how Deleuze and Guattari's concepts can be applied to the creation and interpretation of contemporary art.

8. Smith, D. W., & Protevi, J. (Eds.). (2015). The Cambridge Companion to Deleuze. Cambridge: Cambridge University Press.

This collection of essays includes contributions from various scholars on the key concepts of Deleuze's philosophy, including schizoanalysis and its applications.

9. Thoburn, N. (2003). Deleuze, Marx and Politics. London: Routledge.

Thoburn explores the intersections of Deleuze and Marx, providing insights into the political implications of schizoanalysis and its critique of capitalism.

10. Zepke, S., & O'Sullivan, S. (Eds.). (2008). Deleuze, Guattari and the Production of the New. London: Continuum.

This edited volume includes essays that explore the creative and transformative potential of Deleuze and Guattari's concepts, including schizoanalysis, in various contexts.

Additional References on Contemporary Issues and Applications

11. Braidotti, R. (2013). The Posthuman. Cambridge: Polity Press.

Braidotti engages with Deleuze and Guattari's concepts to explore the implications of posthumanism, including the role of schizoanalysis in understanding contemporary technological and social changes.

12. Bryant, L. R., Srnicek, N., & Harman, G. (Eds.). (2011). The Speculative Turn: Continental Materialism and Realism. Melbourne: re.press.

This collection of essays includes discussions on the relevance of Deleuze and Guattari's concepts, including schizoanalysis, in contemporary philosophical debates.

13. Guattari, F. (1995). Chaosmosis: An Ethico-Aesthetic Paradigm. Bloomington: Indiana University Press.

Guattari's solo work further develops the ideas of schizoanalysis, exploring their implications for aesthetics, ethics, and politics.

14. Lorraine, T. (1999). Irigaray and Deleuze: Experiments in Visceral Philosophy. Ithaca: Cornell University Press.

Lorraine examines the intersections of Deleuze and Irigaray's philosophies, providing insights into the gendered dimensions of schizoanalysis.

15. Patton, P. (2000). Deleuze and the Political. London: Routledge.

Patton explores the political implications of Deleuze and Guattari's work, including the application of schizoanalysis to contemporary political theory and activism.

16. Protevi, J. (2009). Political Affect: Connecting the Social and the Somatic. Minneapolis: University of Minnesota Press.

Protevi discusses the connections between social and bodily experiences, drawing on Deleuze and Guattari's concepts, including schizoanalysis.

17. Thoburn, N. (2016). Anti-Book: On the Art and Politics of Radical Publishing. Minneapolis: University of Minnesota Press.

Thoburn explores the role of radical publishing in political movements, drawing on schizoanalysis to understand the interplay of desire, media, and activism.

These references provide a robust theoretical foundation for understanding schizoanalysis and its applications across various fields.

They offer insights into the concept's implications for contemporary philosophy, political theory, art, and cultural studies, highlighting the ongoing relevance and potential of schizoanalysis in addressing complex social and technological changes.